Flying Scotsman and the Story of Gresley's First Pacific Locomotives

Flying Scotsman and the Story of Gresley's First Pacific Locomotives

TIM HILLIER-GRAVES

PEN & SWORD
TRANSPORT

AN IMPRINT OF PEN & SWORD BOOKS LTD.
YORKSHIRE – PHILADELPHIA

First published in Great Britain in 2023 by
Pen and Sword Transport
An imprint of Pen & Sword Books Ltd.
Yorkshire - Philadelphia

Copyright © Tim Hillier-Graves, 2023

ISBN 978 1 39905 953 4

Typeset in Palatino by SJmagic DESIGN SERVICES, India.
Printed and bound by Printworks Global Ltd, London/Hong Kong.

Pen & Sword Books Ltd incorporates the imprints of Pen & Sword
Books Archaeology, Atlas, Aviation, Battleground, Discovery, Family
History, History, Maritime, Military, Naval, Politics, Railways, Select,
Transport, True Crime, Fiction, Frontline Books, Leo Cooper, Praetorian
Press, Seaforth Publishing, Wharncliffe and White Owl.

For a complete list of Pen & Sword titles please contact

PEN & SWORD BOOKS LIMITED
George House, Units 12 & 13, Beevor Street, Off Pontefract Road,
Barnsley, South Yorkshire, S71 1HN, England
E-mail: enquiries@pen-and-sword.co.uk
Website: www.pen-and-sword.co.uk

or

PEN AND SWORD BOOKS
1950 Lawrence Rd, Havertown, PA 19083, USA
E-mail: Uspen-and-sword@casematepublishers.com
Website: www.penandswordbooks.com

CONTENTS

PROLOGUE

've lost track of how many times I have seen *Flying Scotsman* but remember the first time only too clearly. For such a famous locomotive this isn't unusual. Anybody who is interested in railway history and has lived through her first hundred years will probably say the same. But it goes beyond this, because many people for whom the railways are no more than a means of going from one place to another seem fascinated by her as well, so firmly established is she in the national psyche.

I saw her first on a sunny afternoon at King's Cross when I was just six. I was waiting with my grandfather to catch a glimpse of a much-favoured A4. Instead, with the words 'It's *Flying Scotsman*' echoing over my head I turned to find what I hoped would be an A4 at the head of this famous train only to see a very grimy old engine pulling a rake of much cleaner carriages. I wasn't impressed in the slightest. Nevertheless, and to my great displeasure, I was tugged along the platform to the cab and to see the footplate crew at work. Still no reaction, only a mild request from me to move somewhere where the 'streaks' lived! To say

I wasn't gripped by the national fixation for 4472/60103 would be an understatement, but by the 1950s all the early Gresley Pacifics were, to my young mind, 'old hat' and been eclipsed by later, racier models that were much more to my liking. It was, in many ways, a state of mind encouraged by the speed of social change that followed the Second World War. People looked around and wanted more, not least from the country's transport system. So steam gradually departed, even my beloved 'streaks', to be replaced by something more suited to the modern world.

No. 4472 very early in her career doing what she did best – thundering along the East Coast Mainline with a rake of gleaming teak carriages. (BS)

Yet absence makes the heart grow fonder and in the years following its departure, people began to grow dewy eyed when remembering the heavily polluting giants of steam. What did they wish for? Was it a desire to recapture lost days, enhanced by beneficial hindsight? Or was it the need for a return of their steamy magnificence in the face of the blandness of what followed, plus the rapidity of social change, which some found uncomfortable? Looking back, through rose tinted spectacles can be very reassuring. Steam locomotives helped fulfil this need, with No. 4472 playing a key part in this process. So her 100th birthday (not out!) is an important celebration of this beautifully engineered reminder of Britain's industrial heritage.

It is hard to say when No.4472 first began to acquire iconic status, for that is what she did. The whys and wherefores of such a process are often hard to discern and sometimes it can just be a matter of luck. She had seventy-eight A1/A3 sisters, any of which could have taken up this mantle, but didn't. And she wasn't even the best of the class either, if Bert Spencer, Gresley's talented assistant, is to be believed. He later wrote:

> Although a good engine of the type, and was often used in the early days for publicity purposes, she was far from being the best of the A1s or A3s. There were far better engines that should have been preserved. *Papyrus*, *Shotover* or *Spearmint* are three that spring instantly to my mind, if driver's reports and my own personal experiences are anything to go by.

So what was it that made this engine stand out from the crowd? It can't simply have been that she was a lucky survivor and played to our desire to have an active connection with the past. The truth, it seems to me, runs much deeper and has its roots in the excellence of the LNER's PR team's work in selling the company and its services. They did far better than they realised and created something unique – a legend that still resonates with us today.

After a shaky start, my relationship with *Flying Scotsman* improved as the 1960s arrived. By now a worldly wise 10-year-old, whose head would not be easily turned, I was near Hadley Wood, on the northern edge of London, when the engine came thundering into view and I received a wave from the footplate and a brief, but piercing blast from her whistle. How easily we can have our heads turned by flattery and suddenly the engine acquired heroic status in my mind. It probably also helped that she was in a highly burnished state and looked superb as she headed south towards King's Cross. This would be my last sight of her in active service, because in little over a year she would enter preservation and her second life would begin as a tourist attraction. But as a fellow enthusiast recently said to me, as we stood watching this famous engine, 'She's a cellophane wrapped package of nostalgia and advertised like any other consumer goods. She's lost her soul'. An ignoble end for such a famous engine, perhaps, but better than the cutting torch and reduced to scrap like all her sisters.

Before the first of the A4s arrived in 1935, the A1/A3s dominated the LNER's high profile express trains. Here, No. 2578 *Bayardo*, built as an A1 by North British in 1924, pauses with the Queen of Scots Pullman service in July 1934. In 1928 she was rebuilt as an A3 at Darlington. (BS)

60103 in BR service, near Hadley Wood, not long before entering a well-earnt retirement. (THG)

that few civil liberties were enjoyed then and a type of feudalism still existed, with wealth and power vested in a tiny number of people who were reticent about releasing it to others.

For this reason, the story of *Flying Scotsman* and the other A1/A3 Pacifics is much more than frequently reviewed engineering and operational issues. It is about life itself and the human aspiration that makes something truly worthwhile a reality. It is about the way ambition and intellectual curiosity are stimulated and channelled to further a cause or an idea. It is about the way that human skills are honed and employed to produce something new, even revolutionary, then make it work day in day out. And it is about the way a business manages change without bankrupting itself in the process, doing what it can to sell its products and, hopefully, guaranteeing success in an increasingly competitive world. It is also about art and aesthetics and its influence on design. But most of all, it is about a workforce with few employment rights in a society expecting unquestioning loyalty and obedience labouring to produce something extraordinary with great pride despite the limitations placed on their lives. It is all these things and more that came together to create *Flying Scotsman* and all the other high profile Pacifics produced by Gresley.

To my mind, this surviving engine is a memorial to more than the sum of its engineered parts. It is a symbol of an age, a society and culture of which those who follow 4472 in preservation probably have

For myself, I would rather have her 'cellophane wrapped' and packaged in the hope that she will evoke memories of the people who created and worked on her in the 1920s, '30s and '40s and the times in which they lived – warts and all. Their world has gone, but that doesn't mean we should simply let it go without trying to understand how they lived and what it meant to exist in a country still recovering from the ravages of the Great War. Here times were hard, poverty rife and state help virtually unknown, unless you count the only too numerous workhouses. And if we are honest, we should recognise

no personal knowledge and little understanding. The celebration of *Flying Scotsman's* hundredth birthday allows us to recall these days, warts and all.

It is a story that begins in the last years of the nineteenth century when a young Herbert Nigel Gresley took his first tentative step into the world

of engineering, as he began a Premium Engineering Apprenticeship with the London and North Western Railway at its Crewe Works.

Flying Scotsman, now restored to LNER green and sporting her old number, enters her new life in preservation. (THG)

Chapter 1

TIME AND TIDE AND NEW IDEAS

In the years before the Great War, the Great Northern Railway, in Henry Alfred Ivatt hands, had attempted to update its locomotive fleet. His Atlantic Class engines were a major step forward. However, there were still many of the fifty-three Patrick Stirling's Single 4-2-2 engines, built between 1870 and 1895, around in 1914 to suggest that much more was needed in the way of modernisation. In the immediate post war years, it quickly became apparent that, with loads increasing, much bigger, stronger engines would be needed than even those developed by Ivatt. The picture to the right captures the only Stirling No. 1 to survive and is shown here in the late 1930s following restoration. (BS)

Gresley's first Pacifics arrived at a very difficult time in Britain's history and were seen by some as a sign that things were getting better. When the guns finally fell silent on the Western Front in November 1918, few believed that the war was truly over. Only when the peace was endorsed at Versailles in 1919 did the warring nations finally believe that the 'war to end all wars' was finally over. By then, the full impact of the conflict and its legacy were only too apparent. So, the relief and joy that followed the end of hostilities proved to be a short-lived affair. Four years of bloodletting accompanied by unbearable levels of sacrifice were the primary cause of the deep depression that cast a pall over the 1920s, with millions physically and mentally scarred

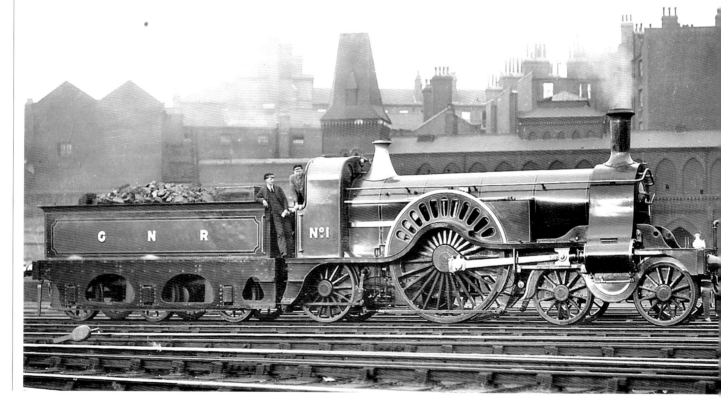

for life by war and unable to see a future free from pain and anguish. And then there was the grief of three quarter of a million families who had lost fathers, sons and husbands to consider.

Yet politicians, as they are wont to do, sought to put a gloss on these awful events, offer bland words of hope and plan for the future without giving sufficient thought to the consequences of a war that had left few without trauma of one sort or another. The unfulfilled promise of 'homes fit for heroes', chanted by the government as a mantra to appease the returning servicemen, summed up the barren state of political thinking and the wasteland the war had created.

Coupled to these deep wounds came the financial consequences of a deluge that consumed the country's wealth as quickly as it did the flesh and bones of its manhood. A once rich nation – for the lucky few anyway – now hovered close to bankruptcy with huge debts that only a prolonged period of austerity could hope to manage. However, those who returned from

the war expected much more than the flowery words of politicians and a stale status quo. Instead, they called for huge social and economic change in recognition of the sacrifices they had made in the name of King and Country.

Sadly, this pressing need for change fell on the deaf ears of the

country's ruling class, who seemed to expect a return to the Victorian world of wealth for a few and submissive deference from the rest, for pre-war Britain had been a place where most individuals had few rights – social, economic or political – and the freedoms we take for granted today simply didn't

In 1919, the return of the war's survivors was celebrated by a 'Victory Parade' (left) through the streets of London. But storm clouds soon gathered and workers, including many ex-servicemen, soon resorted to strike action when the changes they demanded met an unrelentingly cold response from government. Very soon, troops and police in large numbers were on the streets threatening a violent response under the banner of 'restoring order' (below left and right). The 1920s would see great strife as a result and many of these differences would go unresolved to the detriment of the country as a whole. (THG)

A DEMONSTRATION OF MILITARY FORCE: THE ARRIVAL OF TROOPS IN GLASGOW TO TAKE THE SITUATION IN HAND—MARCHING PAST THE CITY CHAMBERS.

Herbert Nigel Gresley in the post war years and beginning to bring his big engine policy to fruition. He was a clever engineer, an astute businessman and an exceptional leader leader who was able to view the future in practical terms and judge what was best for the business. He then argued his case, gained acceptance for his proposals and brought them into service with a sure touch, supported by an exceptional team. (THG)

exist. The pre-war years had seen some pressure groups attempt to improve the lot of the masses by both peaceful and violent means. But the end of the war brought with it much deeper sense of unrest prompted by a greatly inflamed sense of injustice. Extending the vote to women over the age of 30 and at least another seven million men, many of whom had fought in the trenches, showed a willingness, albeit a grudging one, to change, but it only tackled the tip of an iceberg when it came to establishing a fairer society.

To say that the two decades following the Great War were difficult would be something of an understatement. And then there was the rest of the developed world to consider. Here all, except the United States, had suffered equally or worse than Britain. Having sought to isolate itself from events in distant Europe, the USA was eventually drawn into the conflict with Germany's unrestricted U boat war being the catalyst. As a result, it had used its considerable wealth and growing population to help force a decision on the Western Front. In so doing, it flexed its industrial muscle, probably for the first time, and set a pattern for post-war growth that would see it begin to dominate world markets and become an economic power house.

In this role, they would be a key driver in determining the speed of revival. However, the downside of this dominance soon became clear – if the USA's economy shivered, all would catch cold. So, European nations, struggling to rebuild their economies in the face of huge losses in manpower and crippling debts, fell victim to a slump in business on the other side of the Atlantic. The 1920s and '30s would see both of these positive and negative influences come into play, adding to the woes of already crippled nations.

For Lloyd-George, Britain's prime minister, the end of the war presented huge challenges and seemingly endless problems to resolve. And with so many dead or mentally or physically damaged, he didn't even have the luxury of a large, fit workforce to help restore industry and so reduce the national debt. Then there was the

country's infrastructure, including the railways, which had been overworked and overstretched by the needs of war and was now in a dilapidated state, requiring expensive repair and renewal, to consider. All this would inevitably be a charge to an economy drained by war, making anything the Chancellor of the Exchequer might wish to achieve at best restricted and at worst impossible. All in all, there was a perfect storm of troublesome issues brewing that would severely challenge a country in a healthy state, let alone one exhausted and ridden by social divisions.

In the fifty years before the war, the dominant state of Britain's industries and their ability to exploit worlds markets supported by a vast merchant fleet had brought great wealth to the country, if not the majority of its people. This had fed a boom in manufacturing and such things as mining, but also encouraged the rapid and speculative expansion of the rail network in a largely impulsive way, with little thought being given to a central grand strategy. As a result, when war was declared in 1914, Britain was served by a plethora of privately owned companies, both large and small. Some of these were built with serious, long-term economic intent whilst others simply owed their existence to speculators who invested to make a quick killing on the stock market and then move on to pastures new. Yet many, against all the odds, managed to survive, though the depth of their struggle was only too apparent to anyone prepared to read annual reports and consider the level of debt they had incurred along the way.

Those that flourished, such as the Great Western, North Eastern and Great Northern Railways did so because they had a solid customer base, both freight and passenger, and were managed by men prepared to speculate on projects where commercial benefits could be identified. They weren't risk averse, but the chances they took were carefully calculated ones. Then the war came, and all these businesses came under government control with freedom of action being subordinated to a single aim – to win the war at all costs

by marshalling Britain's industrial might to defeat the enemy.

In practical terms, this meant that all planning and development had to be focussed on war needs, whether for freight or passenger traffic. So, out went any plans aimed at increasing profits and in came nationalisation in all but name. For the GNR in particular, this proved particularly frustrating because they harboured many ambitions, key amongst them the construction of a more powerful fleet of locomotives to meet its ever increasing trade. This was a

programme very close to the heart of Gresley, who had been appointed Locomotive Engineer in 1911 as a replacement for Henry Alfred Ivatt.

Within Britain's railway industry, Gresley was seen as a man of ambition and ideas. He had risen to this senior position when only 35 against some very stiff opposition. But he very quickly demonstrated his ability to think for himself unconstrained by the strictures of other more traditional minded souls in the industry.

At heart, he was a scientist who was eager to push back the

The sprawling mass of GNR's Doncaster Works, photographed in the early 1920s, was Gresley's base and the centre of activity for the company until 1923. After amalgamation, Doncaster's status diminished but it would still play a crucial role in the development and construction of the Gresley Pacifics. (THG)

Bert Spencer has written on the back of this print 'King's Cross in the early '20s as passenger numbers increased following the war'. This growth encouraged the GNR to consider developing their locomotive and rolling stock fleets. In Gresley, the company had just such a man to take on this task. (BS)

To do this he was prepared to consider new and novel ideas. To say he was hidebound by tradition would be a wholly misleading conclusion, although he recognised the hold it had on many more conservative souls in his business and was prepared, at times, to accede to their established ideas if no better solution presented itself. He was, after all, considered to be a good, well-grounded businessman, with a weather eye for the politics and manoeuvrings of a large commercial concern trying to balance many needs.

In Gresley, the GNR had a man of many talents who would, in due course, become a giant in the railway world, serving the GNR and then the London North Eastern with great creativity and a strong business sense. With hindsight we can see where he succeeded and where some of his ideas may have gone astray, but in the 1920s and '30s this was far from clear. So, to appreciate how this talented man performed when at the height of his powers, it helps that some of his contemporaries later described the impact he had on the world he inhabited

For many years Oliver Bulleid sat at Gresley's right-hand acting as his Principal Assistant, particularly at King's Cross in LNER days. Working so closely together, he could observe his leader at work and later wrote:

[Gresley] was more than the Locomotive Engineer of one company. His constant search for improvements, his awareness of developments in all locomotive engineering, and his interest in all advances in engineering practice in fields

boundaries of what was possible – scientifically and economically. And by nature, he was someone who would always seek new, possibly more effective solutions to the age-old problems of increasing a locomotive's power and improving their economy, speed and efficiency.

however remotely related to railway work, were reflected in the adaption to his locomotives of the work of other engineers.

He was the best Chief I had been under and our relations were the happiest. He was incapable of ill-temper, but what I appreciated most was his wide interest in all engineering. He was always ready to adopt any suggestion, but only after consideration. It could be felt that if he agreed to try anything it would almost certainly be a success. He had a wonderful memory, was extremely observant, and amongst other things could read a drawing in a way given to few. Disloyalty was the one thing he did not tolerate. After all the head of a department deserves loyal, unremitting service and obedience. He has also to be given every possible help to lighten the burden he assumes.

He gave me orders when he should. He asked my opinion if he wanted it. He expected to receive suggestions and to be given particulars of any development in any field which might not come to him direct.

He was a great man, scientist and leader. But like all great men he was a pragmatist and told us 'when you run out of ideas then copy the best'; very good advice.

The locomotives were the major part of his work, but one tends to forget the giant strides he made in carriage design as well and the particular interest he took in this aspect of railway life. He saw more than the locomotives he saw the entire train.'

To add to this subtle assessment, we have an account that Bert Spencer wrote towards the end of his life. As the Chief Mechanical Engineer's principal advisor on locomotive matters for sixteen years, and a very talented design engineer in his own right, he was well qualified to comment. He also had the opportunity to observe the creative dynamics at play in the offices at King's Cross and, in particular, how Gresley and Bulleid worked together to drive various development programmes forward:

I admired Sir Nigel tremendously and never found him inconsiderate or too busy to listen and discuss my ideas. He had the ability to think broadly and absorb a great deal of information before reaching conclusions. He sought the advice of those he respected and would always consider other possibilities, modifying his own plans accordingly if the arguments put forward held value. But once a decision was

made he pursued a course of action with great determination, taking stock and reviewing progress all the time. When a job was complete he insisted on a programme of testing to make sure the locomotive was as good as it could be and used whatever information he collected to modify the design. It was a constant frustration to him that the authorities were so tardy in building a test centre where better solutions might have been developed. He believed that Churchward achieved greater success because the GWR invested in such a facility and the LNER struggled to match their achievements because we had none.

He inspired confidence and led us all with a sure touch, often in very difficult circumstances. He was a great man and it was a privilege to work for him.

Gresley and Bulleid were like chalk and cheese. Each of them

Apart from being a talented engineer, Gresley was also someone who had the ability to move easily through the different strata of society. He had an easy, self-assured way of dealing with people from all backgrounds and could persuade anyone, by the strength of his argument, to take a particular course of action. This proved to be an invaluable skill when it came to developing new ideas and getting backing from his General Manager, Chairman and Directors, for such things as his ambitious Pacific programme. Here he greets, in his own confident way, the highest in the land – King George V and Queen Mary. (BS)

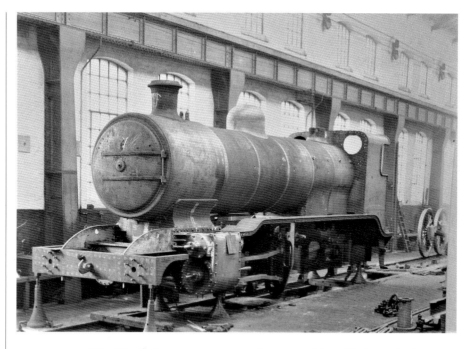

The mixed traffic 2-6-0 H2, the first of which, No. 1630, is photographed here when under construction at Doncaster early in 1912, was Gresley's first effort at locomotive design following his promotion to Locomotive Engineer. It was rather a modest affair by comparison to what came later, but it allowed him to develop and test his emerging ideas. However, as Brian Haresnape wrote in his book *Gresley's Locomotives*, 'many design features followed Doncaster traditions as established under Patrick Stirling and Henry Ivatt, in particular the cab, footplate fittings and tender, but the new engine was sufficiently different in appearance to have a "modern" air about it'. (BS)

was very skilled in their own way, but without the CME's careful handling his assistant could have wasted much time on work that probably wouldn't have led anywhere. His was a lively mind and was always engaged by some new idea, many of which served us well, but Gresley often had to rein him in before he became too distracted by an idea which was likely to lead to a dead end. There were disagreements and lively discussions, as you would expect from two such forceful men who held many strong opinions and could produce fresh ideas with little apparent effort. I think Gresley used me as a foil or filter to keep Bulleid's ideas in check and found that keeping him busy greatly reduced his ability to stray.

Gresley was not an accomplished draughtsman, but would develop ideas based on his wide knowledge of engineering, then sketch them out very roughly. These he passed to me to produce slightly more detailed drawings and a brief for the Chief Draughtsman and his team to consider. This became a much more regular process when we began developing the W1, the P2 Mikado and then the streamliners. I kept many of his sketches and remember well him calling to me in his slightly gruff way, 'Spencer, here's something I want you to look at, get me out some drawings will you!' and then being handed several sheets of paper, some lined, covered with rough sketches. A few days later we would pore over these plans and gradually his ideas would take shape at which point he would call in the Chief Draughtsman and Bulleid to get their point of view. More

often than not he wouldn't give them any forewarning of what he would lay before them, believing that first reactions were always more revealing.'

So, those who worked closely with Gresley, and were able to record their memories of their time together, clearly held in him the highest regard as a man, a leader and engineer. And his contribution wasn't simply a 'flash in the pan', as Spencer later wrote. It was sustained, determined and carefully considered. He had his faults of course, sensitivity to criticism being one of them, as Eric Bannister, Spencer's assistant recalled:

HNG was a pleasant man to work for. He did not like interruptions to his train of thought, so Bert Spencer and I waited until he asked us – with the well-known twinkle – for our opinions. We presented the facts as we found them, knowing HNG would make some comment which would automatically cause a re-assessment of opinion and so lead to further conversation. He would always consider carefully before reaching a decision and we were never kept in suspense because of the 'third copy' procedure. When I first went to King's Cross, BS warned me that HNG did not appreciate criticism of his marine big-end nor of his conjugated valve motion, but otherwise he encouraged original thought.

Spencer, as a great admirer of Gresley and his work, was more likely to be circumspect in his

assessment, but what of others in the railway business who owed the CME no favours or allegiance. Here, we are more likely to find a more critical appraisal of Gresley. Ernest Cox, who rose to senior rank as a Design Engineer with the LMS and then British Railways, provided just such an assessment. In his book *Locomotive Panorama,* he wrote that Gresley was:

An individualist of the deepest dye, he had no sympathy at all with the painstaking improvement of the breed, but wished with brilliant and dramatic improvisations to solve the remaining problems of steam by quite other means. To him novelty was everything. If it would not work then this could not be the fault of the idea itself, but only of the incapacity of those who tried to carry out or use it. The cross he had to bear was that his developments with conventional practice were successful, sometimes brilliant, whereas his exercises in the bizarre often failed.

All who are interested in locomotives have their own pet hobby horses, the inmates of railway design offices as much as any other … Gresley was no exception, and his addiction to the use of three-cylinders for everything was an abiding obsession. Similarly, he thought nothing of the Belpaire firebox. Not only would he not use it on any of his own creations, but he aimed to get rid of it as replacement boilers were required on engines which he inherited.

It would seem abundantly clear from the evidence which remains that the conjugated valve gear was wholly Harold Holcroft's [a talented mechanical engineer who was employed by the GWR, and trained under the guiding hand of George Churchward, before moving to South Eastern and Chatham Railway then the Southern Railway] … Whether Gresley thought he had made a new and personal deviation by placing the 2 in 1 levers in front of the cylinders, instead of behind as Holcroft advocated cannot be known, but the fact is equally clear that Gresley came to think of this gear as his own.

Gresley, like many other innovators, found that his own work had been forestalled by a previous patent.'

Cox pulls few punches and expresses the view that Gresley was seemingly a determined and obstinate man who, when convinced he was right, would follow his chosen course and be blind to other possibilities. Worst still, some ideas he pursued as his own might well be credited to others. But what of Gresley himself and his view of all that happened. Sadly, he didn't live long enough to record his thoughts or memories in a way that many retired people in high profile positions do. This creates something of a vacuum, although the recollections of those close to him may, if considered judiciously, help explain some of the whys and wherefores, but not provide the complete picture as only an autobiography can do.

Luckily, Gresley was a man who belonged to many learned institutions. Through them he took the opportunity to present papers

Above left and above right: **Gresley's single** Class 461 2-8-0 engine, which appeared in 1918, was the first time he used three cylinders coupled to an early version of his conjugated valve gear, rather than three independent sets of valve gear. It was an experiment seen by some as Gresley's most 'outstanding advance'. As Bert Spencer, from whom these photos came, later wrote 'this engine played a very important part in Gresley's career and he looked back with pride at the achievement. These photos of 461's cylinder and saddle block were part of a small, special collection he kept in his desk at King's Cross'. (BS)

on a range of subjects, or simply commented on issues raised by fellow members, particularly where it concerned the development of locomotives. Together these form some sort of legacy for a career that might otherwise have lacked the voice of its chief character. What follows is an amalgam of the key elements of his developing design philosophy, as presented at a meeting of the Institution of Locomotive Engineers in 1918, and the influences that came into play throughout his working life. He begins with a brief description of the industry as it appeared when he began his apprenticeship under Francis Webb, CME of the London and North Western Railway, during October 1893:

It is now 25 years since I started at Crewe Works in an atmosphere of compounds in the locomotive engineering profession … But there was no lack of enterprise in those days; a triple expansion engine was tried, an 8 figure firebox, and several boilers with a water space underneath and at the sides of the ashpan were built … Then I remember an attempt to do away with coupling rods, by the provision of a friction wheel, held up tightly between the coupled wheels by a steam cylinder, and which was to be released when once the engine got away with its train … I could quote many other experiments of great interest, some of which have failed, and some succeeded, but all added to our experience.

The locomotive of today is a very different machine to those to which I have just referred. The improvement is chiefly due to a kind of continuous evolution. During the past ten years this has been greatly accelerated by the introduction of superheating. I am not going to say much about superheating beyond this - its full advantages have not yet been appreciated.

The power of an engine depends upon its capacity for boiling water. The boiler is therefore without question its most important feature, but many engineers still compare the power of engines by their tractive force only and not the boiler. As a measure of the power of an engine, tractive force is useless unless the boiler is able to supply the necessary steam for long and continuous service.

A boiler which will supply steam when an engine is notched up to 20% cut off, and which fails to do so when the engine is let out on a long incline and has to work at 50 or 60% cut off, is too small for the cylinders on that particular work, although it might be quite large enough were it only on shunting duties.

Tractive effort, per se, is useless as a comparative measure of the power of engines. On the GNR there are two very instructive examples of this fallacy.

Mr Ivatt's first Atlantic engine had comparatively small boilers according to present day practice. The heating surface was 1,442 square feet and a grate of 26.75 square feet. The large boiler Atlantics have

2,500 square feet of heating surface and 31 square feet of grate. Except for the boilers, the engines are identical so far as boiler pressures, cylinders and wheel diameters are concerned. Therefore, the tractive powers are equal, but the large boiled Atlantics have proved to be much more powerful as express engines and are able to haul much heavier trains and keep time.

Then later on when the 2-6-0 type was introduced the first ten had smaller boilers – 4ft 8in. diameter. The later ones had boilers 5ft 6 in. diameter, but the grate area was the same in each case, and the engines in other ways were identical. During the last year's work the ten engines with the smaller boilers consumed about 5lbs. more coal per mile for the whole year than the engines with larger boilers.

Talking about fireboxes, it may be of interest to record that the wide fireboxes of the Atlantic engines introduced by Mr Ivatt are more economical from the point of view of life, and I think also from the point of view of efficiency. Recently I had to condemn one of these large fireboxes which had run 420,000 miles. Although the first engine of this type was built 16 years ago none of the boilers have been scrapped, and the first boiler is still running. This is fair proof of satisfactory design and work done in connection with the wide firebox and large boiler.

The work done by these engines is as heavy as that done by any passenger engines in the

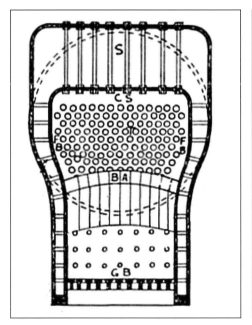

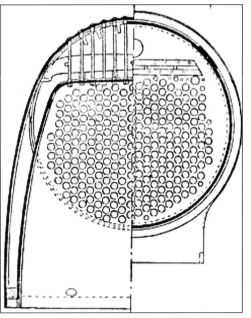

Gresley's rejection of the widely used and accepted Belpaire firebox (invented and introduced by Belgian Alfred Belpaire during 1864) often attracted criticism from fellow engineers who felt that it offered many benefits that may have made his engines even better. But Gresley was unmoved and simply stated that this form of firebox 'offers no advantage over the direct stayed round topped boiler, whilst undoubtedly its first cost is greater'. (Above Left) The cross-section of a typical Belpaire fire box highlighting the increased area for evaporation and the larger volume of water that could be contained above the box. (Above right) Gresley's solution – a flat-topped inner firebox with round-topped outer shells. He argued that this gave as good a thermal performance as the Belpaire and did not suffer from any significant problems. (Below) Bert Spencer's sketch of the Gresley firebox solution as attached to the boiler and firebox of an A1 Pacific. (BS)

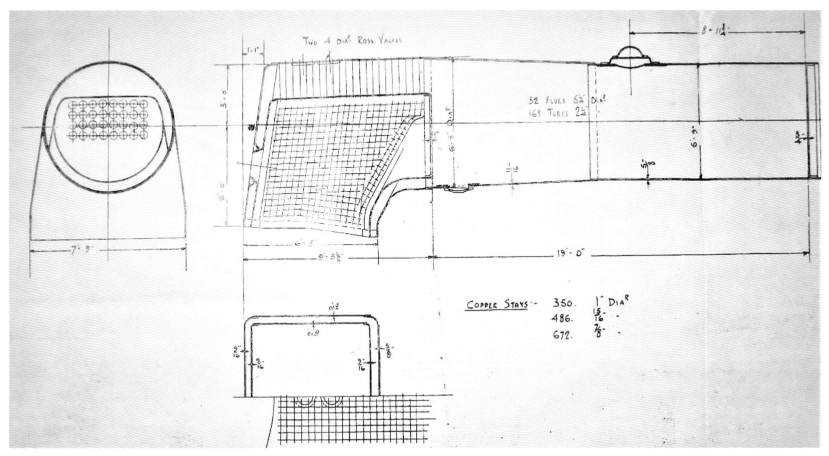

Mechanical lubricators
(in this case a yet to
be painted Silvertown
Lubricator fitted to a
Class O2 2-8-0) were
greatly favoured by
Gresley who commented
that 'there was a marked
decrease in the number
of hot boxes, due to their
use'. He also strongly
supported the adoption
of the Walschaerts valve
gear with his engines,
for external cylinders
at least (as can just
be seen in the photo
above), coupled to his
conjugated valve gear.
A notable exception
was the first P2 2-8-2
with which he opted for
rotary cam poppet valves
instead, the remaining
members of the class
reverting to Walschaerts
for the external cylinders
and his derived motion
for the third. (BS)

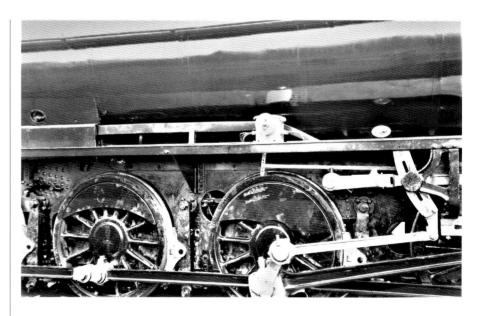

country, and the trains hauled by them often exceed 500 tons behind the tender today. These engines have the biggest boilers and smallest tractive power of any working on the principal railways of this country.

Then there is the much debated question of Belpaire and round topped boilers. I have tried to find some explanation for the apparent conviction of certain engineers in the superiority of the Belpaire type. There must be some explanation of this. I venture to suggest that this conviction is the result of experience. In the case of almost every railway which has adopted the Belpaire box, the firebox roof of the old round topped boilers were stayed with roof bars, which are well known to be objectionable on account of the difficulty in keeping the firebox top free from dirt.

Naturally, when they introduced Belpaire boxers with direct roof stays, many of the troubles disappeared and the improvement was put down to the adoption of the Belpaire type boiler. On the other hand, the use of general stays in round topped boilers has been the general practice on other railways. To such the Belpaire boiler offered no advantage; in fact, on one line it was tried and abandoned. I have, therefore, come to the conclusion that, from a maintenance standpoint, the Belpaire boiler offers no advantage over the direct stayed round topped boiler, whilst undoubtedly its first cost is greater. This view is supported by the experience of American and Continental engineers, where the use of the direct stayed round toped boiler is generally adopted for all new engines.

Another feature worthy of note in modern engines is the tendency towards greater accessibility of working parts. Outside cylinders and particularly outside Walschaert valve gear, offer great advantages. It is possible to secure better cross-bracing of the frames, to say nothing of easier oiling, inspection and maintenance of motion. With such an engine it is not necessary to put it over a pit before leaving the shed and the essential parts can be better examined in a good light, a very important consideration.

The use of mechanical lubricators for axleboxes has also tended to simplify the work of the enginemen, the oiling of all boxes being controlled by one lubricator. There has been a marked decrease in the number of hot boxes and an economy in the consumption of oil, due to the fact that when an engine is standing no oil is being used. It is an important point that the mechanical lubricator should be connected to a point in the motion which has a constant travel and not to a valve spindle, of which travel is reduced as the engine is notched up.

Having outlined some of the ideas central to his work, Gresley turned his eyes to the future and offered a precis of the issues he believed important and needed addressing as part of a wider review of motive power needs. At the time, the issue of standardisation was being widely discussed and before proceeding further Gresley briefly stated where he stood on this issue. 'I am a strong advocate of standardisation in principle, but not necessarily of standardised locomotives.'

To this he received a mixed response, as you might expect from an issue that at the time had given rise to much debate and provoked strong feelings for and against. In the event, the policy he adopted throughout his career steered away from developing standard classes of engines, though not necessarily their constituent parts wherever this proved practical. So he quickly moved on to less provoking design issues focussing, in particular, on engine size and boiler capacity:

A few months ago I was reading a very interesting address, given to one of the American Societies, in which the writer said, with regard to locomotives, that it has been comparatively easy to make them bigger and heavier, but a greater and far more difficult problem faces us today, viz., that of making every pound of weight justify itself in terms of power. Undoubtedly engines are approaching their maximum weights and sizes in this country, but are a long way from attaining their maximum power. We can, and shall have to, get more power per unit of weight.

The most efficient boiler is one which absorbs the maximum amount of heat from the coal burnt per unit of weight; to produce more power without increasing the weight is one of the problems to be faced. How is this to be done? One obvious way is to pre-heat the feed water; very little has been done so far in the matter of really satisfactory feed water heating. Many arrangements have been applied, but none have yielded such striking

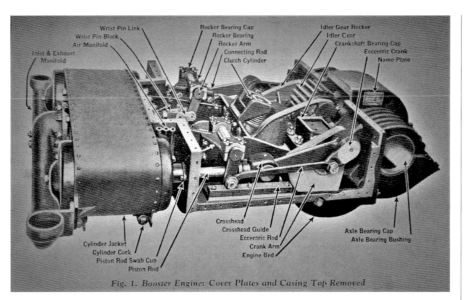

Fig. 1. *Booster Engine: Cover Plates and Casing Top Removed*

results as to justify their general adoption. In most cases, owing to the heaters getting blocked up, their efficiency is so much reduced that there is no return for the extra cost of fitting and maintenance.

But the possibilities are far greater than is generally recognised. It is calculated that roughly three quarters of the heat which is generated in the firebox of a locomotive is wasted up the chimney. This doesn't mean that a locomotive boiler has an efficiency of 25% only – the efficiency is somewhere nearer 70%, because of the heat wasted up the chimney, more than two-thirds is in the exhaust steam and the rest in the flue gases.

One area of research that Gresley did not touch on during various presentations concerned boosters and articulated bogies being fitted to locomotives in an effort to improve their tractive effort, aid pick up when starting with heavy loads, especially on steep inclines (above left – a typical example shown in diagramatic form). He began experimenting with these ideas in 1923 by converting a single Ivatt Class C7 4-4-2 (No. 4419) and then decided that the two new P1 2-8-2s heavy freight trains should also have boosters fitted (below left). In 1935 the programme was extended again and two more C7s (Nos. 727 and 2171) were modified with some positive results (improved riding of the engines and 'with the assistance of a booster a load of 746 tons was started with a drawbar pull of 12½ tons'). Spencer later wrote that 'Gresley was loth to give up the idea and when the Pacifics were being developed wished to experiment by fitting a booster. After much discussion at King's Cross the matter was dropped on the basis that a booster might be more hindrance than help when such fast, high powered engines were operating. However, articulation remained key to Gresley's work with carriages'. (BS)

Left and below: **Using feed-water** heaters in steam boilers was a firmly established principle in 1918 when Gresley addressed the ILocoE, but at that time had not been exploited to any great extent by designers. The concept is a simple one – to keep the water level in a steam boiler constant to ensure safe and efficient running. This is achieved by having a continuous flow of water from a tank or tender into the boiler, but the danger is that this will be much cooler than that already there, causing thermal shock to the boiler's metals. So, pre-heating the water to the highest possible temperature before it enters the boiler would, in theory, improve its thermodynamic efficiency and reduce long term damage. A pre-heating unit in a locomotive also had the benefit of capturing steam exhaust from the cylinders, which was lost to the air, and re-cycling it to heat the water as it passes from the tank into the boiler. It was an idea that Gresley had contemplated for many years, but it wasn't until he became the LNER'S CME that he began to test the theory in a more practical way. In 1927, these trials resulted in four ex-Great Eastern Railway B12s, including Nos. 8517 and. 8523 (shown here), being fitted with French built ACFI water heaters as an experiment. In due course, fifty-two more B12s were similarly modified and then two A1s and the first P2 2-8-0 in 1934. (THG)

The economy to be obtained by the introduction of a really satisfactory feed water system is second only to the economy which has resulted from superheating … but to secure the ideal result the temperature of the feed water must be pre-heated to that of the water already in the boiler; troubles such as leaking tubes and broken stays would then practically disappear, and the amount of water evaporated per pound of coal would increase to a surprising extent.

The locomotive boiler should not be required, as it is today, to heat up its feed water, and should only be called upon for evaporation and superheating; but the problem is by no means easy.

Interestingly, this brief reference to superheating was Gresley's only word on the subject at this stage. By the end of the war, its importance to locomotive engineering was only too apparent and the means of achieving it well advanced in development and operation. He couldn't claim credit for its discovery, of course, as it had begun development many years earlier in Germany, but he recognised its value and potential. When he spoke in 1918, he had become a strong advocate of the concept and had begun to adapt it for use in GNR engines.

In simple terms, the superheater re-heats the steam generated by the boiler and enhances its thermal energy so improving its efficiency. The first practical superheater was developed by Wilhelm Schmidt

during the latter part of the nineteenth century and he saw it applied, most notably, to a Prussian State Railway S3 class 4-4-0 engine in 1898, which then became the first S4 in the process. The benefits of the invention were then demonstrated in Britain by George Churchward at Swindon during 1906. However, he thought the Schmidt type could be improved and introduced his own version in 1909 which became known as the Swindon No. 3 superheater.

Henry Ivatt at Doncaster began his own superheating experiments in 1908 and by 1911 when he retired had progressed sufficiently to begin trials work, which Gresley developed further. Rather than simply try one option, the new Locomotive Engineer, as good scientists do, experimented with three different types for comparison purposes. So, the first twenty-five Class 521 0-6-0s (which became J6s when the LNER came into existence) goods engines were built with 18-element Schmidt superheaters. Another six of the class were then fitted with 'Doncaster straight tube' superheaters two years later and a further five received Robinson designed superheaters in the same year. All three types had identical tube arrangements and heating surfaces and only differed in the way the elements were secured to the header. A fourth design was also introduced in 1913 with engine No. 563 being built with the Gresley 'twin tube' superheater. This design had only seventeen elements, but this still enabled a 10 per cent increase in superheated heating surface to be achieved. Following trials with all these types,

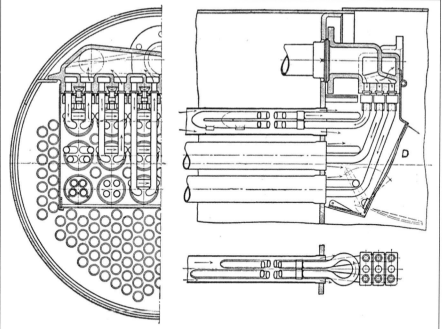

the LNER eventually chose the Robinson superheater as a standard fit for the J6s . But this was just the beginning of the story and over the coming years Gresley and his team would revisit the concept on many occasions, refining it to good effect in many classes of locomotives, perhaps most impressively in the Pacifics, as we shall see.

Gresley then moved on to discuss the ways in which the problem might be solved, analysing the benefits of exhaust or live steam heaters, with or without top feed, but stating a preference for the live version. However, in the time available he couldn't develop the debate any further and quickly moved on to the design of grates, which he believed had 'shown no marked improvement for many years', adding:

This is a very important point in locomotive design to which no special attention has been paid, yet in giving the leading dimensions of an engine the grate area has always been one of the cardinal points. Grates cannot be made much larger, but they can be made more efficient. American engineers have been devoting considerable attention to this subject. Conditions requiring the maximum power demand that air spaces between the bars shall be large as the character of the coal burnt will permit without actual waste of unburnt coal through the spaces between the bars. I know lately some considerable progress has been made in the design of grates and also ashpans. In the arrangement of the ashpan itself, unless properly designed, the advantage which might be expected from an improved grate may be nullified.

Considerations of ease of maintenance have largely influenced firebox design. If more units of work have to be obtained per unit of weight out of locomotive boilers, the fireboxes will have to designed to give more complete combustion and possibly with the provision of combustion chambers and auxiliary air supplies.'

With this the paper ran to its conclusion, touching on such things as the use of pulverised coal, which was becoming a part of life in wartime when the quality of the coal available was slipping, and rolling stock design. However, by this stage his primary thoughts had been fully voiced and he ended with a heartfelt appeal to those present that captured the sombre mood of the time:

The energies of everybody here must be concentrated on the work of the moment – the winning of the war. When this is accomplished, I say, will be the time for the locomotive engineers to bring their broadened experience to bear on the problem of transportation, and apply the engineering knowledge, experience, and, most important of all, the engineering adaptability, which this, the greatest of all wars, has taught us.

On occasions such as this, where a speaker is addressing an audience and not presenting a paper, it was traditional for the listeners to remain silent at the end of the session. So on this occasion it was left to Colonel Kitson Clark, the Vice-Chairman, to summarise the speech and thank the presenter. However, in response, Gresley did pick up a number of the comments made whilst he had been speaking, some of them spoken *sotte voce* perhaps, and added one final comment before the session ended:

'There is just one point. It is in reference to an observation made by my friend on the left. He asks, 'Why not a wide firebox?' The answer is that we have not had an engine to build which was big enough. If, and when, it is necessary to build an engine of this type it will certainly be considered.

In 1918, when he spoke these words, Gresley had such an engine in mind for, as we shall see, the war years were not entirely barren ones when it came to the development of bigger engines, with some planning going on to produce such a beast.

Strangely enough, during his presentation Gresley made no mention of his emerging thoughts on the number of cylinders and type of valve gear to be employed on his locomotives. The absence of any comment on this aspect of design is interesting, especially in the light of the introduction of his first three-cylinder engine that year with his version of a conjugated, 2 to 1 valve gear attached. Does the absence of any word on this subject imply some sensitivity to criticism that he might have plagiarised Harold Holcroft's ideas when creating his own form of conjugated valve gear, as suggested by Ernest Cox? Or does it suggest that, with his first prototype three-cylinder engine soon to appear and face public scrutiny, he preferred to remain silent until its potential had been tested? Either way, it is interesting to describe how Gresley reached this position and how his and Holcroft's joint effort shaped the path of locomotive design in the LNER.

The story of how the 2 to 1 valve gear evolved really begins before Holcroft was born and when Gresley was merely a child. During the late 1860s, David Joy, a mechanical engineer and inventor of note, investigated and developed a radial valve gear, which he patented in 1870 (though one source suggests it may have been 1879). During his career he appears to have worked for Shepherd and Todd, E.B. Wilson, the Nottingham and Grantham Railway and the Oxford, Worcester and Wolverhampton Railway as Locomotive Superintendent, amongst others. During this period, he experimented widely

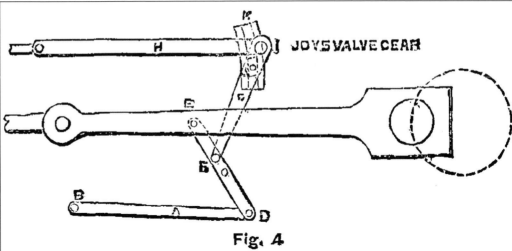

JOYS VALVE GEAR

Fig. 4

with different elements of engine design, with one primary example arriving early in his career when Chief Draughtsman for Wilsons. In this post he played a leading role, with James Fenton the Works Manger and E.B. Wilson himself, in the development of *Jenny Lind* the first of a successful class of ten 2-2-2 steam locomotives built for the London, Brighton and South Coast Railway in 1847. This gifted designer then sought to link three cylinders in an engine for use at sea and it was this work that seems to have evolved into the radial valve gear solution he then patented in the 1870s.

By the time this patent had been accepted, Joy was a man of some status in the industry and had demonstrated a very keen creative edge in many areas of design. So, in his lifetime he created a rich legacy of ideas for others to consider, but it was his work in producing the radial valve that may have caught Holcroft's eye and, perhaps even that of Gresley himself. And they had to look no further than the records held by the Institution of Mechanical Engineers for a primary source of material to inform their studies on this and many other issues. For example, during 1880, Joy presented a paper to fellow members entitled 'A New Reversing and Expansive Valve Gear' and this remained compulsive reading for those who followed. However, his death in 1903 opened his research up for others to explore. Quite independently, or so it seems, Holcroft had been developing his own conjugated valve gear, apparently encourage by George Churchward to do so. It was a proposal the young engineer then sought to turn in to a patent. But all was not plain sailing, as his memoirs recall:

The Record Office said that time was getting short in which to lodge the complete specification at the Patent Office, so had to be attended to at once. During my absence [in North America during 1909] they had made an extensive search and found that David Joy had applied a form of conjugated valve gear for operating the middle valve of triple-expansion marine engines, and therefore my claim could not be for entire originality, but would have to specify particular ways of operating the middle valve. I set to work, but, what with the need to make haste and some loss of enthusiasm over the device not being entirely original, all possible forms of in which the invention could be applied were not fully exploited, with the result that Gresley found a loophole a few years later on, which a little thought [by Holcroft] might have closed.

'What might have been' is an often contemplated and invariably fruitless issue when all outcomes are known and disappointment might be felt even more keenly. Nevertheless, it was Holcroft's inability to take the design forward and complete the application, that lay at the core of the issue. It was, after all, this lack of action that allowed this incomplete patent to

(Above left) David Joy, the inventor in old age. In the 1870s, he patented his radial valve gear that was a precursor to Gresley's 2 to 1 valve gear that he used with his three-cylinder engines, most notably the A1, A3 and A4 Pacifics. (Above right) His patented valve gear design in which the valve of one cylinder, in a three-cylinder engine, was activated by the combined motion of the gears operating the valves of the other two. Though unlikely to have been fitted in a locomotive by Joy, this solution undoubtedly had a clear link to both Gresley's and Holcroft's 2 to 1 valve gear designs. (RH)

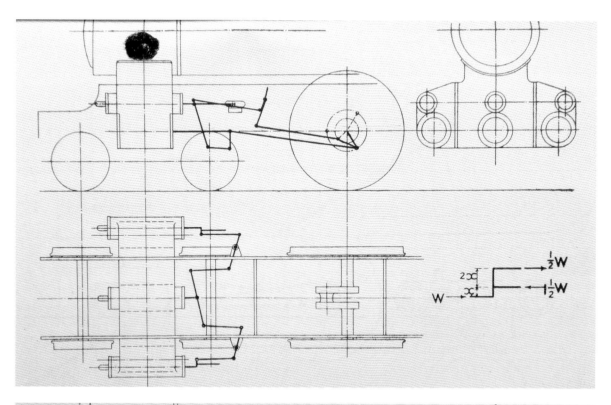

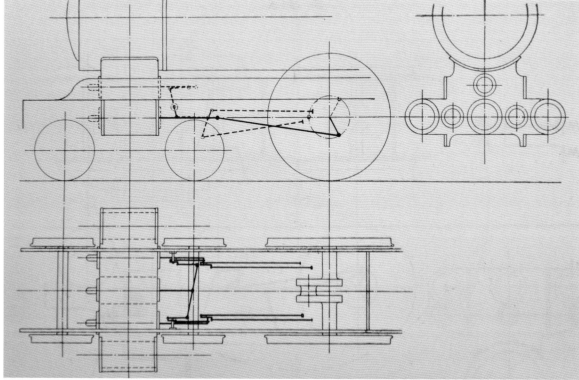

(Above) **Harold** Holcroft in old age. His work in creating a 2 to 1 valve gear for use with three-cylinder engines was not deemed sufficiently different from the work of David Joy by the Patent Office. Officials there suggested further work was needed to show a clearer divergence between his and the Joy design. But Holcroft failed to do this and his application was allowed to lapse. In due course, a Gresley solution appeared and received a patent in 1915, with his first engine so configured appearing in 1918. In November that year, Holcroft presented a paper to the ILocoE entitled 'Three Cylinder Engines'. In his submission he talked about the 2 to 1 concept, but only briefly mentioned Gresley's recently produced single 2-8-0 No. 461. Instead, he focussed on describing two proposals he had been pursuing separately (above left and lower drawings). Presumably these designs include the modifications he could and should have made when the originality of his patent application was queried. (RH)

lapse and enable others to pursue the concept further. This Gresley did a few years later, resulting in his patent, number 15769, which was submitted and accepted during 1915.

Did he know of Holcroft or Joy's work and did he use it as a basis for his own conjugated valve gear, so leaving a suspicion of plagiarism hanging in the air? Holcroft never publicly stated that Gresley had benefitted from his work, but during a presentation to the ILocoE he made on 2 November 1918, then repeated at several other locations including Leeds, some words of bitterness can be noted. In a paper entitled 'Three Cylinder Engines' he mentioned Gresley's work, adding a slightly barbed comment;

A 2-8-0 engine has now appeared on the GNR, in which the elimination of the third valve gear has been accomplished by a special arrangement of valve gear of Mr Gresley's. The possibility of constructing three-cylinder engines with two valve gears was, however, fully realised at Swindon some years ago, but not until the four-cylinder engines were firmly established.

So long after these events, and with no word from Gresley, it is difficult to reach any firm conclusions, but in my book *Gresley and his Locomotives* (Pen & Sword Transport, 2019), I attempted to put the whole matter in some sort of perspective. In the intervening years, and after much thought, I tend to stand by what I wrote then:

'On the moral question of 'adopting' other people's ideas, altering them slightly then taking credit, the issue is clouded by the nature of science and invention itself. Engineering contains many examples of seemingly unrelated discoveries being brought together to create new, probably unguessed

outcomes. The Wright Brothers didn't invent each part of the first powered aircraft, but they did absorb lessons learnt and discoveries made in a number of fields. Their skill lay in spotting the potential of different inventions and combining them successfully to achieve manned flight at Kitty Hawk in 1903. Likewise, neither Holcroft or Gresley invented the steam locomotive, or their many parts, they simply developed ideas, from many sources, then attempted to take them to a new level.

So where does the credit really lie and who can rightfully claim ownership of an idea, especially in a highly competitive world, where incremental advances can barely be measured at times? It is a grey area, but I don't think sufficient 'evidence' exists to allow Gresley's reputation to be tarnished by such an accusation. In any case his accomplishments, were far wider than this one issue. So it is important to view the totality of what he achieved, often in the most trying circumstances, to fully understand his greatness, for that is what it was. And engineering was only one part of the picture.'

However, this wasn't the end of the story, which had one final twist in its tail that might have acted as an olive branch to placate Holcroft. By the time of the younger man's 1918 paper, Gresley, with the war over, was considering the next step in the GNR's locomotive programme – in this case a new version of the 2-6-0 introduced in 1913. As part of

this work, he and his team had to consider the performance of engine No. 461 to see how this first three-cylinder engine was coping with its duties, by comparison with a standard 01 2-8-0, No. 456. In the weeks that followed, a number of trial runs took place over various routes, though these tended to focus on heavy coal trains operating between London and Peterborough, on occasions with a borrowed GWR dynamometer car in tow. Here, 461 proved itself superior to the O1s, but as Bert Spencer, then a draughtsman at Doncaster, wrote, 'the performance of the conjugated valve gear was not as good as it could have been and, after much head scratching, Gresley sought the advice of a number of engineers on ways it might be improved'. One of these proved to be Holcroft, perhaps as a result of his presentations, one of which Spencer, but not Gresley, attended. Holcroft recorded what happened next:

Gresley wrote later and invited me to meet him at his King's Cross office in London at 2.30 pm on January 19th, where I presented myself for what proved to be an historic occasion. Gresley was very frank and went straight to the point; he said that the performance of his 2-8-0 and No 461 had satisfied him as to the superior results obtained by the use of three cylinders. Now that I had given him the key to the solution of the problem of applying his simple combination to any type of engine, it was his intention, henceforth to build nothing but three cylinder engines.

Gresley's ideas concerning three cylinder engines with conjugated valve gear are made plain in these two diagrams. The drawing on the right, prepared by Bert Spencer, shows the layout of the valve gear on engine No. 461. The drawing below shows the modified version fitted to the 2-6-0 H4 (later becoming the K3 when the LNER was formed). Many years later, Holcroft recorded that this version was designed and adopted 'subsequent to a meeting [between him and Gresley] at King's Cross in January 1919 … and first applied to K3 No. 1000 in 1920'. His emphasis on collaborative working is noteworthy as is the claim for some credit for the design which harked back to his own lapsed patent. (DN)

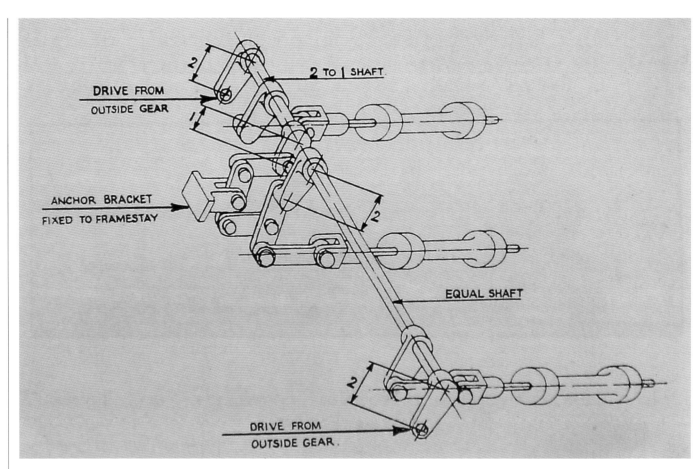

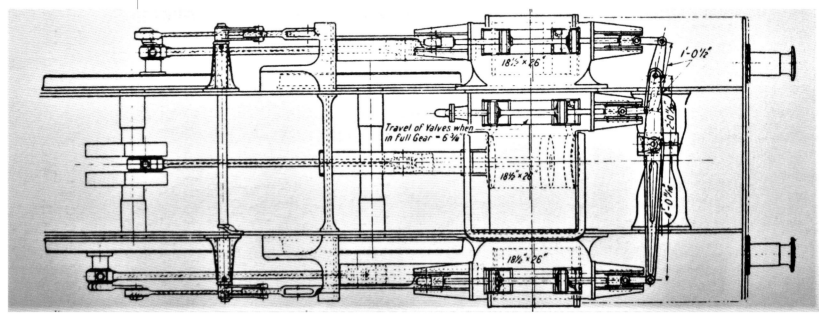

We then got down to details, and I pointed out that placing the inside steam chest in a horizontal position at the side of its inclined cylinder and giving the steam ports a twist in so doing would present no difficulties. The passage of steam would not be affected by the shape, whilst any skilled patternmaker could deal with the shaping of the ports. As regards the crank axle, this would have to be moved round through an angle of approximately 7 degrees in relation to the two outside cranks to give six equal pulses and exhaust beats.

The position of the combination was then discussed; my proposal was to locate it behind the cylinders so that it would not obstruct withdrawal of piston valves or the inside piston. Gresley, however, preferred that the levers should be placed in front of the cylinders, as the connection to the valve spindles would be simpler and more direct. I pointed out that the setting of the inside valve would be affected by the lengthening by heat of the outside valve spindles and that the gear would have to be dismantled before it was possible to withdraw piston valves or inside piston. Gresley thought that the lengthening of the spindles would be offset by making allowances for it when setting the valve. As to removal of piston valves for examination, he was prepared to uncouple the connections to the spindles and to lift the

combination bodily out of the way. This was how matters were left.'

Probably as a result of these discussions, the first of the new class of mogul, the H4, which appeared in 1920, carried a modified valve gear which seemed to combine Gresley and Holcroft's ideas successfully. It was a model, with further refinements, that would feature in Gresley's other three-cylinder engines. But why did he stick so determinedly, some might say stubbornly, to this concept and largely ignore the possibilities inherent in using either two or four-cylinders instead?

Luckily, he chose to air his thoughts on the subject when delivering a paper, entitled 'Three Cylinder High Pressure Locomotives', to the IMechE in 1925, when invited to do so by Vincent Raven, who was President that year. Whether he felt the need to justify the course of action he had taken is unclear, but he may have been aware that some members of this institution, and the ILocoE, were less than enthusiastic about the path he had taken. In the circumstances, he may have felt that his professional reputation had been impugned and saw such a public response as a valid course of action to take.

He made clear from the beginning of his presentation the benefits he felt were secured by using three cylinders and the value of adopting the 2 to 1 solution rather than having three sets of independent valve gear and listed them in a very simple way:

'*Uniformity of Starting Effort.* Three-cylinder engines show a marked superiority over two-cylinder in giving a more uniform starting effort. In starting a heavy train from rest the ideal condition is a perfectly uniform turning-moment at the wheel-rim. With widely fluctuating crack effort, in some positions the engine may be unable to start, and at other crank angles the effort may be so much in excess of the mean that the limit of adhesion is passed and slipping commences.

[During comparability tests] the relative starting efforts of two, three and four cylinder locomotives were based on the first few revolutions from rest with the full steam-pressure on the pistons, the regulator fully open and the reversing lever in full forward gear. Figure 1 (reproduced on page 30) shows the calculated mean and minimum value of crank effort for all ratios of connecting rod to crank during revolutions with two, three and four-cylinder engines of equal cylinder volume, all cutting off at 75% of the stroke and being identical in all respects, except cylinder arrangement. The much more uniform turning moment by the three-cylinder engine is clearly shown.

Increased Mileage Between Repairs. Another practical advantage in the use of three-cylinder engines is increased mileage between general repairs. The following figures show the experience of the

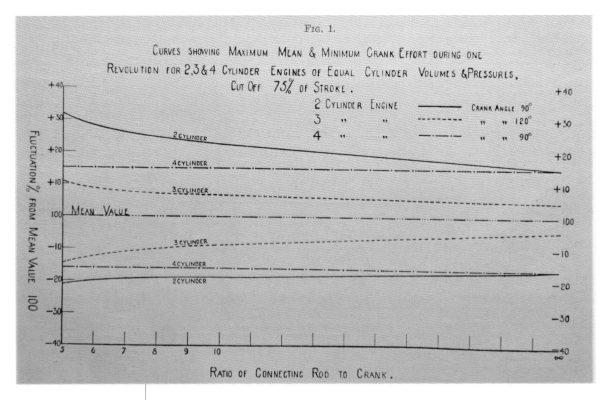

FIG. 1.

CURVES SHOWING MAXIMUM MEAN & MINIMUM CRANK EFFORT DURING ONE REVOLUTION FOR 2,3&4 CYLINDER ENGINES OF EQUAL CYLINDER VOLUMES & PRESSURES. CUT OFF 75% OF STROKE.

LNER with engines of both types. The three-cylinder 'Atlantics' [in this case thought to be ex-NER locomotives, probably of the Class Z/LNER Class C7 type of which 50 were built to a Vincent Raven led design] averaged 73,000 miles between repairs, compared to 56,000 for the two-cylinder Atlantics used on the same section (between Newcastle and Edinburgh).

Although there is no equivalent two-cylinder locomotive to make a comparison with the three-cylinder Pacific engines used on the railway with which the author is connected, it may be of interest to say that these engines have been running up to 120,000 miles before requiring general repairs. These higher mileages are attributable principally to the lower pressures transmitted through the pistons and connecting rods, and to the better balancing which can be obtained with three-cylinder engines. This further re-acts on the question of tyre wear, which is reduced.

During his presentation to the IMechE during 1925, Gresley sought to demonstrate the advantages of using three-cylinders in locomotives over comparable engines with two or four-cylinders. One key assertion was that they showed a 'marked superiority over two-cylinder in giving a more even starting effort' (presumably over a four-cylinder engine as well?) To prove this point, he produced various charts, with the two shown here (Figs 1 and 2 in his paper) demonstrating a key part of his argument. (RH)

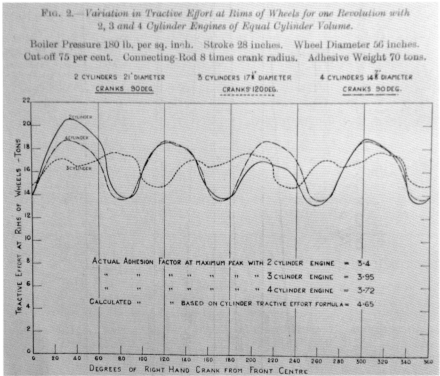

FIG. 2. — *Variation in Tractive Effort at Rims of Wheels for one Revolution with 2, 3 and 4 Cylinder Engines of Equal Cylinder Volume.*

Boiler Pressure 180 lb. per sq. inch. Stroke 28 inches. Wheel Diameter 56 inches. Cut-off 75 per cent. Connecting-Rod 8 times crank radius. Adhesive Weight 70 tons.

Steady Running at High Speeds and Decreased Hammer-Blow. The three-cylinder engine has proved itself to be very steady running at high speeds; in this respect it is superior to two-cylinder engines, but probably not as good as the four-cylinder type. The effect of the revolving parts can, of course, be neutralized by other revolving weights, but the reciprocating parts can only be properly balanced by

other reciprocating weights moving in a directly opposite direction; this is impractical, and therefore, a portion of the reciprocating masses is balanced by revolving weights. This decreases the disturbance in the horizontal plane, but introduces one in a vertical direction… this is usually referred to as 'hammer-blow', and if large, has a bad effect on the track and bridges. So to keep it in safe limits, it is only possible to balance a proportion of the reciprocating parts.

With the three-cylinder arrangement the parts are lighter per cylinder, so the weight of the excess counterbalance can be reduced. Further, owing to the equal spacing of the cranks, it is not necessary to balance the same proportion, so the excess counterbalance can be still further reduced.

Decreased Fluctuation in Smoke-Box Vacuum. A further advantage with the three-cylinder engine is the more uniform smoke-box draught action, which reacts favourably

on coal consumption and boiler repairs. If a two and three-cylinder engine both use the same volume of steam per-revolution, then for equal diameters of blast-pipe the

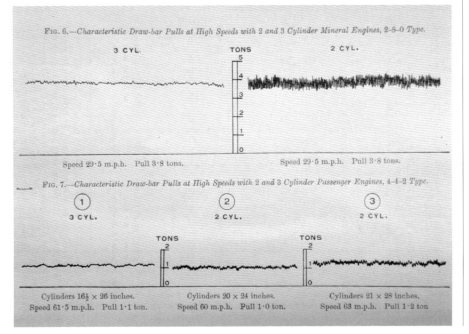

FIG. 6.—*Characteristic Draw-bar Pulls at High Speeds with 2 and 3 Cylinder Mineral Engines, 2-8-0 Type.*

3 CYL.   TONS   2 CYL.

Speed 29·5 m.p.h.   Pull 3·8 tons.   Speed 29·5 m.p.h.   Pull 3·8 tons.

FIG. 7.—*Characteristic Draw-bar Pulls at High Speeds with 2 and 3 Cylinder Passenger Engines, 4-4-2 Type.*

① 3 CYL.   ② 2 CYL.   ③ 2 CYL.

Cylinders 16½ × 26 inches.   Cylinders 20 × 24 inches.   Cylinders 21 × 28 inches.
Speed 61·5 m.p.h. Pull 1·1 ton.   Speed 60 m.p.h. Pull 1·0 ton.   Speed 63 m.p.h. Pull 1·2 ton

Fig 5 was produced by Gresley to help demonstrate that a three-cylinder engine could produce a reduced fluctuation in the smoke-box vacuum which would 'react favourably on coal consumption and boiler repairs', in comparison to a two-cylinder engine of a similar type undertaking identical duties. In this case, Gresley compared two and three-cylinder versions of his 2-8-0 freight locomotives. (RH)

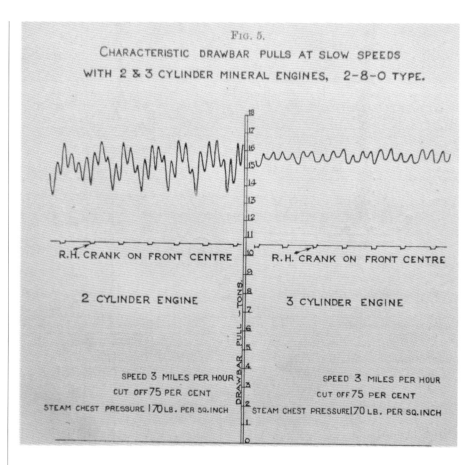

individual exhausts of the two-cylinder engine, which occur four times per revolution, will be heavier than those given by the three-cylinder one, and will not allow of such efficient combustion as the more frequent and lower impulses given by the three-cylinder type.

At slow speeds when working hard, at the instant when steam escapes from blast-pipes there is a small plenum in the smoke-box; it is followed instantly by the maximum vacuum, which falls again to zero before the next impulse. Under the conditions shown in Fig 5 at 3mph the maximum vacuum with the two-cylinder

engine was 10 inches and 7 inches with the three-cylinder, preceded by pressures of 1 inch and ½ inch respectively … It is not anticipated that there would be much variation at high speeds, as the impulses would follow so rapidly that there would no time for the vacuum to drop.

From this it is clear that Gresley considered that the advantages gained by using three cylinders, rather than two or even four, greatly outweighed the complexity of the valve gear he patented. He believed that three cylinders achieved the same power as two larger cylinders, but created far less wear, so

reducing maintenance requirements and achieving longer life.

By the time of this presentation, Gresley and his team had considerable experience of operating his and the inherited three-cylinder engines. As a result, he could have presented much more supporting evidence to back up his assertions, but he chose not to and his evidence was quite light fare, which must have left a question mark in the minds of those who heard or later read his paper. Nevertheless, he had made his point and continued, in a single-minded way, to develop engines with three cylinders and conjugated valve gear until the end of his career.

It wasn't the end of the matter, of course, and there would be many other twists and turns along the way, in particular the long lap valve issue, but it was a critical debate that didn't go away and came to the fore again after Gresley's death in 1941. As the Second World War took its toll on the motive power fleet, it was found that the condition of his three-cylinder engines appeared to have deteriorated more quickly than the two-cylinder locomotives, so much so that Gresley's successor, Edward Thompson, felt it necessary to commission a study by William Stanier and Ernest Cox to consider the issue and recommend solutions, if the problem was found to be as serious as some believed. As we shall see, this was a move that proved highly controversial and left ripples that still resonate with railway historians and enthusiasts to this day.

Gresley ended his presentation by adding a few paragraphs about the version of conjugated valve gear he and his team had developed

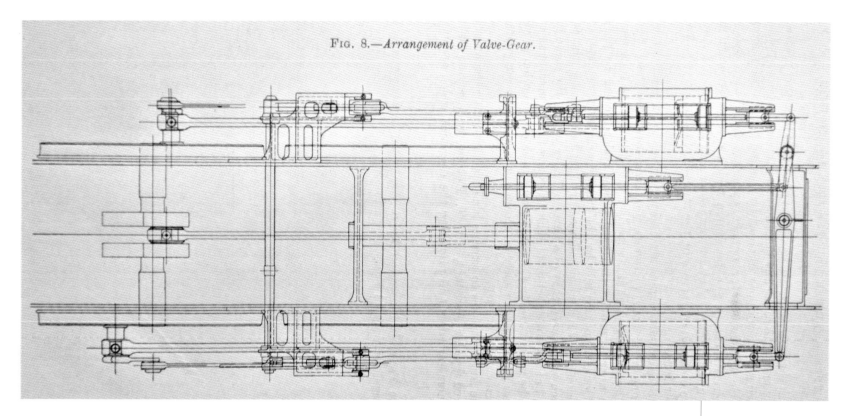

FIG. 8.—*Arrangement of Valve-Gear.*

over the previous ten years. Interestingly, he makes no mention of any contribution made by Harold Holcroft or for that matter claims outright credit for himself. Apart from describing how the valve gear worked, he simply said, 'Other combinations of levers may be used to produce the same effect, the axes of the pins may be turned round and rocking shafts substituted, but the arrangement shown in Fig 8 is the simplest. I have applied it to about 140 three-cylinder engines and it is giving entire satisfaction.'

There are two other issues worth mentioning at this stage, one because it reflects Gresley's openness to new ideas, the other because it demonstrates his ability to look beyond his immediate area of interest to other areas of science for inspiration and ideas.

In some quarters, Gresley was criticised for his apparent inability to embrace other forms of motive power when developing locomotives for the GNR, then the LNER. Arthur Stamer, CME of the North Eastern Railway, who was in the audience in 1918, was one of them. During the presentation, he expressed surprise that Gresley hadn't touched on this issue, particularly electrification, when discussing future developments in motive power, especially when the GNR and NER were making good progress in this field. If Gresley responded to Starmer he did so in private, with any comments he made to his future Deputy CME now lost to time. Perhaps he did not wish to become a hostage to fortune or, more likely, he simply realised that the chances of it happening in the foreseeable future

were slim. Yet years later, when he was elected President of this Institution, he stated emphatically, to crush any dissent on the issue, 'I should remind our members that this is an Institution of Locomotive Engineers, not an Institution of Steam Locomotive Engineers; all kinds of locomotives, steam, oil and electric are our concern.'

There doesn't seem to have been any trace of regret in these words, because he goes on to say that electrification has proved to be a viable option on the Southern Railway and on the Continent, too. But despite this, he believes there was still a place for internal combustion engines, such as diesel, as well as steam traction, if both continued to be developed and made more efficient. This is very much the voice of a forward-

At the end of his speech, Gresley presented this drawing (Fig 8) to demonstrate the way the conjugated valve developed adding, 'I have applied it to about 140 three-cylinder engines, and it is giving entire satisfaction'. He makes no claim for initiating the design, but neither does he fully describe its evolution or Holcroft's part in the process. (RH)

When Gresley became CME of the LNER he inherited some very advanced electrification projects, principally initiated by the NER's last two Locomotive Superintendents, Wilson Worsdell and then Vincent Raven. When the war came, plans were also in place to extend electrification to the mainline between York and Newcastle, but the conflict soon put paid to this work which remained in abeyance until 1920. This then led to the development of a new mainline prototype 2-Co-2 (4-6-4) engine designed and built at Darlington where it first appeared , as No. 13 (above), in May 1922. For reasons that aren't entirely clear, though were probably linked to lack of funds, the LNER's managers decided to delay the project unil the depressed state of the country improved significantly. This wasn't to be until the late 1930s, when progress was again delayed by the coming of another war. Contrary to the occasionally expressed view that Gresley was not a fan of electrification, he was, in fact, a strong advocate who, when the opportunity arose, enthusiastically developed his own programme. If the circumstances had been different, the A1 Pacific programme might have been greatly restricted and electrification come to the East Coast Mainline instead. (RH)

Sitting alongside the issue of motive power for locomotives sat the concept of streamlining, both internal, to improve such things as the flow of steam through passages, and external, to harness aerodynamic effects to make the progress of a moving object through air more efficient. By 1918, both these issues were beginning to be understood, but it is the latter which seemed to engage the scientist in Gresley and teased his desire to explore and experiment.

During the Great War, rapid advances in aeroplane design, driven by the need to make fighter aircraft faster and more manoeuvrable, highlighted the benefits of streamlining in trying to reduce drag. This research soon received wide publicity, leading people such as Gresley to consider how these emerging principles might be applied elsewhere. However, it soon became apparent that the aerodynamic effect might only become truly effective when objects, such as a train, were moving at fairly high speeds, although in the early 1920s it was far from certain what these might be or the benefits that could be derived from adopting a more streamlined shape.

It is probably true to say that at this stage there was little expertise in this field and few proponents of this new science, outside the world of aviation, to refer to for guidance. In Gresley's case, it wasn't until late in the 1920s, when he was introduced to Frederick Johansen, a young scientist working for the National Physical Laboratory in Teddington, that he made such a connection. By this stage, Johansen was beginning to make a name for himself in

thinking man eager to embrace change in any form, provided it is practical, affordable and improved upon what was already available. He grasped the strengths and weaknesses of all three technologies, but, being a pragmatist, he realised that the change from steam to diesel or electric on the LNER would be

a slow process – especially so in the dire financial circumstances that gripped Britain, and much of the world, in the 1920s and '30s. But when given the opportunity to develop electrification projects, he did so with great enthusiasm, only to see his efforts curtailed by the coming of another war.

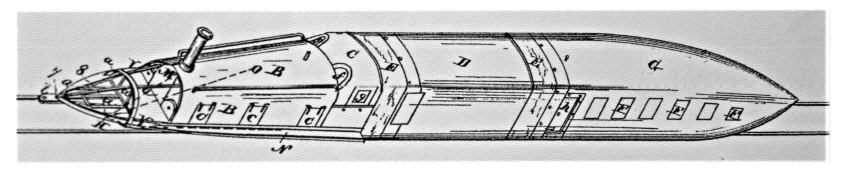

By the early 1920s, Gresley's interest in aerodynamics had been aroused and he was probably even then considering how these principles might be applied to locomotive design. At this stage, very little research into applications beyond the world of aviation had been undertaken but this would change over the next fifteen years. However, for those prepared to search, there was a bank of mostly conceptual work undertaken in the USA as far back as the 1860s. (Above) Samuel R. Calthrop's 1865 patented design for a fully streamlined steam powered train. It was an idea that appears to have gone no further than the drawing board. (Right) In the early 1900s, William Riley McKeen's first streamlined, lightweight, petrol driven rail car appeared. He wrote that the design would 'improve adhesion and reduce wind drag with the outer surface so formed to utilize the wind pressure in driving the car toward the track while the knife edge bow sliced through the atmosphere so reducing air resistance. At the same time, the spheroidal shape of the rear end prevented a vacuum forming at the back of the railcar'. In essence, he and Calthrop had captured the key issues in ways of improving the aerodynamics of a moving object, but lacked the wherewithal to explore the concept more fully. (JC)

Below: **While working** at the National Physical Laboratory, Frederick Johansen experimented with the aerodynamic shaping of trains. One of his early, wind tunnel tested, designs, shown here, was remarkably similar to McKeen's work in the USA early in the twentieth century. However, Johansen would refine his designs considerably when asked by Gresley to do so and significantly influence locomotve design in the process. (BS)

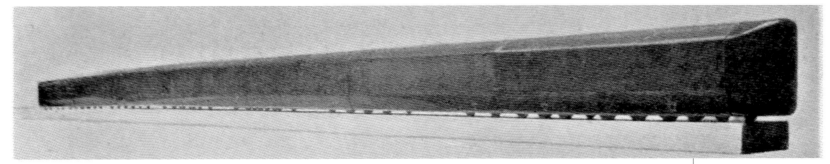

the fields of hydrodynamics and aerodynamics and was undertaking detailed research on behalf of such companies as Supermarine, becoming an expert in wind tunnel testing along the way.

In due course, Gresley would make use of Johansen's emerging ideas, and the facilities at his disposal, when developing the streamlined shapes of his single 4-6-4 W1, six P2s, thirty-five A4s and two 4-6-0 B17s. In addition, his work also contributed much to solving the more general issue of drifting smoke and the limiting effect this had on a driver's forward visibility. In this case, streamlining a loco's entire body could help, but such a radical solution was hardly practical when it came to freight or some types of passenger trains, such as commuter services. So here Johansen focussed on modifications to smokeboxes and chimneys, with cut-outs and deflectors of different types, developing and wind tunnel testing many variants for Gresley to use, as he did for the Southern Railway and London, Midland and Scottish. It was this work that fed into the development of Gresley's A1 and A3 Pacifics in the 1920s and onwards from there.

So here we have, described in a very broad way, some of the key engineering issues and principles that Gresley felt were important when designing locomotives, but how did he turn these theories into practice? The first point to note is that it wasn't a quick or easy process, but one measured by the GNR's commercial needs and the state of its finances when it came to new investments. But as good businessmen the company's directors would have been only too aware of the old maxim 'it is necessary to speculate to accumulate', especially so when competitors were more than capable of stealing a march by building bigger and better locomotives at any time. Even with the conflict at its height, and subduing their

bread-and-butter trade, all the railway companies were looking forward to a time when these restrictions were lifted, competition returned and investment in trains and the railway's infrastructure was again possible.

In truth, Gresley had only three years before the war to begin his development programme, but in that short time, as funding and time allowed, he began to experiment with both locomotives and rolling stock. He later wrote that Ivatt's locomotive programme had been so successful that the need for more engines when he took over was not a pressing one, so muting the commercial imperative that underpins any business. However, with the conflict over, and the railways avoiding the issue of state control or other interference for the time being, they returned to a peacetime existence. Funding any new projects would be problematical, as would restoring their infrastructure, but at least the companies were gradually released from the crushing burden of war. And this allowed Gresley

to take up the reins of locomotive projects he had developing when the war started, which he believed were essential to the GNR's future success. From the beginning, he had managed these issues in a measured way. There had been no sudden rush to build new, more advanced engines between 1911 and 1914, but whatever a man such as the singular Gresley attempted would always be interesting, even when shorn of a big budget and a certain amount of freedom to experiment.

Gresley's first engines to emerge, following his promotion to Locomotive Engineer, appeared in 1912 and 1913 respectively and passed through the GNR's workshops alongside such established designs as the N1 0-6-2 tank engines and J2 mixed traffic 0-6-0s. The first of the 'Gresley engines' was the two-cylinder H2 2-6-0 mixed traffic locomotives, though some believe that these may have been on the drawing board when Ivatt was still in charge and Gresley on long term sick leave. Either way, he played a significant role in their development and the engines that

Gresley's promotion to Locomotive Engineer in 1911 did not lead to a sudden change in the pace of either new construction or the speed in developing new locomotives. Much of the work undertaken by his predecessor, Henry Ivatt, had given the company a more modern fleet and this seemed to be meeting the immediate needs of a company not particularly rich in resources. However, having selected such a young and dynamic individual for this central role, the chairman of the board was clearly planning for the future and ways of expanding trade and here a more advanced fleet of locomotives and rolling stock would prove crucial. So, quite slowly to begin with, Gresley began experimenting and developing his own ideas or adapting those then current in the industry on such things as number of cylinders, conjugated valves, size of boilers and much more. In July 1912 the first visible sign of this work came with the construction of engine No. 1630, the first of ten 2-6-0 two-cylinder H2s, at Doncaster (captured in this photograph when new). The prototype wasn't a huge departure from types already developed by Ivatt, but sufficient was included to suggest that more changes were on the way as Gresley considered the future. (RH)

1913 saw two new Gresley engines appear. (Top) The GNR had a pressing need for bigger, freight locomotives and here Gresley looked to George Churchward and the Great Western Railway for inspiration, seeing in their 1903 introduced Class 2800 2-8-0s a concept worth exploring. The use of a pony truck allowed a larger boiler to be utilized with power being transmitted to the wheels via two cylinders and Walschaert valve gear, with a high degree of superheat provided by a 24-element Robinson designed superheater. No. 456 was the first of a class of twenty locomotives, six of which were built by the GNR and fourteen under contract by the North British Locomotive Company. (Below) Next came a modified 2-6-0, the H3, still with two cylinders but this time the boiler was increased in size from the 4ft 8in on the H2 to 5ft 6in so following Gresley's dicta that 'the power of an engine depends on its capacity for boiling water'. So successful was this Mogul that seventy-five were built between 1913 and 1921. (RH)

emerged reflected the evolutionary process Gresley described in his May 1918 paper to the ILocoE.

The first H2 (or K1 as it became under LNER management), No. 1630, was completed in August 1912 and soon entered a period of evaluation before nine more were ordered a year later. In due course, Gresley reviewed his design and decided that a bigger boiler was needed; a move that mirrored Ivatt's work on his Atlantics a

decade or so earlier. But in this case, the H2's 4ft 8in diameter boilers, with an 18-element superheater, producing a pressure of 170lb per sq in, and a tractive effort of 22,070lbs, were discarded. In its place came a 5ft 6in diameter boiler with a 24-element superheater, though still producing 170lb of pressure, generating a tractive effort of 23,400lb. However, the modified 2-6-0 still retained two cylinders, though by this stage Gresley was

undoubtedly considering other options including three cylinders. This new engine, designated H3 (later the K2), first appeared in 1913 and over the next eight years seventy-four more were added.

The second new design, the first of twenty O1 2-8-0 heavy goods engines, appeared in 1913, brought out to supplement the Ivatt 0-8-0 'Long Toms' which to Gresley seemed short of stamina for the ever-increasing weight of freight

Having begun to match three cylinders with conjugated valve gear with the single Class 461, Gresley adapted these principles to the GNR's growing fleet of 2-6-0s, in this case the H4 (later the K3) of which 193 would be built between 1920 and 1937 (ten by the GNR, the rest by the LNER). This photograph captures the recently built prototype, No. 1000, pulling a fast freight. Apart from three-cylinders and a refined version of the 2 to 1 conjugated valve gear, developed with the help of Harold Holcroft late of the GWR but by then with the South Eastern and Chatham Railway, the engine had a 6ft diameter boiler. (BS)

trains they had to pull. Having seen Churchward's Class 2800 2-8-0s, introduced and operating so successfully on GWR metals, he was determined to explore the benefits such a type might offer.

The 2-8-0, or Class 01 as it became known, was another design that would undergo change. It adopted many features included in Gresley's Moguls – two cylinders, 21in by 28in, coupled to Walschaert valve gear and a 24-element superheater. And the design also mounted the largest boiler so far built by the GNR and owed much to Ivatt's work in this field. It had a combined heating surface of 2,654sq ft and the engines produced a tractive effort of 31,860lb. This exceeded Ivatt's Q series, including those modified by Gresley during 1913 and '14, by replacing their saturated type boilers with superheated versions, by a margin of between 2,000 and 5,000lb.

Although the O1 proved successful, their number was insufficient to meet the growing amount of freight traffic the GNR was now attracting. It had become

apparent that something stronger was needed to haul these heavier trains.

In May 1918, Gresley added a three-cylinder version, the O2, constructing one single locomotive, No 461, to test the principle. In many ways this was his most ambitious design so far, because it brought together many ideas he would use regularly in the future as he searched for greater efficiency and better performance. The war made speculative new construction very difficult, but didn't stop him or his team considering the future as a paper exercise at least. But as the hostilities wound down, and a return to normal business began, Gresley was encouraged to develop his thoughts and begin building locomotives again. 461 became the focal point for these efforts and came to be considered a test bed for new ideas. In this, he basically took the O1 design and fitted three smaller in line 18in by 26im cylinders with external Walschaert gear connected to the inside cylinder by a conjugated valve gear.

In the trials that followed, primarily hauling heavy coal trains between London and Peterborough, the engine showed itself to be superior to the O1s. And, as the trials progressed, Gresley began the process of refining his ideas, seeking out Holcroft along the way to discuss the concept, for which they shared credit.

Although proving to be a success, No. 461 didn't immediately lead to more O2s being built. Ten were eventually constructed for the GNR by the North British Railway Company in 1921, then fifteen more followed from the Doncaster Works during 1923/24, with another forty-one gradually appearing, in three more batches, by 1943. It

wasn't a massive programme, but the railways had had to absorb many hundreds of ex-War Office 8Ms when the conflict ended, so the need for more GNR O2s was hardly a pressing one. But No. 461's real significance lay in the way it encouraged Gresley to push ahead with his proposals for more three-cylinder designs. This he did with great enthusiasm with a new 2-6-0 Mogul that appeared in 1920 and with it the distinctive look of a 'Gresley engine' began to take shape.

Evolution will often see a number of small, almost imperceptible, changes being made before a perceived master work appears. And so it was with Gresley as he gained expertise, grew in confidence and explored new ideas and options. The new mixed traffic engine was a step change that came to be seen as marking a boundary between the past and the future. It was a feeling visually reinforced when the first of the new H4 (K3) class engines, No. 1000, appeared in the early months of 1920. With an immense 6ft diameter boiler, the largest to appear on a British engine up to that time, the new locomotive was, to say the least, imposing. However, it was a project that had taken quite a long time to come to fruition. This was partly due to restrictions imposed by the war, but also the need to develop the concept of a three-cylinder engine with a conjugated valve gear to an acceptable level. There were also concerns that an engine with such a large boiler might be too large for the loading gauge permissible on the railway. As these problems were gradually resolved, the design came together and, as O S Nock reported in his classic book *Locomotives of*

Sir Nigel Gresley, word soon spread through the railway world that something special was on the way – '… after the Armistice the news got about that a "super" main line locomotive was under construction at Doncaster; everything pointed to a Prairie at least, if not a Pacific, and then No.1000 came out. This remarkable engine created quite a stir at the time …'

If this heightened sense of expectation did really exist, it may well have been actively encouraged by Gresley and the GNR. As events would soon show, the art of Public Relations had been more widely embraced by a country grown used to high levels of propaganda of one sort or another during the war. And with these new-found techniques, reputations were built and prestige enhanced, not solely with the aim of increasing demand or profits. In Gresley's new Mogul engine there was much to be exploited, even though only ten were built initially and then were employed solely on fast freight duties for a time. Here they proved themselves to be effective engines, especially during the 1921 miners' strike, when severe wage reductions were imposed on workers. Many engines of different types, the H4s amongst them, were pressed into service to ensure that

an adequate supply of coal was maintained.

Once this was over, they took up the other duties for which they had been designed and began pulling passenger trains between Doncaster and London. With their immense strength, and a tractive effort of 30,031lb, loads of 600 tons were not uncommon. As records show, even with nineteen carriages they could keep to scheduled times, maintaining an average speed of 50mph in the process. However, their riding qualities were described as 'lively at speed', which may well have been an understatement. Nevertheless, the crews must have relished being able to ride on the footplate of such strong engines, with their reserves of power, no matter what the load.

In many ways, all these classes of locomotives, no matter how successful, are now perceived as a series of steps in Gresley's rise to prominence. Stride by stride he seemed to be heading for something of greater significance – something that would come to define his career. However, at the core of Gresley's strategy lay the ambition for bigger, more powerful engines and a desire to explore the Pacific concept, a type for which there appeared to be a growing demand.

When peace was finally declared in 1919, the railways could again look to the future and consider ways in which they could serve communities undergoing rapid change. One of the pressing issues to be addressed was the ever growing requirement of people commuting into towns and cities, for work and pleasure, as hinterlands rapidly expanded. It was a level of traffic that was expected to rise as the economy returned to normal and servicemen were demobbed and returned to work. Or, at least, this was the hope, because no one could predict with any certainty how quickly Britain's industries would recover. Nevertheless, businesses have to plan well ahead and assume that the economy will continue to grow, recession be avoided, and demand increase.

It was this desire to meet such a demand that lay at the roots of Gresley's plans for both locomotives and rolling stock. Only time would tell if the market could support such expansion and, if so, where this might lead. In 1921, the GNR were prepared to gamble and in Gresley they had a man who would take up this challenge and, within the financial restrictions imposed upon him, develop bigger and better solutions, including a new Pacific class of locomotive.

BIGGER AND BETTER

As 1920 dawned, it was clear to many in the railway industry that change was in the air. Although central government had released control of the network back to individual businesses, four years of their direct management had revealed much about the state of the industry – its inefficiencies and, in some cases,

its poor financial controls. For every company such as the GWR, North Eastern and Great Northern there seemed to be a number that survived on a wing and a prayer. Many in Whitehall thought it was time for change to ensure that the railways were fit for purpose. Nationalisation was on the cards, as it would be again in 1945, but this time the powers that be, which

were wedded to the concepts of free trade and market forces, baulked at such an idea and looked for an alternative. While these issues were debated, Gresley got down to the serious business of developing new locomotives and rolling stock.

At the same time, his Board of Directors considered the thorny issue of funding these projects while paying to restore infrastructure to

For the GNR, the immediate post war years were a time of re-establishing many business practices overtaken by the conflict. Travelling for pleasure had virtually ceased to exist, most services being packed with troops going to or from the war or those commuting to work, but most of these were over relatively short distances. When it came to industry, only those supporting the war effort could claim any priority, while other businesses had to tag along as best they could. 1920/21 saw the beginnings of a revival and a bustling King's Cross (above left) captures the mood of the time with a multitude of trains, including a Gresley Mogul and 0-6-2 tank engines, for both long and short haul traffic, in evidence. (Above right) The GNR's PR Department soon began the process of advertising their holiday services, but in the first instance used many pre-war style posters such as this. They would soon have more modern, Art Deco style images to use, reflecting a modernising country. (RH)

its pre-war condition, with minimal government support. The problems were many and varied and not helped by the shortage of skilled workers as the loss of three quarters of a million men hit home, let alone the huge number of ex-servicemen severely maimed by the war who were now unable to do the work for which they had been trained. It would take British industry many decades to recover from this loss, which would only partially be made up by women workers.

If the railways faced an uncertain future, it was an uncertainty felt by many people and industries at the time. Any expectation that the population had of better living conditions, higher pay or an end to the slums that blighted most towns and cities, were soon dashed, although promises of better times ahead came only too easily to the lips of the country's leaders. With huge levels of national debt to service, austere housekeeping measures would trump all other considerations until the economy picked up. As history shows, it would be a long haul, with many ups and downs along the way.

Nevertheless, by 1920/21 some businesses, particularly the bigger railway companies, found their revenue increasing in a modest way suggesting that the worst might be over. It was also true to say that many people lucky enough to be in work felt the time was right to begin spending again – on their homes, social lives and, possibly, holidays. It wasn't a sudden rush, after four very difficult years such a thing was unlikely, but there were signs that consumer spending was increasing in certain quarters, though not for the masses just yet.

So, now, some companies probably thought, might be the time to begin investing in the future again. The risks were certainly high, but so would the profits if these forecasts came true.

For the GNR and Gresley this meant building bigger, more efficient locomotives capable of pulling increasingly heavy loads without the need for costly double-heading, especially over long distances. If anything, this was a message that had been driven home during the war years when the need to move men and materials in vast quantities to feed the front line had quickly exposed many operating weaknesses. For the Great Northern, Gresley's five large O1 2-8-0s built in 1913 had begun to show the way, but the impact of such a small number of engines could not hope to make a significant inroad into

such a colossal undertaking. But the point had been made and now was the time to develop these bigger engines to pull both heavier and longer passenger and freight trains. For Gresley, this meant developing ideas he had been rehearsing in one way or another for some time. So he focussed on building more 2-8-0s and considering a large new passenger engine, with a Pacific type one possibility. And here he could look to developments elsewhere in the world for inspiration. It's probably true to say that there was much for him to observe and consider.

In many ways, engineers in the USA had been at the forefront in developing many locomotive designs over the years with 2-6-0 and 2-8-0 classes, amongst others, being central to their efforts. Designers elsewhere may have

By 1921, Gresley's policy of building large 2-8-0 goods engines had proven itself, allowing the GNR to increase its freight traffic considerably. By that year, twenty-one, including the singleton engine No 461 above, were in service and would be followed by another twenty-four between 1921 and 1924. If a clear demonstration of the benefits of having bigger engines was needed, this programme certainly provided it. (BS)

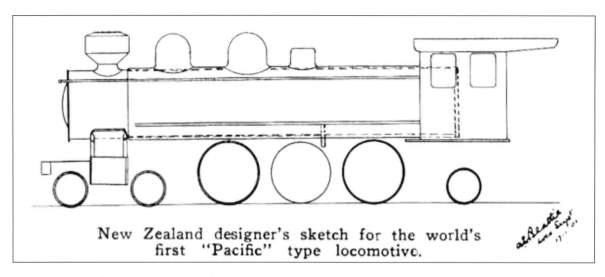

New Zealand designer's sketch for the world's first "Pacific" type locomotive.

The New Zealand Q Class that appeared in 1901 is considered to be the first serious attempt by designers to produce a Pacific locomotive. (RH)

taken this research further, but the conceptual work can often be traced back to developments in the States and the 4-6-2s were no different. It was, of course, an evolutionary process as engineers sought to improve performance with bigger boilers and fireboxes, which was found to be best achieved by extending the frames and providing trailing wheels so helping to distribute weight more evenly.

One of the first steps in this process took place in 1887 when engineers from the Baldwin Locomotive Works, employed by the Lehigh Valley Railroad to construct and maintain its engines, decided to fit a new firebox to one of its 4-6-0 locomotives and found that this caused a severe imbalance which could only be counteracted by fitting a rear bogie. However, after this initial work, Baldwin's

chose to take the concept no further for reasons that aren't entirely clear. However, two years later the Chicago, Milwaukie and St Paul Railway decided to revive this research and rebuilt an existing 4-6-0 locomotive with trailing wheels in an attempt to reduce its high axle loading. Whether the company were encouraged in this by Baldwin's isn't clear, but there would undoubtedly have been a business relationship of sorts between them that might have encouraged the project. Once again, further development wasn't pursued, and all remained quiet on the Pacific front until 1896 when six 3ft 6in gauge Q class 4-6-2 tank locomotives were introduced by the Western Australian Government Railways. Unfortunately, any test data or reports describing how these engines performed do not seem to have survived nor, for that matter, any drawings or photographs.

However, the next development of note in the Pacific story occurred on the other side of the Tasman Sea in New Zealand and appears to have had no direct connection with the narrow gauge Q Class engines built for use in Australia.

During 1901, the NZ Railway's Chief Mechanical Engineer, Alfred Beattie, appears to have issued a specification to Baldwin's for thirteen new engines. Having considered this requirement, and concluded that the boiler and firebox could only effectively be mounted if a trailing bogie was fitted, engineers in the States suggested that 4-6-2 solution be adopted. In the negotiation that followed, Baldwin's managers seem to have persuaded Beattie that it would be prudent to accept this solution and allow them to build the new engines as Pacifics and from these discussions the first major class of 4-6-2s emerged.

From the few reports written in these early years, it seems that this wheel arrangement was seen as allowing larger boilers to be fitted, offered greater strength and stability particularly when travelling at speed, helped produce a higher tractive effort and, possibly, increased their efficiency and economy. It is also interesting to note that within three years of the Beattie 4-6-2s appearing, an inventory of locomotives in the States reveals that 233 Pacifics had entered service, 85 of which were four-cylinder compounds. Sadly, these records are very thin in detail, making it difficult to understand how and why this sudden boom in numbers took place. However, a boom it was and by 1930, 6,800 Pacific locomotives had been built for domestic use, with another 500 or so going for export. With so much going on, it would have been surprising if Gresley, and many other engineers around the world, hadn't been influenced by what was happening in the States.

How word of these developments spread across the Atlantic to Europe is unclear, but the engineering world is one informed by the work of many institutions and societies. Membership of these bodies helped spread new ideas across international and political boundaries and opened up many discussions that could take new ideas further forward. So, as the first decade of the twentieth century passed, word filtered through from

An inventory of main-line steam locomotives in the United States completed during 1904 identified 233 Pacifics in service across the country. Other than this broad summary, the information provided is very slight so giving few guides to the design of the engines involved. Intriguingly, two photographs have come to light and show two Union Pacific Railroad Pacifics in service during 1904, numbered 112 and 119 (shown above). (JC)

During 1907, the French engineer George Solacroup, with the help of Alfred De Glehn, introduced the first European 4-6-2s when building two prototype Pacifics for the Compagnie Du Paris-Orleans, of which he was Chief Mechanical Engineer. These four-cylinder compound engines proved so successful that the PO would build another 277 Pacifics, while other French companies built an additional 1,087 4-6-2 engines of varying types over the years. (BS)

New Zealand and the USA that the 4-6-2 concept was an idea for designers in Europe to explore and develop as they saw fit. In France, George Solacroup, Chief Engineer of the Compagnie Du Paris-Orleans, was probably the first to take up

this particular baton. With the help of Alfred De Glehn, he produced a four-cylinder compound Pacific in July 1907, beating similar projects in Britain and Germany into production by, in one case, a very narrow margin indeed.

The German Baden IVf 4-6-2s were nearly the first Pacifics built in Europe and might have appeared in 1905 except for some production or design problems at the J.A. Maffei Works in Munich. During these delays, the Compagnie Du Paris-Orleans stole a march and produced two prototype Pacifics in July 1907 a few weeks before the Maffei engines appeared. The IVfs were a mixed success, their main operating problem being caused by the comparatively small size of their driving wheels. It was a shortcoming apparently corrected with the IVhs that came out in 1918. The attempt at streamlining the IVfs is interesting, a coned nose and wedge-shaped cab being the most obvious developments. Even at this stage, the concepts being explored by aerodynamics and hydrodynamics were entering the minds of railway engineers. (BS)

Solacroup's aim was a simple one. He wished to increase the boiler and smokebox dimensions of his 1903 built 4-6-0s (Class 4000) because he had come to believe that they were underpowered. Faced with the limitations imposed by this design on the size of the firebox and boilers they could carry, he decided to experiment with a 4-6-2 design instead. In doing so he introduced a trapezoid shaped firebox – wide at the rear and narrow at the front – which allowed the heating surface to be increased. This interestingly shaped smokebox he found could be comfortably fitted between the driving wheels and this allowed its weight to be distributed further forward giving the engine a better balance. Unlike Gresley, Solacroup saw merit in having a Belpaire firebox and appears, from the few photos available, to have installed them in these two Pacifics. In addition, the HP cylinders that lay outside were served by piston valves that drove the second coupled axle, while the LP cylinders were inside the frames with slide valves that drove onto the forward axle.

The result of this work were two prototypes that, although displaying a few teething problems, including a faulty exhaust nozzle, proved to be successful and encouraged the company to build another 277 Pacifics over the years, while across in France, others saw the design's merit and eventually produced another 1,087 Pacifics, making it one of the most numerous types of steam locomotive on the country's network. Designers in Germany soon followed suit and it was left to George Churchward at Swindon to introduce the type to Britain, even though he was, by all accounts, a less than enthusiastic contributor to the story.

The first French 4-6-2 only narrowly beat the first German Pacific into production. The Baden Class IVf was built for the Grand Duchy of Baden State Railways, based on a design produced by the Bavarian Company J.A. Maffei in 1905. However, due to manufacturing delays, the first three locomotives were not completed until 1907, a few weeks after Solacroup and De Glehn's Pacific appeared. The Baden IVfs

were four-cylinder compound locomotives which adopted many design principles explored in Germany by the Prussian State Railway's CME August von Borries, especially those contained in his successful 1899 introduced four-cylinder compound engines. After this initial batch of Baden IVf locomotives, a further thirty-two were built under license by Maschinenbau-Gesellschaft Karlsruhe and delivered during the years 1907 to 1913.

Although deemed a sound investment and successful in the mountainous regions of the Baden State Railway, their small driving wheels led to comparatively high revolutions per minute which caused some overheating and damage at high speed on level track. As a result, twenty modified Baden IVhs were built by Maffei and introduced between 1918 and 1920.

A year after the Class IVfs appeared, perhaps the most successful early German Pacific, the Bavarian S 3/6 class of the Royal Bavarian State Railways, designed by company engineers Anton Hammel and Heinrich Leppla, rolled out of the Maffei Works in Munich. This was a larger version of the Baden IVf class, retaining the four-cylinder compound arrangement, but suitably modified to overcome the perceived shortcomings of the earlier engines. Altogether, 159 of these locomotives were built between 1908 and 1931 and were deemed such a success that they were placed on display at the Exposition Universelle et Internationale de Bruxelles during 1910.

Interestingly, Oliver Bulleid was the exhibition's Mechanical and Electrical Engineer and in this important role had access to all the items on display and would have observed an Ivatt Atlantic alongside the German Pacifics. It isn't known whether Gresley visited Brussels to see the various locomotives on display. He may well have done, of course, and been influenced by what he saw there. But of equal importance to the future direction of the GNR's of locomotive policy was the fact that in 1912, Bulleid became Gresley's Personal Assistant and began advising him on design matters. It was a partnership that would profoundly affect railway history and so it is important to understand the dynamics of their relationship. But, equally so, it is appropriate to understand the external influences that may have come into play in the offices at Doncaster, as Pacifics were developed in the States, France and Germany in the early years of the century. Then there is the work of George Churchward to consider and how his sole Pacific engine, which began running in 1908, may have influenced Gresley's thinking.

Exposition Universelle et Internationale de Bruxelles en 1910
Locomotive expresse à quatre cylindres du type **Pacific**
construite par J. A. MAFFEI, Munich.

Timbre de la chaudière	. . . . .	15 Atm.	Surface de chauffe du foyer	. . . .	14,6 m. c.
Diamètre des cylindres à h. p.	. .	425 mm	Surface de chauffe des tubes	. . . .	203,8 "
Diamètre des cylindres à b. p.	. .	650 "	Surface de chauffe du surchauffeur	.	50,0 "
Course de pistons	. . . .	610/670 "	Surface de chauffe totale directe	. .	268,4 "
Diamètre des roues motrices	. . .	1870 "	Surface de grille	. . . .	4,5 "
Diamètre des roues porteuses	. .	950/1206 "	Poids en service	. . . .	86,5 "

Amongst his papers, Bert Spencer kept this postcard and other items from the 1910 Brussels Exhibition. He was only 12 at the time, and still at school, so was unlikely to have attended. This suggests they were part of Gresley's collection of papers that he took with him to Doncaster following the CME's death in 1941. Before taking up a new post there, he received a personal instruction from Edward Thompson to 'maintain Sir Nigel's papers and continue working on the ideas he had pursued regarding locomotives'. It is speculative, of course, but it is interesting to consider how the Pacific designs initiated by French and German designers may have influenced the CME's thinking, alongside those developed in the USA. (BS)

It seems that during 1906/07, the GWR 's designers began giving very serious thought to the idea of a Pacific and a year later a single experimental locomotive, 'The Great Bear' appeared. Its development has been the subject of much speculation because Churchward was thought to have been a less than enthusiastic supporter of the project from the first, mainly because it went against his stated preference for 4-6-0 classes of locomotives. However, it is likely that Gresley, who was a great admirer of Churchward, would have closely followed the progress of the GWR project. From any information he could glean he could then form

his own ideas on the design's strengths and weaknesses, as he worked towards his own solution.

Some observers, including the railway writer W.A. Tuplin, believed that the idea may have been forced on Churchward by his Board of Directors, led by Alfred Baldwin, who were eager to build the biggest passenger locomotive in Britain. If so, it was a project the GWR's publicity department seemed eager to trumpet. However, was this reason enough to sway such a man as Churchward? Probably not, but there is the possibility that he was promised something else to sweeten the pill

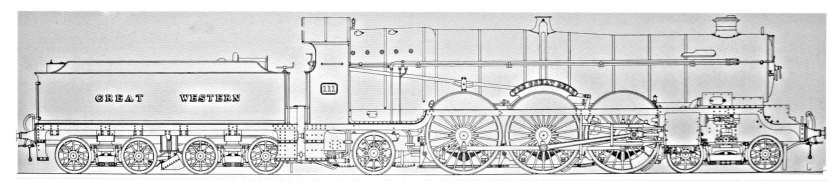

For a Pacific to be built at Swindon when Churchward had a clear preference for 4-6-0 engines indicates that the development path it took might not have been a straightforward one. For such a strongminded and dominating figure, he was unlikely to have acquiesced without good reason and during the course of his Pacific's life he displayed a somewhat ambivalent attitude towards it. Wherever the truth might lie, it was certainly an impressive looking engine, but in practice had limited route availability due to its axle loading and in service proved to be disappointing and not an improvement on existing classes. One critic observed that 'its excessive tube and barrel length of 23 feet made for bulk rather than efficiency', adding that 'the axle boxes of the trailing wheels tended to become overheated due to their proximity to the firebox, which did not endear it to the footplate crew or staff in the workshops'. However, it was to some a handsome engine as the two pictures above suggest. (BS)

so, perhaps grudgingly, acquiesced. Such is the way in any business.

However, O. S. Nock, the noted observer of railway matters, offered a different view when he wrote, in his book *The GWR Stars, Castles and Kings*:

The conception was entirely due to Churchward, and not to outside influences that pressed the project upon him… The suggestion of a super locomotive was accepted by the Board and on 30th January 1907 a sum of £4,400 was voted for the construction of it, while a subsequent vote of £800 was made to cover additional expenditure … Churchward had already shown himself one of the most far-sighted of British locomotive engineers, and such was the upward surge in traffic resulting from the enterprising new services out into operation since 1906 that he foresaw the time when his four-cylinder 4-6-0s would be extended to their limit. It was not his nature to allow himself to be overtaken by circumstances, and the building of a Pacific was a step towards the provision of still greater power.

To this he later added that this four-cylinder, superheated locomotive was built 'primarily as an exercise in boiler design', with Churchward seeking to experiment before developing newer more powerful 4-6-0s.

If this is so, Churchward seemed to display a certain ambivalence to the project when in 1906, with the design in its infancy and still unfunded, he pointed out to his

Directors that a 4-6-2 class engine would be bigger than required at that time, but that such a design was currently being prepared. These words tend to suggest a lack of enthusiasm on his part, but also seem to indicate an acceptance of the inevitable. However, it was not an experiment he repeated, and it is perhaps most telling that he chose not to build any more of the type, focussing instead on the next stage of his 4-6-0 programme. Wherever the truth of the matter might lie, it was a project that caught Gresley's eye, although in 1908, when the *Great Bear* appeared, it would be some years before he felt able to follow suit. It is also clear that Nock's statement contains words that Gresley might himself have used when justifying the construction of his first Pacifics.

So, how much influence did the GWR Pacific have on Gresley's plans for the future? Here, Bert Spencer is probably our best guide, having sat beside Gresley for so many years at King's Cross and absorbed so much information from his leader. He later wrote:

Sir Nigel occasionally spoke about Churchward's 'Great Bear' and it certainly lay at the heart of his own plans for just such a locomotive. Whenever the subject of the Pacifics came up the CME would occasionally recall a letter he had received from the GWR man in 1922, when the first of the GNR's engines appeared, suggesting he could have had their 4-6-2 for a very good price and not built his own! I suspected that the two men had discussed the GNR's plans and at some time

Gresley had acquired many of the GWR's drawings. There was an album of photographs of the engine as well, taken during construction and then running on various duties. It had a dark green leather jacket and GWR embossed in gold centrally on the cover and resided in the CME's office. I believe it was a personal gift from Churchward and was passed to Arthur Peppercorn in due course, who, I seem to remember, kept it when he retired in 1949. It wasn't unusual for 'rival' companies to share information in this way. When speaking to Tom Colman [the LMS's Chief Draughtsman] years later he recalled that Stanier had a set of drawings and album too from Churchward, though he didn't say if Churchward's work had been used in any way.

With so much development work going on round the world, and many examples of 4-6-2s to consider, when did Gresley first come to see a Pacific as the way ahead for the GNR? Was it a sudden flash of inspiration or a slowly emerging belief that this concept could meet the company's developing passenger needs? Engineering, it seems, rarely has eureka moments. In truth, advances tend to follow a slow evolutionary process in which many ideas are considered and tried until a combination is found that meets a given or projected need. In some cases, this may take many years to come about and will have taken designers down many dead-end streets as they struggle for solutions. The Gresley Pacifics

were just such a case and, as we have seen, there was a great deal going on elsewhere to consider as he made his way along this particular path.

In some ways, Henry Ivatt did some of the groundwork for Gresley in producing a bigger engine. In the early years of the nineteenth century, he and his team began exploring designs for such a locomotive to pull ever increasing loads more effectively. Much of this effort focussed on a new locomotive primarily to pull fast freight trains, but, undoubtedly, it would have had a mixed traffic capability. As a result of this, his Chief Draughtsman, William Elwess, produced a 2-6-2 tender engine four-cylinder compound design in 1907 that carried an Atlantic type boiler and wide firebox. Such a locomotive, if built, could have shone a light on the need for an even bigger engine, with a Pacific being the natural outcome. Instead of this, the 2-6-2 tender engine concept was not fully explored by the GNR or LNER for nearly three decades, until Gresley's V2s appeared in 1936.

While this was going on, Gresley sat on the periphery of locomotive design at Doncaster. As Carriage and Wagon Superintendent, he would probably have been aware of ideas being developed but had no need to be directly involved, unless Ivatt or Elwess sought his opinion on some matter. This they may have done, Gresley being noted for his grasp of the key issues involved, but these conversations, if they took place, would have been in private and so in the margins of any work being undertaken. Post 1911, when Gresley replaced Ivatt, this would

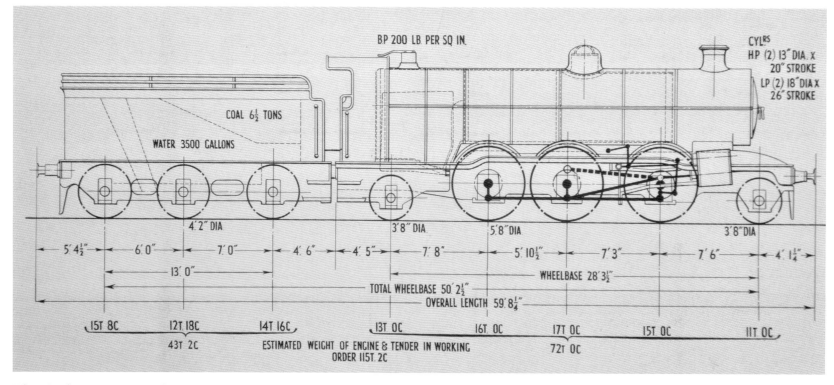

BP 200 LB PER SQ IN.

CYL^RS
HP (2) 13" DIA. X 20" STROKE
LP (2) 18" DIA X 26" STROKE

COAL 6½ TONS

WATER 3500 GALLONS

4' 2" DIA.   3' 8" DIA.   5' 8" DIA.   3' 8" DIA

5' 4½"   6' 0"   7' 0"   4' 6"   4' 5"   7' 8"   5' 10½"   7' 3"   7' 6"   4' 1¼"

13' 0"   WHEELBASE 28' 3½"

TOTAL WHEELBASE 50' 2½"
OVERALL LENGTH 59' 8¼"

15T 8C   12T 18C   14T 16C   13T 0C   16T 0C   17T 0C   15T 0C   11T 0C
43T 2C   ESTIMATED WEIGHT OF ENGINE & TENDER IN WORKING   72T 0C
ORDER 115T. 2C

When Gresley was Carriage and Wagon Superintendent at Doncaster, Henry Ivatt embarked on designing a mixed traffic 2-6-2 tender engine which he believed was necessary to pull increasingly longer and heavier fast freight trains. As a result, this design appeared during 1907, but never got beyond the drawing board for reasons that aren't entirely clear. However, cost may have been a factor, so might its axle loading and perhaps a lack of ambition amongst company's Directors in the face of less than expected revenue returns. Its long term value to the GNR may have been that it formalised the thoughts designers may have had on the way locomotive design should move – bigger and better. It certainly set down a template for Gresley to explore a few years later when considering a 4-6-2 engine with some elements of the Ivatt 2-6-2 finding their way into early options explored in a proposed GNR Pacific in 1914/15. (RH)

all have changed, with Elwess and his team dancing to a quite different tune.

On promotion to Locomotive Engineer, and before ringing in any changes he wished to make, Gresley had to convince his Chairman, William Jackson, 1st Baron Allerton, that his ideas were viable and could be kept within a restricted budget. This businessman and politician, who was responsible for first recruiting Gresley to the GNR's ranks and then promoting his career, was not averse to risk. However, the practicalities of running a business so dependent on market

forces would generally dictate prudence and minimal risk. As a result, Gresley's design ambitions tended to be more theoretical than practical, resulting, as we have seen, in few new locomotives. Then came the war and all was put on hold as Britain struggled to build a huge army to fight on continental Europe and help bring the war to a successful end.

It was during this period that the first designs for a new Pacific began to appear, building on the work Ivatt and Elwess had begun a few years earlier with their proposed 2-6-2 tender engine. While the chances of building even a single

4-6-2 during the war were slim, to say the least, it is likely that Jackson gave his protégé the freedom to experiment. And so the idea of a GNR Pacific was born, with the reality coming only when peace had returned and business had begun to pick up again. Sadly, by this time, Jackson, the great facilitator, was dead, passing away suddenly in 1917, leaving Sir Frederick Banbury to take up the reins as Chairman and allow Gresley to complete his work: until the creation of the LNER that is, when William Whitelaw took over. Although he worked well with each Chairman, the partnership with Whitelaw proved to be most productive of all, for both men.

If war hadn't come in the summer of 1914, progress on a new Pacific might have been more rapid, with its final form being very different to that which eventually appeared in 1922. By then, Gresley's work on three cylinders coupled to a conjugated valve gear, by then tested in his single Class 461 2-8-0 and then, in modified form, his 2-6-0 Class H4s, had been refined considerably, allowing him to work these ideas into other new designs.

So what might the 1915 Pacific have looked like if it had been built during the war? In looks it gave the impression of being a stretched version of Ivatt's proposed 2-6-2. In the 4-6-2's case, the four cylinders would have been 15in by 26in and would have driven on to the second axle. Piston valves were to be adopted, with the inside valves being activated by rocking shafts driven by external Walschaerts valve gear.

The boiler would have had a diameter of 5ft 6in and, following established practice at the time, would not have been tapered. The tube heating surface would have been 2,402sq ft, with 730sq ft of superheater surface and 150sq ft for the firebox. This was supported by a grate area of 36sq ft. and it was predicted that such a boiler would have produced a working pressure of 170lb and 21,139lb of tractive effort. Such a big engine was projected to have a wheelbase of nearly 34ft with a total weight producing an 18-ton axle load.

Although these proposals seem to have advanced a long way, the ever-worsening war situation ensured that that no metal would be cut, or frames laid until it had been fought to a successful conclusion. So, without a working engine how

The three company Chairmen who exercised the greatest influence on Gresley's career between 1905 and 1938 and played an active part in his emergence as a leading designer, but also in allowing him to develop a big engine policy to meet growing traffic needs. Each man seems to have recognised his potential as an engineer and leader and allowed him to flourish. Their trust would be repaid many times over. (Left to right) William Jackson, Baron Allerton, recruited Gresley and speculatively promoted him to senior rank when fairly young and largely untried. Sir Frederick Banbury, who succeeded Jackson in 1917 and oversaw and approved the successful development of the A1. William Whitelaw, who was chosen, over at least three other candidates, including Banbury, to be the first Chairman of the LNER and then led the CME through the most active and creative part of his career, producing the bulk of the A1s then the exemplary A3 and A4 Pacifics along the way. (THG)

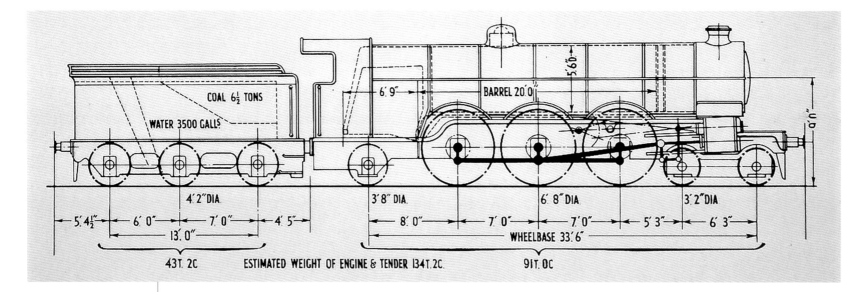

Though there may have been drawings of a proposed Pacific appearing earlier than this one, the first found in surviving records seems to be this diagram which was issued in 1915. It shows a locomotive that seems to have stretched Ivatt's proposed 1907 2-6-2 design to include a four wheeled front bogie. Gresley, it is suggested, believed this proposal was a combination of Ivatt's Atlantics and Churchward's four-cylinder engines. If so, it made an interesting combination and suggests in which way his thoughts were moving in 1915 before the full impact of his work on three-cylinder designs with a 2 to 1 valve gear had been realised. (BS)

can we assess the design and place it an historical context? Truth be told, we can't, but there are some indicators that we might consider when reaching any conclusions.

In his excellent book *Nigel Gresley. Locomotive Engineer*, E.A.S. Brown, when describing this project, provided an interesting summary. In 1961 he wrote that it 'gave the impression that Ivatt's influence was still strongly felt at Doncaster. Gresley is understood to have described the design as based on a combination of Ivatt's Atlantics and Churchward's four cylinder engines.'

Then we have experiments Gresley authorised, live trials to test out the effectiveness of his proposed four-cylinder Pacific. To do this, he authorised the rebuilding of two-cylinder Atlantic engine, No.279 in 1914/15, with four 15in diameter cylinders, a 24-element Robinson superheater with a 427sq ft heating surface and a boiler producing a slightly lower pounds per square inch of pressure (down from 175 to 170). Although the tractive effort was increased and the engine's

acceleration on the level and rising gradients was recorded as being good, overall, the improvements expected didn't materialise. It suffered, or so it seems, from, as Bert Spencer recalled many years later:

… a shortage of steam at times that meant the engine struggled even with moderate loads. This seems to have convinced Gresley that four cylinder engines were not the way ahead. Of course, by this time his experiments with the derived valve gear linked to three-cylinders were far advanced and had been patented so dominated his thinking.

It would be another five years, or so it seems from available records, before Gresley's next Pacific design appeared. By this time, his thoughts on the number of cylinders and valve gear to be employed had developed somewhat, informed by the construction of engine No. 461, which proved to be a useful test

bed for his ideas. In the meantime, Gresley took stock of what was happening elsewhere in the railway world, especially when it came to engines of the Pacific Class, to see if there were any ideas he might explore and possibly use in his own designs. In the States, there was just such a development taking place which might have had implications for what he was doing himself.

By 1920, the number of 4-6-2s in North America had risen exponentially with the Pennsylvania Railroad (PRR) becoming a leader in their use. This company was also advancing rapidly into the world of locomotive testing with the establishment of a purpose-built centre at Altoona in 1904. This was an event that Gresley was unlikely to have missed and in due course would become the strongest advocate for such a facility being built in Britain, though would not see its completion in his lifetime. While he watched and waited, an experimental 4-6-2 was constructed by the American Locomotive Company; a group formed in 1901 when seven

small locomotive builders merged with the Schenectady Locomotive Manufacturers of New York. Then, in 1905, under the presidency of Alfred Pitkin, they added the Rogers Locomotive Works of Paterson of New Jersey, the second largest locomotive builders behind Baldwin's, to their number. So armed, such a powerful company

had the resources to speculate and test new concepts. A new Pacific, given the number 50000, was just such an exercise and according to a published report this new engine was:

The first, example, of the 'heavy' Pacific, designed and built to handle the passenger trains

which were approaching 800/900 tons behind the tender, and at a time when such heavy trains were required to operate at speeds in the 60mph range and was the prototype for many future designs, including the K4s.

This locomotive had 79-inch drivers, a boiler producing 185 psi and a starting tractive effort

With the war hindering the business of engine design, Gresley could only develop his ideas for his first Pacific very slowly. In 1915 he had advanced sufficiently with a four-cylinder version to want to test some of his theories. This he did by converting a two-cylinder Ivatt Atlantic (No. 279, later on 3279, shown here) to four cylinders. The results were mixed and probably confirmed him in the belief that three cylinders would prove to be a better solution, accompanied by his conjugated valve gear, which that year he patented. No 279 remained in this condition until rebuilt as a two-cylinder engine in 1937. (RH)

Photos of the American Locomotive Company's experimental Pacific, No. 50000, of 1910 are few and far between. This rare picture appears to show the engine in its as built condition. A slightly heavier version, given the Class No. K29, was ordered by the PRR in 1911 and from this the first K4 Pacific eventually emerged three years later. (JC)

of 40,800 lbs. The grate area was 59.7 square feet, the firebox dimensions 114 x 75 inches. The tube length was 22 feet, and the total heating surface 4048 square feet … It is the first engine to have rationalised proportions of boiler, firebox and cylinders.

In the tests that followed, some in the Altoona Test Centre, the concept was proved to be sound and, having observed its development, the PRR decided to order a slightly heavier version for testing in 1911 to which they gave the classification K29. From this work, the company

The single K29 Pacific under undergoing trials in the Altoona Test Centre during 1912. If Gresley observed the development of this new Pacific with some interest, as he did the K4 that followed, the test centre would probably have been of equal, if not greater importance. He was convinced that just such a facility was needed in Britain if locomotive design were to advance in a more measured way. It was a cause that he championed until approval was finally given for such a facility to be built at Rugby in the run up to the Second World War. The new conflict frustrated these plans, and it wasn't until 1948 that it finally opened, when the end of steam was in sight and its use of rapidly reducing benefit. (JC)

Above and below: **Some railway** historians have recorded their belief that the PRR K4 Pacifics marked a step change in the design of 4-6-2s. This is a matter of opinion and these will always vary according to the views and loyalties of the person passing judgement. For myself, I tend to trust the views of Bert Spencer, Gresley's closest aide, who wrote that 'the K4, and the work that preceded it, keenly influenced the creation of the A1s'. Either way, the K4's proved to be very successful in service resulting in 425 being built by 1928. (JC)

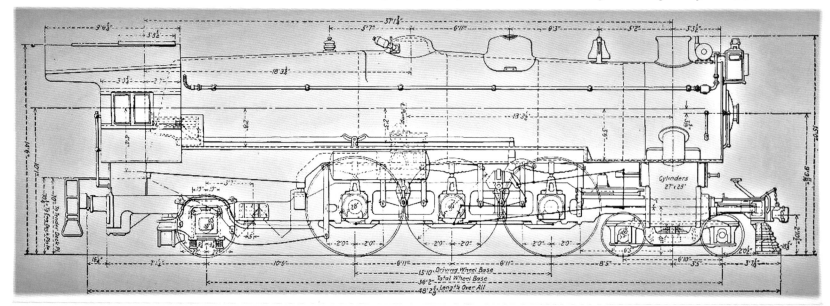

designed and built their K4 Pacifics, which emerged in 1914, with 425 being built by 1928. When asked late in life about the influence of the K4 had on Gresley's own Pacifics, Bert Spencer simply wrote:

The work undertaken by the Pennsylvania Railroad in constructing the K4 encouraged Gresley in his efforts to develop his own 4-6-2. Although there were many other examples of the type that had received some publicity it was this class, and the two engines that had preceded it [No. 50000 and its heavier derivative] that impressed him most. In fact, it was the detailed account that appeared in a 1916 edition of 'Engineering' that he studied closely and kept amongst his papers, and it was this that seemed to encourage him to look beyond his 1915 Pacific design. By this time, I was a draughtsman at Doncaster and it was common knowledge that the K4, and the work that preceded it, had keenly influenced the creation of the A1.

The K4 was designed by a team lead by the PRR's Chief of Motive Power, J.T. Wallis, with Chief Mechanical Engineer Alfred W. Gibbs and Mechanical Engineer Axel Vogt taking day to day responsibility for the project. Initially, it was developed alongside the L1 2-8-2 Mikado, and as will often happen in these situations, they shared many common features including the boiler. However, as we have also seen, it drew more heavily on the design of the

experimental American Locomotive Company Pacific and the K29 that followed. It is also recorded that the K4 design adopted some ideas explored by Gibbs when producing his E6 Atlantic – in particular its heat-treated, lightweight machinery, a three-bar slidebar and crosshead and cast-steel trailing truck.

The two-cylinder K4 carried Walschaerts valve gear and piston valves, which drove to the middle axle. A large 7ft 5in diameter boiler, tapering to 6ft 6½ in, containing tubes 19ft in length, and generating 205psi, was used and to this was attached a firebox which incorporated a combustion chamber 3ft long, measuring 70sqft. This combination is recorded as producing 44,460lb of tractive effort and reports suggest this greatly enhanced the K4s' steaming capability. Equipment, which has been described as quite basic by some observers, did include lightweight three-bar crossheads, a screw reverse, which was soon upgraded to power reverse, and a tender that could carry 7,000 gallons of water and 12½ tons of coal. Although the design would be modified over the years, it was this prototype that received wide publicity during 1916 and which Gresley may have found so illuminating, according to Spencer.

It is interesting to speculate why this was so, especially with so many other noteworthy examples available for scrutiny, including Churchward's *Great Bear*, which was physically within easier reach. So, was it the specifics of the K4 design that influenced Gresley or were broader, more conceptual issues at play here? There were, of course, some key differences between

the two designs. Chief amongst them was the Wallis, Gibbs, Vogt preference for two cylinders, which was hardly in line with Gresley's thoughts at that time but had proved itself an effective solution during the trials at Altoona. However, with his work on three-cylinder designs successfully advancing by 1920, it was unlikely that the PRR preference would find favour with Gresley, though as Spencer related, 'three-cylinders were not everyone's cup of tea at Doncaster and some felt that two or four would have better suited such a large express locomotive as the A1'. If so, any contrary voices failed to alter the direction in which the Locomotive Engineer was travelling and three cylinders and the 2 to 1 valve gear remained his firm, and apparently unalterable, choice.

For Spencer the K4's chief influence on Gresley lay in:

The overall balance of its design, in terms of the ratio between the size of boiler tubes (which followed the Pennsylvania 19 footers), heating surfaces and cylinder volumes, was what caught his eye. Then there were such things as the use made of lightweight materials for many components such as the crossheads that impressed as did their use of tapered boilers, rather than one of a parallel type, which had found favour with the GNR up to that time. By adopting this alternative design, the boiler was made more efficient, when coupled to a wider firebox, because the passage of steam was improved and the loss of heat as steam

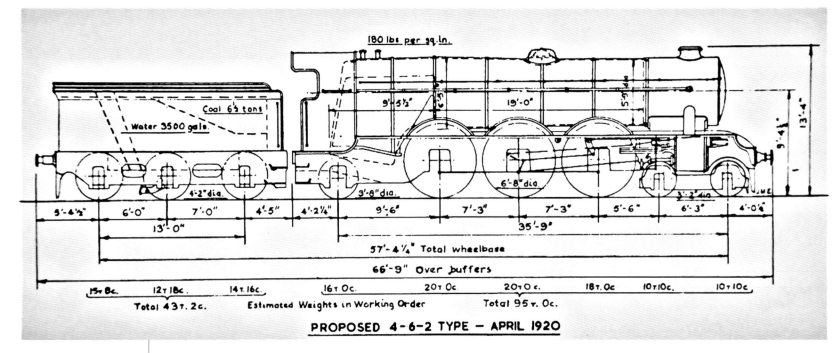

PROPOSED 4-6-2 TYPE – APRIL 1920

There were probably interim designs between the 1915 Pacific and the 1920 version, but, if they exist, they don't seem to have come to light yet. This new version still has a slight Ivatt look about it – the cab's design being chiefly responsible for this – but underneath there were many differences. Chief amongst them was three cylinders and conjugated valve gear and a boiler that adopted the design principles that had evolved in the States with the PRR's K4 Pacifics. The final stage of the A1s' evolution is now on course and with further refinements added to the design will finally appear in 1922. (BS)

passed through the tubes was reduced. In addition, with its downward sloping tapered front end, the engines were made lighter which increased the rate of acceleration, reduced coal and water consumption and lowered the axle loading which greatly pleased the Civil Engineers when they came to consider the merits of the A1s hammer blow and weight on structures that might need strengthening.

It is probably true to say that although the K4s boiler was of a very large diameter and as a result, far too large and heavy for Britain's loading gauge, it could be adapted for use in a scaled down form to suit our needs, which is what happened at Doncaster.

This would seem to be the crux of the matter as far as Gresley

was concerned. Here was a design that identified a new way of doing things and contained sufficient flexibility for him to adapt its working principles to his needs. It would also have helped considerably that these engines, and the two prototypes that preceded them, had been extensively tested at Altoona, as well as being assessed in day to day service. So, it would seem that his 1920 Pacific design absorbed many lessons learnt by his colleagues in the States, with his own specific ideas added, including three cylinders and conjugated valve gear. And with this Gresley gradually moved his design forward, gained approval from Banbury and the Board to build the first batch of engines and proceed to the final stage of his 4-6-2 programme and begin construction of the first two locomotives.

As the new decade began it must have been with a keen sense of

anticipation that the draughtsmen at Doncaster began the final stages of the Pacific project, with the aim of getting both engines in service during 1922. With such a stimulating project to absorb them it must have seemed that the gloom that had descended during and after the war was finally lifting a little, although there would still have been daily reminders of the terrible price that had been paid for victory all around them. But this was a positive step towards better times and here again Spencer again caught a flavour of the atmosphere in the Drawing Office:

[We were] aware that something was in the wind and a high degree of secrecy was the order of the day. We heard rumours that the North Eastern Railway were working on their own Pacific at Darlington and we were imbued with a sense of

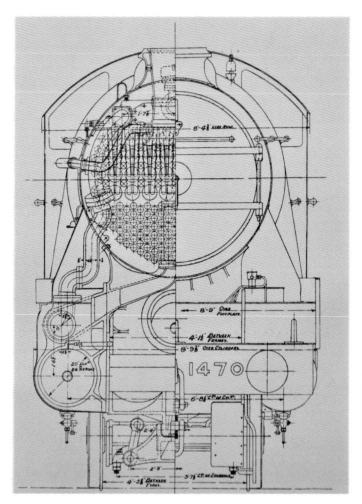
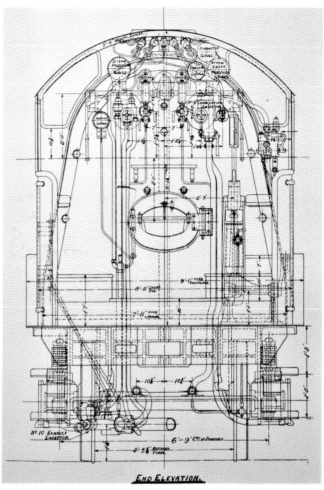

END ELEVATION.

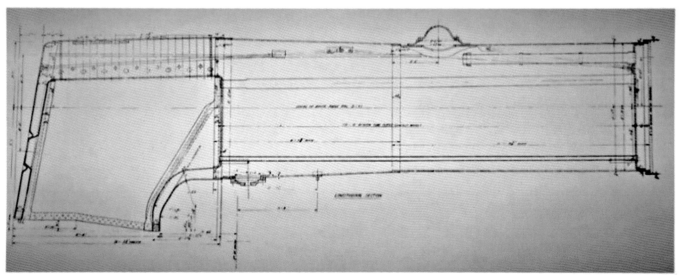

This page and overleaf: Amongst his collection of papers, Spencer kept a number of drawings showing the layout and fine detail of the first two A1 Pacifics, far more than any other locomotive he worked on except the A4s. These are just six of many drawings he kept from this period. At the time, he was a junior draughtsman at Doncaster, and this was his first major project so was undoubtedly memorable for that reason. However, when he came to describe the project, in his 1947 paper to the ILocoE, his words were brief and understated, which belies the impact working on such a project must have had on him. These drawings cover the most important elements of the A1s design – its general arrangement, plus boiler, cylinders, smokebox, cab and tender. (BS)

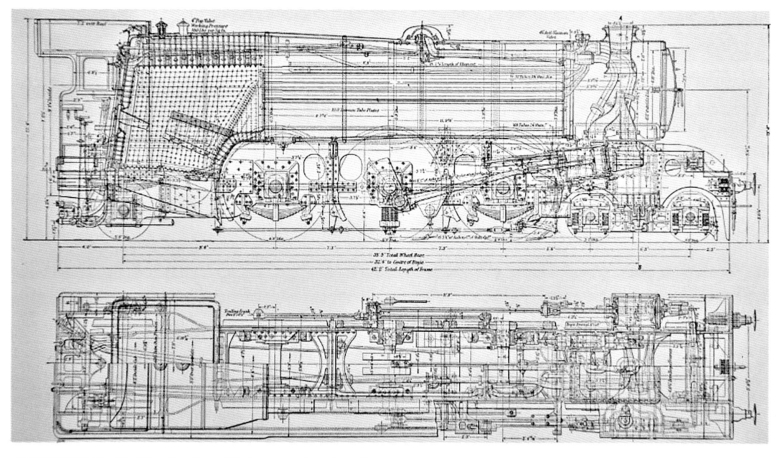

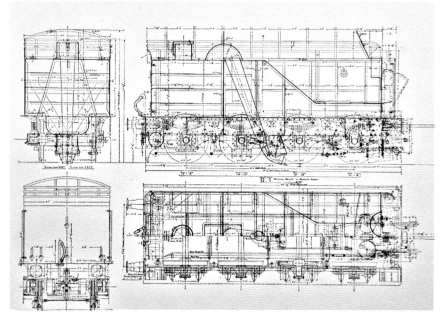

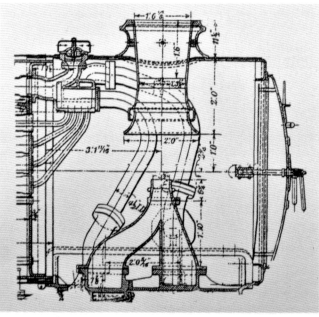

rivalry and wished to be first. Of course, by this stage the GWR's *Great Bear* had been running for many years, so the GNR's Pacific would not have been the first in the field, but Swindon had abandoned theirs and were only concerned with building more of their impressive 4-6-0s.

However, in his 1947 presentation to the ILocoE, he tended to play down this major step forward and the huge impact the A1s had. In fact, his words barely caused a ripple, so understated were they:

The increasing necessity on the GNR for an express passenger engine of greater power than the Atlantic type led to the adoption of a 4-6-2 type three-cylinder engine. The first of these engines, No. 1470 *Great Northern*, was the forerunner of the LNER streamlined Pacifics, was completed at Doncaster Works in April 1922. Classified A1, these engines had 6ft 8in diameter wheels and 20in x 26in cylinders. The design incorporated the form of Gresley gear employed on the H4/K3 and later 02 Classes, the outside cylinders being placed horizontally over the bogie, and the centre cylinder being inclined at 1 in 8 and located over the rear axle of the bogie. As in the case of the H4/K3 and 02 Classes, the drive from all three-cylinders was taken by the second pair of coupled wheels.

As the project moved to completion, the working relationship between Gresley and his draughtsmen

FOUR STAGES IN THE CONSTRUCTION OF A "PACIFIC" LOCOMOTIVE AT DONCASTER WORKS

The Frames in Position.

Cylinders and Valve-chests attached.

The Boiler and Firebox mounted.

The Finished Locomotive.

Photos: L.N.E.Ry.

seemed to become even closer. He was someone who certainly took a 'hands on' approach as Spencer later recalled:

Gresley always paid close attention to all parts of a design, whether large or small. He took a particular interest in the cab arrangements for No.1470 and a full-size wooden model was erected in the pattern shop at Doncaster before the engine was built. This was inspected by all and sundry, but particularly the 'top link' drivers and firemen who were encouraged to voice their opinions, and these we considered in refining the layout. But before building this model there was much discussion over of the most

suitable height at which to place the firehole of the new class in relation to the cab footboards. To obtain a better idea of this Sir Nigel had chalked upon one side of a Drawing Office desk an oval shape representing the fire hole. Then towards this he shovelled imaginary coal with his walking stick until he was certain that we had the correct height for a fireman off average build. When the wooden model and then the locomotive were built he would examine them with the same critical eye, making changes as necessary. He was a perfectionist.

Gresley would often visit the Drawing Office and happily discuss with one and all his ideas. He liked to give tasks to the

Spencer also kept a series of photos and articles, of which this is one, showing No. 1470 being built at Doncaster. As an up and coming designer, he was clearly fascinated by the project, was eager to learn from all he saw. He later wrote that 'working beside a skilled leader and his team was a wonderful experience and taught me much at an important stage in my career'. (BS)

Engine No. 1470, now named *Great Northern* and resplendent in its GNR livery, photographed at Doncaster having only recently been built in 1922. This colour scheme, which Spencer thought 'suited the engine very well', will quickly give way to the LNER's more familiar green. An opportunity will soon be taken to photograph No.1470 beside the Atlantic engines she will be superseding, making the increase in size of the company's high profile new passenger locomotives only too apparent. (BS)

young and inexperienced men, to test them and see how they would react. It may have been one of the ways he learnt himself when starting out and it certainly worked. He would set aside time in his very busy schedule to listen to their answers and proposals, with the full agreement of the Chief Draughtsman, who might in other circumstances have felt by-passed.

He believed that learning didn't have a limit and should be pursued as a matter of course through education and the study of other people's work in many fields of research. We were encouraged to join relevant bodies such as the IMechE and IlocoE, participate in their work and keep up to date by reading their journals as well as the 'Engineer', 'Gazette' and other magazines, but also follow the course of various patents, files of which we retained. I was also encouraged, early in my career to submit and comment on others. We were also encouraged to attend institution annual dinners where contacts could be made and renewed.

Gresley's influence on my career was only very slight

No. 1470 *Great Northern*, possibly in April 1922, drawing a crowd at King's Cross. Although the first of the class, she will soon be eclipsed by the arrival and ever increasing fame of No. 1472 *Flying Scotsman*, and quickly slip from the public view. Why this is so is not clear, but Spencer's suggestion that 'she wasn't one of the best' may offer some explanation for this. In 1945, she will be rebuilt by Edward Thompson and his team into a new form of Pacific in an attempt to eradicate problems believed to have developed with Gresley's valve gear. In addition, this work acted as a rehearsal for the development of the next stage of the LNER's Pacific programme. This was a move that later attracted much criticism for the apparent destruction of Gresley's 'masterpiece'. The truth of these claims has been long discussed and will probably never be satisfactorily resolved. (RH)

at the beginning and was limited to a few special tasks. For example, he asked me to consider the layout of the Pacific's cab. In this I adopted a side-window layout similar to those seen on some Great Eastern engines. I was pleased with the result and showed Sir Nigel during one of his visits. He liked it and ordered it to be fitted in place of a traditional GNR cab. After that the number of small tasks he set me increased.

All this work came together in April 1922 when the first engine, numbered 1470 and soon named *Great Northern,* rolled from the works at Doncaster and quickly drew the attention of a railway press eager to see Gresley's long awaited 'big engine'. From the accounts that have survived, they were clearly impressed and, when the locomotive was put on display at King's Cross the same month, the plaudits only increased. The tone of the reception can best be gauged by a report that appeared in May's edition of *Transport and Travel Monthly*:

The greatest advance in British locomotive practice for many years is that just made by Mr. H.N. Gresley, the Locomotive Engineer of the GNR. The new departure is the introduction of the 4-6-2 type locomotive for express passenger traffic.

The following are the chief dimensions of this locomotive. Diameter of six coupled wheels – 6ft 8in, diameter of bogie wheels – 3ft 2in and trailing wheels – 3ft 8in.

Cylinders – three with a diameter of 20 in and 26 in stroke. Boiler which is massive has a total heating surface of 3,455 sq ft, with a diameter of 6ft 5in at its broadest which tapers down at its front to 5ft 9in. The grate area is 41¼ sq ft. A working pressure of180 lbs per sq in. The boiler is equipped with a Robinson superheater having 32 elements. The wheelbase of the engine is 35ft 9in, wheelbase rigid – 14ft 6in, wheelbase of engine and tender – 60ft 10 5/8 in. Tender with eight non-bogie wheels carry's 8 tons of coal and 5,000 gallons of water.

The outside cylinders are placed horizontally over the bogie and drive to the middle pair of coupled wheels, the inside cylinder, at an inclination of 1 in 8, is located over the rear axle of the bogie and also drives to the middle wheels – by means of a balanced crank-shaft. Walschaerst valve motion is provided for the outside cylinders. The valve spindle of the inside cylinder is coupled to that of the two outside cylinders by a simple arrangement of levers patented by Mr Gresley, which gives a steam distribution for the inside cylinder similar to that of the outside ones [interestingly no mention is made of Harold Holcroft's contribution].

A new type of cab is fitted with side windows, the roof extending back over the tender. The footplate is roomy and the general arrangements of the cab and fittings are excellent [thanks to Bert Spencer's design

work]. The regulator handles are duplicated, one on each side of the firebox back-plate, and connected by a cross shaft, the handles being arranged to pull forward. A very clear outlook is provided, and padded seats are available for both driver and fireman.

The total weight of engine and tender in working order is 92 tons 9 cwt, of which 60 tons are carried by the coupled wheels. The total weight of the tender loaded is 56 tons 6 cwt.

Mr Gresley is to be complimented most heartily upon this fine design of locomotive.

In October, a correspondent in the *Railway Gazette* added an even more gratifying report based on trials carried out by No. 1471:

It must be perfectly obvious to everyone who follows such matters that in these new Pacific type express locomotives the GNR have at their disposal a class of engine which, with train loads of 500 or even 550 tons, should be able to make a non-stop run between London and Grantham on schedules of 1hr and 45 minutes. Or, alternatively, of taking loads in excess of the best pre-war timings without any question of assistant engines arising. The performance of engine No. 1471 demonstrates what is possible with skilful designing to achieve in the way of locomotive output within the restricting limits of British loading gauge. The results of the tests are a matter on which

the GNR and Mr Gresley are to be congratulated.

One can only imagine Gresley's reaction at seeing these and many other complimentary articles, providing, as they did, a clear affirmation of the quality of his work.

Once 1470 was in traffic, followed by 1471 in July, a period of testing followed. Interest in its performance was inevitably of great concern and many, including Gresley, would have sought time on the footplate to observe how well the engines worked. Spencer, according to his papers, managed to get three rides beside the driver on 1470 and a couple on her sister:

I handled the controls as instructed by the crew, experiencing the surge in power when the regulator was applied and the wheel slip, which we soon realised was quite common on the Pacifics. For a time, it became a not uncommon sight to see

the second engine running under test with a shelter around its front end to protect the engineers monitoring its performance in this precarious position. They were mostly used between Doncaster and London and proved themselves capable of handling 600 or more ton loads of 20 bogie carriages. During these runs the engines averaged 70mph on the level and could take the steep gradient on Stoke Bank at 45mph.

Following the successful performance of the first two engines the construction of a further ten was authorised by the GNR, all of which left Doncaster Works in 1923, including No. 4472 *Flying Scotsman.*

With the new Pacific safely launched, it had become clear that the network over which it would run was undergoing profound change. Politicians had finally decided how the plethora

Above and right: **Under Gresley's** guiding hand, the ergonomics of cab design advanced considerably. The footplate would never be an easy place to work, but conditions could be made more tolerable and this simple theme lay at the heart of his work. He had, so it is reported, a strong affinity with his drivers and firemen and sort to improve their lives wherever he could. The A1 brought many of his ideas (and those of Bert Spencer) together as the photo above makes clear. Perhaps it was these changes that caused the driver or fireman to smile for the camera while checking out the roomy interior of 1470's footplate (DN)

No.1470 out on the main line early in her career and soon to become an LNER engine. As prototypes she and No. 1471, *Sir Frederick Banbury*, will spend many months being put through their paces to establish the strengths and weaknesses of the design. (RH)

of railway companies should be operated. It hadn't been a quick process. From these deliberations, many senior government officials had reached the conclusion that nationalisation or a scaling down of numbers was essential if the system was to survive as a going concern. Armed with this information, the Minister of Transport, Eric Campbell-Geddes, set up and ran a review to establish the way ahead. This resulted in the 1921 Railway Act which, although falling far short of nationalisation, proposed splitting most of the

100 or so companies into four privately run concerns, with anything left over being absorbed into smaller 'joint railways'. The Act was passed into law in August that year and 1 January 1923 set for this amalgamation to take effect. From that date, the London, Midland and Scottish Railway, the new Great Western Railway, the Southern Railway and the London North Eastern Railway came into existence.

It became clear to Gresley very early in these deliberations that the GNR would be absorbed by a

group that would probably include the Great Eastern, North Eastern and Great Central Railways, plus the Great North of Scotland Railway, North British and the Hull and Barnsley Railway Company. This proved to the case and inevitably meant many changes in responsibilities and extensive rationalisation. If the new companies were to survive, and make good the ravages of war, there would be cuts and a degree of business streamlining. But first the new structures had to be created and a competition

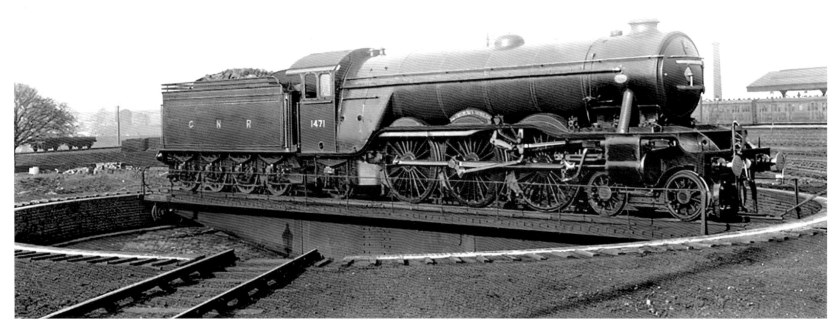

***Above and below*:** **No. 1471** soon after completion in July 1922 as the GNR moved close to amalgamation and the loss of its identity with the formation of the LNER in 1923. Both photographs capture the truly striking form Doncaster achieved in designing and building these locomotives. (BS)

for positions soon began, though some had been canvassing for some months by then, hoping to get the plum posts. Being an ambitious, resourceful man, Gresley observed all this going on and began assessing his chances of becoming Chief Mechanical Engineer of the LNER. For this to happen, he had to overcome some strong opposition from the likes of John Robinson of the Great Central, Vincent Raven at the North Eastern and Alfred Hill with the Great Eastern. In addition, there was always the chance of some 'outside' candidates coming forward to open up the competition even more.

Gresley was a good company man who had learnt how to manage in difficult situations such

as this and soon began a campaign that he hoped might improve his chances of taking the top job and by his performance with the GNR, he had clearly established his credentials. It wouldn't be lost on his fellow challengers that the GNR had, despite limited resources, pushed ahead with a modernisation plan that was now topped by a most imposing new Pacific. Its appearance during these deliberations couldn't have been better planned, but only time would tell if Gresley's case was strong enough and during 1922 this was far from clear.

His main rival for the top job seems to have been Vincent Raven at Darlington. He, like Gresley, had initiated a modernisation plan,

which, coming from a company well placed financially, was rather more ambitious. It was Raven who had pursued the high profile programme that might have seen the East Coast Mainline elecrified in the 1920s. In the meantime, he had introduced electric trains to some areas of industry in the North-East with some success. Undoubtedly, these projects could have been very attractive to the LNER's new board, as well as those in central government and enhanced his case for promotion. In addition, Raven and his team had begun developing their own three-cylinder Pacifiic, though in a timscale slightly behind the A1 programme, with the first, No. 2400, *City of Newcastle*, only appearing in December 1922 to a very muted response,. This may

No. **1471** under test, on 3 September 1922 near Wood Green, with technical staff measuring her performance in the most uncomfortable of positions behind this 'Heath Robinson' style indicator shelter that was fitted around the engine's smokebox. (RH)

not have mattered, of course, and other considerations may have come into play when the powers that be were deciding who the new CME would be. Nevertheless, Gresley's new Pacific was first, received massive publicity and could not fail to impress anyone who saw them blasting out of King's Cross, where the LNER's new HQ would soon be situated.

Whatever forces came into play, Gresley proved to be the chosen one and Raven, after a period, departed the scene, leaving one thought hanging in the air. How would he have taken the LNER forward? Would he have discarded Gresley's designs and built his own Pacifics in greater numbers leaving the A1s to become a footnote in railway history. If so, it is hard to imagine the Flying Scotsman being pulled by a Raven engine and not No. 4472 or her sister A1s, A3s or A4s for that matter. It is also difficult to imagine the Raven Pacifcs achieving the same iconic status as the Doncaster A1s, possibly because Gresley was the true icon and his fast express locomotives simply reflected his star quality. Wherever the truth might lie, the LNER had a CME who would drive the company forward possibly in a way that few could have predicted. But such is the way of great men and women. The years to come would be exciting and dynamic by any standards and shortly after amalgamation the most famous member of the Gresley fleet made its appearance.

No. 1471 apparently in general service before the LNER takes over. Notes on the back of the print suggest she is pulling the 10.00 am train from Leeds to Doncaster. (RH)

SELLING *FLYING SCOTSMAN* AND THE A1/A3 PACIFICS (1923–2023)

The appearance of the first A1s, including 1472 *Flying Scotsman,* in 1922/23 coincided with a rapid growth in a company's ability to sell its products. The need for a strong and aggressive propaganda campaign during the Great War had helped to refine sales techniques and led to a boom in advertising in the years that followed. All this was aided by a growth in newspaper and magazine sales, an ever-increasing number of cinemas and, in time, the coming of radio. It is true to say that the Gresley Pacifics were a key beneficiary of this media explosion.

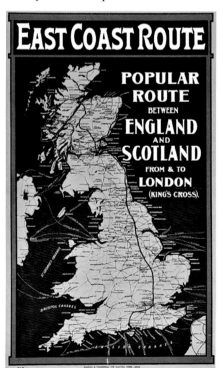

Left and overleaf above:
Before the 1914/18 war, companies such as the GNR produced adverts that had a very cosy feel in targeting their customers. It was humorous but unrefined as the examples here demonstrate. There was little focus on the locomotives and rolling stock, though the GNR did produce a number of postcards of these for sale at stations, but laid little emphasis on speed, comfort or technical advances. The arrival of the first A1, 1472 *Great Northern,* in 1922 changed all this. (RH)

Postcards of the locomotives continued to be produced but now heavily emphasising technical advances being made, aided by an extensive press campaign highlighting the huge improvements in both engines and carriages – speed, comfort and on board facilities. (Below) The gap between the Stirling Singles, built between 1870 and 1895, and No. 1470 is made only too clear in this postcard. (THG)

Below right: **The GNR's** PR managers were quick to exploit the image of the new engines and target a growing market – the long distance, commuting businessmen. (RH)

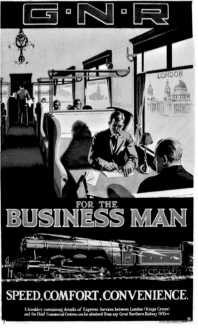

***Above and overleaf spread*: As the** number of A1s gradually increased, so the artwork made available to the public became more lavish and purposeful. The image of these new super-engines was soon fixed in the public consciousness with *Flying Scotsman* at its core. (RH)

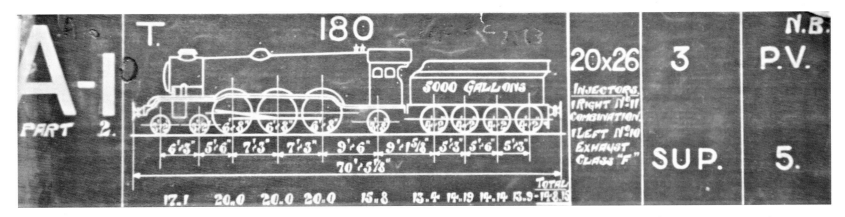

Bert Spencer, Gresley's assistant, kept copious notes and records of all the Pacifics, charting their development, their performances and the many press reports they generated. It was on his advice that good locomotives were made even better, not that this could be gauged from the papers he kept which, as this small, simple diagram above confirms, he carried in a small book in his pocket for years as he went about his business. (BS)

Right, opposite and overleaf: **The British** Empire Exhibitions of 1924 and 1925 at Wembley cemented the A1's reputation, with No. 4472 on display on both occasions, attracting huge interest in the process. Even her arrival at Wembley and positioning for the show drew a crowd and generated many column inches. Perhaps it was at this stage that the locomotive began the transition from being just one of the class to the icon she would soon become. (THG)

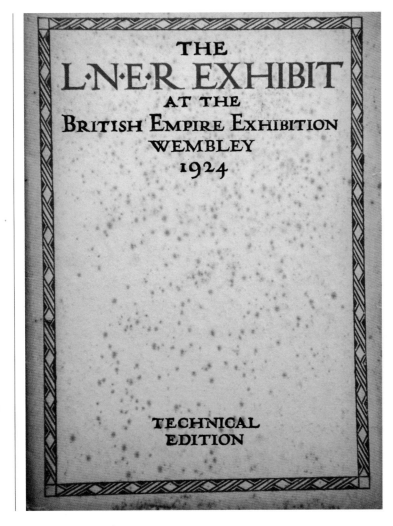

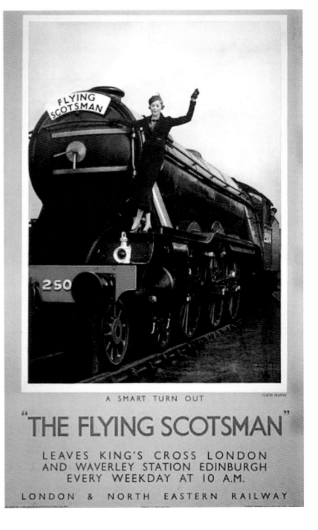

The inauguration of a new service, a record run or the public endorsement by a famous person are all valuable means of selling a company and a product. In the 1920s and '30s, the LNER became very adept at exploiting these events. (Top right) The departure of the first non-stop Flying Scotsman service on 1 May 1928, appropriately pulled by No. 4472, was attended by large crowds and given wide press coverage. (Below) Engine No. 2750 *Papyrus* makes ready to start from King's Cross in heavily overcast conditions on 5 March 1935 attended by a crowd, including many LNER employees. During the day, she will break the 'world speed record for steam when running from London to Newcastle'. (RH)

The flying ace Geoffrey de Havilland, winner of King's Cup Air Race in 1933, shakes hands with Driver Bill Sparshatt, another 'speed merchant', on 17 July 1933, the first day of that season's first non-stop Flying Scotsman service with No. 4472 in charge. On 30 November 1934, Sparshatt will take this engine up to 100mph adding something new to an already glowing reputation. (BS)

"THE FLYING SCOTSMAN"

A book of 130 pages with numerous interesting illustrations dealing with the 63-years' history and development of "The World's Most Famous Train"

At L·N·E·R Offices and Bookstalls
1/-

LNER

THE FLYING SCOTSMAN

THE WORLD'S MOST FAMOUS TRAIN

Third Edition

Above left, above right and overleaf: As *Flying* Scotsman's fame grew so did the appetite for more printed material about her and her sister engines. The cinema soon got in on the act with newsreels then a famous 1929 feature film with the locomotive as star – Ray Milland, Moore Marriott and Pauline Johnson played 'supporting roles' to the famous engine. (THG)

THE INTERIOR OF A LONDON & NORTH EASTERN 4-6-2 THREE-CYLINDER "PACIFIC" EXPRESS LOCOMOTIVE.

NAMES OF PARTS.

1 Chimney
2 Chimney Liner
3 Chimney Petticoat
4 Lamp Iron
5 Hand Rail
6 Smokebox Door Handles
7 Smokebox Door
8 Dart for fastening Smokebox Door
9 Smokebox Door Baffle Plate
10 Smokebox
11 Ring Blower
12 Blast Nozzle
13 Exhaust Pipe
14 Exhaust from Outside Cylinder
15 Exhaust from Inside Cylinder
16 Steam Pipe to Outside Cylinder, Superheated
17 Steam Pipe to Inside Cylinder, Superheated
18 Anti-Vacuum Valve
19 Boiler Lagging Plate
20 Boiler Lagging Bands
21 Dome Casing
22 Dome
23 Regulator Valve
24 Steam Pipe Head
25 Regulator Rod
26 Main Steam Pipe to Header
27 Superheater Header
28 Superheater Fire Tubes
29 Superheater Elements
30 Receiving Passage for Saturated Steam
31 Discharge Chambers for Superheated Steam
32 Fire Tubes
33 Regulator Rod Bell Crank
34 Regulator Bracket
35 Injector Pipe
36 Pop Safety Valve
37 Pop Safety Valve Section
38 Washout Plugs
39 Outer Firebox Wrapper Plate
40 Outer Firebox Back Plate
41 Outer Firebox Throat
42 Firebox
43 Inner Firebox Side Plate
44 Inner Firebox Back Plate
45 Inner Firebox Crown Plate
46 Firebars
47 Firebars Carrier
48 Firebars for Drop Grate
49 Drop Grate Shaft Bracket
50 Firebrick Arch
51 Firehole
52 Firehole Door
53 Deflector Plate
54 Foundation Ring
55 Ashpan
56 Ashpan Damper
57 Ashpan Support
58 Firebox Side Stays
59 Boiler Diagonal Stay Rod
60 Stay Rod Brackets
61 Firebox Cross Stays
62 Smokebox Tubeplate Diagonal Stay Rod
63 Smokebox Tubeplate Diagonal Stay Rod
64 Stay Rod Brackets
65 Boiler Barrel Front Plate
66 Boiler Barrel Back Plate
67 Cab Roof
68 Cab Window
69 Cab Window Slides
70 Stand Pipe for Steam Valves
71 Steam Pipe Elbow
72 Pipe to Steam Stand Pipe
73 Firebox Crown Stays
74 Firebox Backend Stays
75 Firebox Frontend Stays
76 Water Gauge Top Valve
77 Water Gauge Bottom Valve
78 Firehole Door Quadrant
79 Combined Injector Valve
80 Steam Pipe to Injector
81 Steam Pipe to Exhaust Injector
82 Exhaust Injector Supply Pipe
83 Exhaust Injector
84 Drawbar Pin Hole
85 Screw for Drop Grate
86 Bell Crank for Drop Grate
87 Rod for Drop Grate
88 Lever for Drop Grate
89 Control Handle for Ash Pan
90 Ashpan Damper Bell Crank
91 Ashpan Damper Rod
92 Reversing Gear Handle
93 Reversing Gear Screw
94 Reversing Gear Bell Crank
95 Reversing Gear Rod
96 Reversing Shaft
97 Reversing Shaft Support
98 Reversing Gear Radius Link
99 Reversing Gear Radius Link Support
100 Valve Gear Radius Rod
101 Valve Gear Combination Lever
102 Valve Gear Union Link
103 Valve Gear Crosshead Arm
104 Piston Valve Rod Outside Cylinder
105 Motion Bar Inside Cylinder
106 Motion Bar Outside Cylinder
107 Crosshead Inside Cylinder
108 Crosshead Outside Cylinder
109 Piston Rod Inside Cylinder
110 Piston Rod Outside Cylinder
111 Inside Piston
112 Outside Piston
113 Inside Cylinder
114 Outside Cylinder
115 Front Steam Port, Outside Cylinder
116 Back Steam Port, Outside Cylinder
117 Piston Valve, Outside Cylinder
118 Steam Chest, Outside Cylinder
119 Steam Chest, Inside Cylinder
120 Front Exhaust, Inside Cylinder
121 Back Exhaust, Inside Cylinder
122 Front Exhaust, Outside Cylinder
123 Back Exhaust, Outside Cylinder
124 Steam Chest Liner, Inside Piston Valve
125 Steam Chest Liner, Outside Piston Valve
126 Connecting Link Inside Piston Valve
127 Motion Lever for Inside Cylinder Valve Gear
128 Holes in Main Frame
129 Buffer Head
130 Buffer Socket
131 Buffer Base
132 Draw Bar Hook
133 Draw Bar Springs
134 Coupling Links
135 Coupling Screw
136 Wakefield Mechanical Lubricators
137 Wakefield Mechanical Lubricators Connecting Rods
138 Vacuum Brake Cylinder Bracket
139 Vacuum Brake Cylinder
140 Vacuum Brake Cylinder Piston Rod
141 Vacuum Brake Shaft Lever
142 Vacuum Brake Pull Rods
143 Vacuum Brake Cross Stays
144 Driving Wheel Brake Hangers
145 Front and Rear Wheel Brake Hangers
146 Driving Wheel Brake Blocks
147 Front and Rear Wheel Brake Blocks
148 Adjusting Screws
149 Adjusting Screws Turnbuckle
150 Pull Rod Pins
151 Sand Box
152 Sand Box Filling Pipe
153 Sand Box Filler
154 Sand Box Pipe
155 Sand Ejector
156 Sand Ejector Steam Pipe
157 Connecting Rod, Inside Cylinder
158 Connecting Rod, Outside Cylinder
159 Coupling Rods
160 Leading Coupled Wheel Axle
161 Trailing Coupled Wheel Axle
162 Driving Wheel Axle
163 Crank Axle Pin
164 Balanced Crank Web
165 Driving Wheel
166 Leading Coupled Wheel
167 Trailing Coupled Wheel
168 Driving Wheel Centre
169 Leading Coupled Wheel Centre
170 Trailing Coupled Wheel Centre
171 Driving Wheel Tyre
172 Leading Coupled Wheel Tyre
173 Trailing Coupled Wheel Tyre
174 Driving Wheel Spokes
175 Leading Coupled Wheel Spokes
176 Trailing Coupled Wheel Spokes
177 Driving Axle Helical Springs
178 Leading Axle Laminated Springs
179 Trailing Axle Laminated Springs
180 Auxiliary Spring Case
181 Spring Buckle
182 Spring Buckle
183 Hornstay
184 Hornstay
185 Hornstay
186 Spring Hangers
187 Spring Hangers
188 Spring Hangers Brackets
189 Spring Hangers Brackets
190 Driving Wheel Axle Box
191 Leading Coupled Wheel Axle Box
192 Trailing Coupled Wheel Axle Box
193 Driving Wheel Balance Weight
194 Leading Coupled Wheel Balance Weight
195 Trailing Coupled Wheel Balance Weight
196 Main Frame Plate
197 Main Life Guard
198 Lamp Iron
199 Cylinder Drain Cock Lever
200 Quadrant for Control Wires to Cylinder Drain Cock
201 Tube for Control Wires to Cylinder Drain Cock
202 Control Wires to Cylinder Drain Cock
203 Quadrant for Control Wires to Cylinder Drain Cocks
204 Connecting Link, Inside Cylinder Drain Cocks
205 Connecting Link, Outside Cylinder Drain Cocks
206 Connecting Lever, Outside Cylinder Drain Cocks
207 Connecting Link, Outside Cylinder Drain Cocks
208 Drain Cocks, Inside Cylinder
209 Drain Cocks, Outside Cylinder
210 Bogie Wheel Tyres
211 Bogie Wheel Centres
212 Bogie Wheel Spokes
213 Bogie Wheel Springs
214 Bogie Wheel Axle Boxes
215 Bogie Centre Pin
216 Bogie Top Centre
217 Bogie Bottom Centre
218 Bogie Life Guard
219 Guard Plate
220 Bogie Spring Beam
221 Bogie Frame Plate
222 Axles
223 Rear Wheel Tyre
224 Rear Wheel Centre
225 Rear Wheel Spokes
226 Rear Axle Laminated Springs
227 Rear Axle Laminated Springs Buckle
228 Rear Axle Box
229 Axle
230 Exhaust Steam Pipe to Exhaust Injector
231 Exhaust Injector Controls
232 Exhaust Injector Controls
233 Seat
234 Tray
235 Boiler Mud Hole
236 Firebox Water Space
237 Eccentric Crank
238 Eccentric Rod
239 Front Tube Plate
240 Firebox Tube Plate
241 Foot Plate

Above, right and below: **The appetite** for *Flying Scotsman* material continued to be fed throughout the 1930s by luggage labels, children's toys and paperweights, all of which my late uncle, an avid LNER enthusiast, collected. (RH)

Brighton Toy and Model Museum

Driver Sparshatt again, here with Fireman Bob Webster, remained a constant presence on Gresley's Pacifics, No. 4472 in particular, until the end of his career and, in so doing, became part of the folklore surrounding these magnificent engines. (RH)

Above left, above right, left and overleaf: **Preservation for** No. 4472 proved just as dramatic as her active service career with the LNER and BR, though for quite different reasons. Saved from the cutters' torch in 1963 by Alan Pegler (top left and right - *RH*), the sheer cost of maintaining the old engine proved exorbitant and her life until 2004 became a case of 'boom and bust'. Eventually, with the support of a public subscription, she was bought for the nation and returned to steam, which will allow her to see her hundredth birthday in style (and one hopes, her 200th as well). (THG)

Chapter 3
DOMINATING THE LINE

The size of the task that faced Gresley when he became the LNER's first Chief Mechanical Engineer was daunting by any standards. Nevertheless, at 47 he had accumulated a great deal of experience in running a large organisation, while learning how to negotiate the operational, political and financial pitfalls of such work along the way. As an engineer and designer he had few equals, so this part of his work, no matter how large, was unlikely to present problems he could not solve. However, his new empire was vast and would take very careful handling, and a great deal of support from William Whitelaw and Ralph Wedgwood, the General Manager, if it were to succeed. And to be frank, if its constituent parts had struggled to make headway, in the post-war gloom, the new organisation would find it equally difficult, no matter how much support they received from the Ministry of Transport, which, in the circumstances, was unlikely to be great.

Above left, above right and overleaf: **As soon** as the third A1, No. 1472 *Flying Scotsman*, appeared in February 1923, she seemed to attract attention, probably because she was the first of these engines to be completed under the LNER banner. With the first two A1s being named *Great Northern* and *Sir Frederick Banbury* they carried an echo of the old regime which did not sit well with the new company. As a result, 1472, re-numbered 4472 in March 1924, was often chosen for display and publicity photos, but as the top photo shows, she was still a working engine and had to perform well when away from the cameras. The remaining photos are just a few of those appearing in the press at the time. Her most public performance in these early years was probably when placed on display at the 1924 and '25 British Empire Exhibitions at Wembley, where she sat in the Palace of Engineering attracting huge crowds, according to press reports of the time. Aware of the kudos that such a high profile exhibition generated, 4472 was joined by Swindon engines – No. 4073 *Caerphilly Castle* in 1924 and No. 4079 *Pendennis Castle* a year later. The GWR engines were displayed under the provoking banner 'the most powerful locomotive in Great Britain' which seems to have aroused the competitive instincts of some at King's Cross. (BS/RH)

Gresley's first priority in 1923 was to bring together all the disparate parts of his new organisation and make them work as one, supported by a carefully selected team of deputies and assistants eager to do his bidding. Then he had to establish what was needed in the way of locomotives and rolling stock, while determining the fleet's current condition and the extent of the problems he'd inherited. And finally, he had to forge effective working relationships with a host of people from the directors down to the men and women on the shop floor to make sure all worked as one. All this would take time and be profoundly affected by external events over which he had no control, but such a clever, resourceful man wasn't likely to be deflected from the goals he set. It was against this background that the Pacific programme slowly rolled forward, forever competing for Gresley's time and a share of the company's limited resources.

A **new** locomotive for a new age. There is no doubting that these handsome engines could turn heads with their impressive lines and sense of power even when standing still. As the 1920s passed, they came to symbolise much more than a triumph of engineering, but reflected people's aspirations as the post war depression began to lift. Here engine No. 1480 *Enterprise*, which entered traffic in August 1923, gently simmers in the sunshine. (RH)

While all this was happening, the third of A1s, No. 1472 *Flying Scotsman*, slipped quietly into service on 24 February 1923, initially attracting little attention. But this would soon change, probably because she was the first of the Pacifics to appear under the LNER's banner. With the first two A1s being named *Great Northern* and *Sir Frederick Banbury* they carried an echo of the old regime which did not sit well in this new, amalgamated world. As a result, 1472, re-numbered 4472 in March 1924, was quickly selected for public display and, in this guise, frequently appeared in the press and newsreels, then becoming more common as new cinemas sprang up around the country. Undoubtedly, her name helped too, because the Flying Scotsman service had become a well-established phenomenon in the general public's collective mind, conjuring up, as it did, a picture of travel, speed and glamour. If so, her attendance at the British Empire Exhibition in 1924 and '25 at Wembley cemented her position in the public eye.

As her reputation began to grow throughout 1923, she was joined by another nine A1s, with many more being planned. While this was happening, it was proposed that three more Raven Pacifics be built – a leftover of the Raven days at Darlington. Why this programme survived isn't entirely clear, although William Whitelaw's allegiance to the NER, as its last chairman, may offer some explanation. Equally so it can be said that their construction did give the workshops at Darlington something to do while future programmes were worked out. They also offered an alternative solution should the A1s begin to fail for some reason and so could have been built in greater numbers to take up some of the slack if required.

Whatever the reason, Gresley faced a dichotomy – push ahead with two types of Pacific or prove that one was better than the other. He chose to take the latter course and between 25 June and 4 July 1923, comparative trials were held between No. 1472 and Raven's six-month-old Pacific, No. 2400, *City of Newcastle*, which had now been classified as an A2.

Before the trials began, it was discovered that the 2400's radial axleboxes were prone to overheating. No action was taken to correct the problem at the time, but in due course Gresley modified the class by fitting the trucks he'd used on the A1s. In addition, he arranged for a GNR type sniffing valve to be fitted to engines 2402, 2403 and 2404 when built, suggesting that the CME didn't simply intend to write them off, but try, for a while, to make them as effective as possible.

1472 and 2400 undertook three double trips on different days pulling very similar loads between Doncaster and King's Cross. The weather on each day of trials was recorded as variable, but this does not seem to have given one engine an advantage over the other. To make the test runs even fairer, each locomotive was crewed by men familiar with the type – from Gateshead and Doncaster. Fireman C. Fisher, on 2400, subsequently attracted attention and praise for his ability to achieve an average boiler pressure of 200lb on two runs

Vincent Raven's first Pacific. No. 2400 *City of Newcastle*, is rolled out of the works at Darlington in late 1922 painted grey, with some of the men responsible for her existence posing proudly in front of her. By comparison to Gresley's A1s, the Raven class had an old-fashioned look.

(BS)

COMPARATIVE TESTS BETWEEN PACIFIC ENGINES MADE BETWEEN DONCASTER AND KING'S CROSS JUNE – JULY 1923. — SHEET I.

RECORD NO	DATES	TRAIN	Nº OF INTERMEDIATE STOPS	Nº OF CHECKS	DISTANCE IN MILES	TIME MINUTES BOOKED	TIME MINUTES ACTUAL	SPEEDS M.P.H. BOOKED	SPEEDS M.P.H. ACTUAL	VEHICLES	AXLES	TONS	1000 TON MILES ENGINE AND TRAIN	TRAIN ONLY	AVERAGE DRAWBAR PULL TONS	AVERAGE DRAWBAR HORSE POWER	AVERAGE SUPER HEAT	AVERAGE BOILER PRESSURE	AVERAGE STEAM CHEST PRESSURE	AVERAGE CUT OFF %	WEATHER
								ENGINE Nº 1472. G.N. SECTION.													
946	June 25th 10.51 am	Ex Doncaster	3	2	156·06	176	179·23	53·2	52·2	13	56	415·85	63·41	63·19	1·76	549	526	154	100	40	FINE EACH DAY
947	· · 5.40 pm	· Kings Cross	2	6	155·99	180	179·41	52·0	52·18	16	70	518·85	100·78	77·56	1·96	610	543	162	113	38	WIND 4 M.P.H. S.E.
956	July 2nd 10.51 am	· Doncaster	3	4	156·05	176	160·48	53·2	55·2	12	52	376·85	86·57	65·35	2·18	718	542	169	128	40	· 6··· S.W.
957	· 5.40 pm	· Kings Cross	2	4	155·97	180	173·41	52·0	54·0	16	70	520·85	102·64	79·62	2·00	645	–	167	112	40	
958	· 3rd 10.51 am	· Doncaster	3	2	156·06	176	172·66	53·2	54·1	13	62	452·85	97·28	74·06	2·36	763	563	165	129	40	· 16··· S.W.
959	· 5.40 pm	· Kings Cross	2	5	156·02	180	172·38	52·0	54·2	16	70	515·85	102·12	78·90	2·17	702	560	168	124	40	
AVERAGES								53·7					95·83	73·11	2·07	663	547	164	118	40	
								ENGINE Nº 2400 N.E. SECTION.													
951	June 28th 12.52 pm	Ex Doncaster	2	5	156·05	180	180·16	52·0	51·98	12	52	395·85	93·26	70·16	1·71	529	565	197	94	40	WIND 4 M.P.H. W.
952	· 5.40 pm	· Kings Cross	2	4	155·98	180	181·88	52·0	51·5	16	70	517·85	102·10	79·00	2·15	661	585	195	115	40	
953	· 29th 10.51 am	· Doncaster	4	2	156·05	176	176·10	53·2	53·19	14	62	452·85	97·06	73·96	2·14	679	572	198	105	40	· 2··· W.
954	· 5.40 pm	· Kings Cross	2	5	155·97	180	177·60	52·0	52·7	17	74	545·85	106·51	83·41	2·29	722	576	200	110	40	
960	July 4th 10.51 am	· Doncaster	4	1	156·06	176	172·15	53·2	54·4	14	62	452·85	96·75	73·75	2·37	771	566	200	125	40	· 10··· S.W.
961	· · 5.40 pm	· Kings Cross	2	4	156·00	180	173·26	52·0	54·0	16	70	515·85	101·86	78·76	2·12	683	582	194	91	40	
AVERAGES								53·0					97·92	76·5	2·13	673	574	197	106	40	

WATER ON TRIP — POUNDS OF HOUGHTON MAIN COAL USED. — EVAPORATION

RECORD NO	GALLONS TOTAL	PER MILE	PER HOUR	PER 1000 ENG & TRAIN TON MILES	PER 1000 TRAIN TON MILES	LBS PER DRAW BAR HORSE POWER HOUR	LBS PER SQ FOOT OF HEATING SURFACE PER HOUR	COAL TOTAL	LIGHTING UP & AT LONDON	ON TRIP AT LONDON	(TOTAL) PER 1000 ENG & TRAIN TON MILES	(TOTAL) PER 1000 TRAIN TON MILES	(TOTAL) PER MILE	(TRIP) PER 1000 ENG & TRAIN TON MILES	(TRIP) PER 1000 TRAIN TON MILES	(TRIP) PER MILE	(TRIP) PER HOUR	(TRIP) PER DRAWBAR HORSE POWER HOUR	(TRIP) PER SQ FOOT OF HEATING SURFACE PER HOUR	(TRIP) PER SQ FOOT OF GRATE PER HOUR	FEED WATER TEMP DEG FAHT	POUNDS OF WATER PER LB COAL ACTUAL	FROM AND AT 212° FAH
								ENGINE Nº 1472 G.N. SECTION															
946	–	–	–	–	–	–	–	14750	1120	13630	79·9	104·8	47·3	74·0	96·9	43·7	2280	3·92	·613	54·8	61·0	–	–
947	–	–	–	–	–	–	–														60·0	–	–
956	6031	38·65	2137	68·1	92·4	29·7	618	16692	1120	15570	87·2	115·02	53·5	81·5	107·5	49·9	2750	4·00	·789	66·0	60·5	7·3	9·51
957	5347	34·5	1852	52·0	67·2	28·7	536														61·0		
958	6468	41·5	2247	66·5	87·4	29·3	650	17763	1456	16327	89·2	116·3	57·0	81·9	106·75	52·3	2845	3·89	·821	74·8	61·0	7·65	10·8
959	6022	38·6	2090	59·0	76·4	30·3	607														61·5		
AVERAGES	5967	38·3	2081	61·4	80·8	31·0	603	16407	1232	15176	85·4	112·04	52·6	79·13	103·71	48·6	2625	3·94	·741	65·2	61·0	7·47	10·15
								ENGINE Nº 2400 N.E. SECTION															
951	4833	31·0	1611	52·3	69·6	30·7	960	17696	1456	16240	90·6	118·6	56·7	85·1	108·9	52·04	2765	4·52	·936	64·9	62·5	–	–
952	–																				62·5		
953	6309	40·8	2151	65·0	85·3	31·65	743	17778	1120	16658	87·4	113·0	56·99	81·9	105·9	53·4	2850	4·04	·966	66·6	61·0	7·98	10·56
954	6094	44·6	2362	65·6	83·8	32·73	821														61·0		
960	7132	45·7	2480	73·7	96·7	32·3	865	19488	1456	18032	98·1	127·6	62·43	90·8	118·1	57·8	3161	4·31	1·088	75·5	61·5	7·42	9·8
961	6225	39·8	2155	61·1	79·1	31·55	750														61·0		
AVERAGES	6298	40·4	2153	63·5	82·9	31·7	748	18321	1344	16976	92·03	120·4	58·71	85·26	110·96	54·41	2925	4·29	·995	68·9	61·6	7·7	10·18

The CME's summary of the trials held between his A1 and a Raven A2 during 1923. The performances achieved were remarkably similar, though the A1 was deemed to have enjoyed a slight advantage. However, the gap was unlikely to have been as large as Gresley would have wished. As a result, construction of three more A2s went ahead, but so did a further forty A1s which appeared in 1924/25. (RH)

and 197lb over all six journeys. By comparison, the A1 only achieved an average of 164lb, well below its rated 180lb. Despite this the A2's performance, with its higher coal consumption, was deemed to have made the type marginally inferior when all facts and figures had been evaluated.

It is easy to think that a political spin might have been applied to these findings to enhance the A1's reputation. In the event this doesn't seem to have happened, but if Gresley had wished to, he could have pointed to some of the A2's perceived mechanical shortcomings as justification. These were believed to stem from Raven's ambition to get his Pacific into service quickly before amalgamation and so enhance his ability to compete with Gresley for the CME post. In haste, or so the story goes, he took the simple step of basing the new engine on his three-cylinder Z Class Atlantics – stretching the design to suit the 4-6-2 configuration. As a result, the frames were made longer so that a bigger boiler and wider firebox could be fitted and, by necessity, all three-cylinders drove to the leading coupled axle. It was a solution Gresley believed put an undue strain on the axle. He also believed that Raven's use of three sets of Stephenson valve gear caused excessive bearing wear on the driving axle and overheating of the motion to the detriment of the locomotive's performance.

There was also the question of access during maintenance to consider, the A2s valve layout making life more difficult for the fitters. Strangely enough, it was a criticism later levelled at Gresley's conjugated valve gear, especially when their condition deteriorated rapidly under wartime conditions. Finally, the CME also believed that the boilers on the A2 were too long and this created 'cool spots at the front end so reducing their efficiency'. However, as 2400's boiler had consistently produced higher average pressure than 1472, the 'cool spots' assessment may have been a suspect one.

All in all, Gresley found sufficient evidence to support his view that the A1 was a better engine for mass production than

the A2 and convinced the Chairman of the merits of his case. As a result, forty more were ordered in late 1923, but at the same time the construction of the three remaining A2s was also allowed to proceed. One can only assume that Chairman and General Manager were leaving their options open just in case of problems. In the event, the A2s gradually acquired secondary status, then slowly slipped from view.

So, the A1 reigned supreme, but all was not plain sailing as events in 1924/25 soon revealed. All forty of the new engines were in service by December 1924, one batch of twenty built in-house at Doncaster and the rest contracted out to the North British Locomotive Company in Glasgow. With experience gained on the first twelve, various adjustments were made to the design. This work included a revised front buffer plate and modifications to the cab, chimney, dome, safety valves and

the cab roof ventilator to allow it to meet the reduced loading gauge found in northern areas. It was also found necessary to improve the A1s' riding quality by replacing the helical springs beneath the middle-coupled axles with uncompensated plate springs.

With so many more Pacifics in service Gresley's engineers could begin a more detailed evaluation of their performance, with the 2 to 1 valve gear being of particular interest. The team already had experience of this system in other classes of engine, but the higher stresses created by the more powerful A1s were more likely to reveal weaknesses or imperfections. Very early in its development, some critics had questioned the suitability of this valve gear in high speed express engines, asking the simple question 'was it strong enough to take such stresses'. It was a view to which an incident involving Gresley's 2-6-0 No. 1000 during May 1920 gave rise.

A certain amount of over travel of the centre valve had been experienced when the engine was coasting in full gear with the regulator closed. As a result, the valve spindle crosshead had come into contact with the chest cover causing sufficient damage to warrant a revised operating instruction being issued by Gresley. In effect, the maximum cut-off position was reduced from 75 to 65 per cent, which would trim the valve travel in full gear from 6⅜in to 5in. In parallel with this, the drivers were instructed to set the gear at 25 per cent cut-off when coasting at speeds above 25mph. At the same time, the chest cover was modified. It was a balancing

Images of *Flying Scotsman* could be seen in many places during the 1920s and take many forms including this one which links the engine to an even more glamorous picture of global travel. Good PR is about selling a dream and in austerity-hit Britain, this proved even more important to a weary nation. (THG)

act, of course, in which the need to avoid any damage caused by over travel had to be measured against the need to avoid creating a vacuum in the cylinders. So, from day one the big Pacifics had to operate under this restriction, and it was inevitable that thought soon turned to ways of improving their design.

Quite early in this process it had been noticed that the middle cylinder was performing more work than the two on the outside when moving at high speed. This imbalance caused the right-hand cylinder to work harder than the left. To try and reduce or even eradicate this problem, Gresley proposed that the steam lap on the centre valve be increased. Work began in March 1925, when a new

set of piston rings were fitted to the centre valve of engine No. 1474, now numbered 4474. With a steam lap of 15/16in, it was hoped that this would correct the problem and initial reports suggested this was so. But events in April and May that year caused a re-think, which, as Bert Spencer later reported, in his 1947 presentation to the ILocoE, 'had a far-reaching effect on the development of LNER locomotives'. He then went on to describe these events. 'An exchange of engines took place [not an uncommon occurrence between railway companies, but the reasons for this particular event have been the subject of much speculation over the years and so remain an open question] and trials were carried out on both the LNER and GWR

lines between Gresley's Pacific and Collett's 4-6-0 type Castle.'

These trials, and the embarrassing accounts that then appeared in the press which, to all intents and purposes, placed Gresley's engines second, must have acted as a catalyst for change and probably spurred his competitive instincts at the same time. The CME's reaction can probably best be summed up by a somewhat testy memorandum he wrote to the Locomotive Committee on 3 June. In this he criticised the GWR for reneging on an agreement he thought he'd made with his opposite number, Charles Collett, not to go public with the results unless there was 'mutual concurrence' to do so. He added, in the coldest terms, 'this agreement

By the beginning of 1924, twelve A1s were plying their trade along the East Coast Mainline, including No. 1477 *Gay Crusader* which entered service in June of that year; the same month as No. 1478 *Hermit*. (RH)

(Right) One of the two GWR engines, 4079 *Pendennis Castle*, chosen for the exchange trials that took place in May 1925. This engine competed with two A1s – 4475, *Flying Fox* (below with *Pendennis Castle*), and 2543, *Diamond Jubilee* running from King's Cross. In April, No. 4475 had also been due to run from Paddington, but had to be replaced by 4474, *Victor Wild* (opposite below), when the first engine developed a hot tender box. No. 4475 was fit and ready to run the trials from King's Cross, but had to be replaced this time by 2545, *Diamond Jubilee* for the some of the trials work. The second GWR engine, No. 4074, *Caldicott Castle* (opposite above), was used only on GWR metals. By comparison to the A1, the Castles were generally judged to be better, especially their coal consumption and an ability to start heavy loads without a hint of slip. (RH)

has not been kept'. Perhaps, in self-justification, he added:

[The trials], which have caused a great amount of public interest, have shown that each engine was able to undertake the work of the other, and maintain the time schedules with ease … Conclusive results, however, cannot be obtained from such a short trial…I am confident that if the trial had been extended the position would have been reversed … The trials show that the road bed of the LNE is superior to that of the Great Western. The Pacific could not safely be run as such high speeds

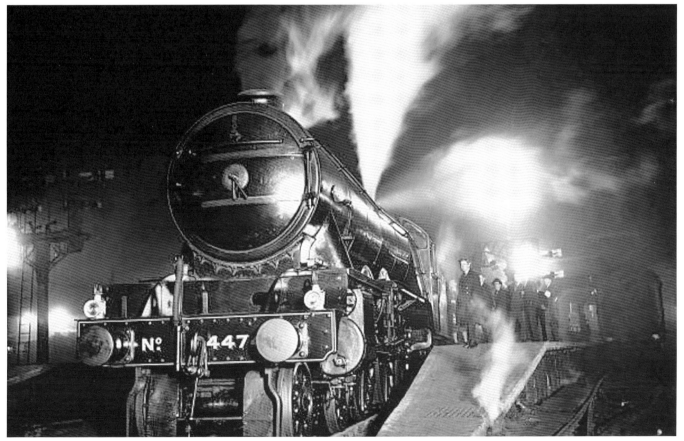

During the debate over the use of long travel valves on the A1s, a number of engines were modified. This was undetaken in an attempt to remove the imbalance caused when the middle cylinder performed more work than the outside pair at high speed. After much 'toing and froing' Bert Spencer's long lap valve proposal was adopted and the A1s' performance was significantly improved. However, Gresley was only finally convinced of this when riding on the footplate of engine No. 2555 *Centenary* (shown here) in May 1927 from Doncaster to London. It was this modification that many believe helped open the way for long distance, non-stop travel, which was a key commercial aim of the LNER's senior managers (RH)

on falling grades on the Great Western road as their engines, probably due to the greater length, weight and height of the Pacific engine. Strict observation had therefore to be observed on speed limits on the curves by the Pacific engine, and consequently higher speeds were required on the upgrades to maintain schedules. The higher coal consumption is partially consequent upon this.

Spencer was an informed witness to these events, but he was much more than that. From as early as 1922, when working in the Drawing Office at Doncaster, he had become keenly aware of an

apparent limitation in Gresley's valve gear. Ever conscious of his responsibility to identify a problem and suggest a solution, he began proposing ways in which their performance might be improved. From these deliberations he became convinced that using long travel valves would be the solution. Gresley, having conceded that the A1s could perform more effectively, during March 1925, directed Francis Wintour, at Doncaster, to fit a modified set of piston rings to the centre valve of engine No. 4474, to create a longer steam lap. During the tests that followed, an improvement was noted and Gresley instructed the Mechanical Engineer to begin modifying all

but one of the remaining A1s, with No. 4475 first in line so that she could participate in the exchange trials, the results of which were soon being gloomily mulled over by the CME, encouraging him to consider other more extensive changes.

As an interim step and, perhaps, as a concession to his insistent young assistant, in February 1926, Gresley agreed to engine No. 1477 (soon to become 4477) being fitted with long travel valves similar to those fitted to the Castle Class. However, testing didn't get underway until August. Spencer, now Gresley's assistant at King's Cross, was not involved in this work and is quoted as having said that 'it was a botched-up job, with more emphasis on using existing components than on getting good valve events'. So, it probably came as no surprise that the hoped-for improvements were not forthcoming.

Following the A1's questionable showing during the exchange trials, Gresley revisited the problem, but still seems to have thought that Spencer's ideas were interesting but not necessarily correct. He seems to have reached the conclusion that the A1's trouble stemmed from the uneven and excessive wear of the broad piston valve rings and the amount of steam that then escaped. He also seems to have concluded that long travel valves would suffer greater wear and a drop in efficiency. All well and good if his modifications to the valve gear had proved successful, but the results were poor.

One can only imagine Spencer's frustration as he watched from the wings, but his constant campaigning was beginning to have an effect. As 1926 moved to a close, Gresley relented and agreed with Spencer's proposal to manufacture a modified version of the long travel valve gear for testing purposes. On this occasion, Spencer was actively involved in all that happened, so, under his guidance, for example, the connection between the foot of the radius link and the eccentric rod was lowered and the radius of the link foot joint was increased from 1ft 6in to 1ft 9in.

Bench testing followed to allow Spencer's design to be refined and on 13 December instructions were given to fit the new valve gear to Pacific No. 2555, *Centenary*, which was undergoing repair at the time.

No. **4480** *Enterprise* **was** the third A1 to be fitted with 'Spencer's' re-worked valve gear and is reported by him to have 'shown the benefits of this modification and the closely supervised trials that followed made sure the results were measured correctly and accurately reported'. (BS)

Work began on 30 December and the engine was back in service on 25 March ready for testing. Whereas trials with 4477 had, Spencer believed, been poorly managed, no such mistake was made with *Centenary*. This attention to detail was crucial and trial running soon revealed that this engine performed better and burned significantly less coal than A1s with the old valve gear (39lb per mile against an average of 50lb).

Even allowing for this success, Gresley still seemed loth to abandon a concept so

Right and opposite:
The General Strike of 1926 marked a very dark time in Britain's history. Years of struggle for equality, fair pay and better working conditions finally exploded when the mine owners forced severe wage cuts and longer working hours on their employees. It was a move that sparked widespread outrage and resulted in a complete breakdown in capital and labour relations (right and opposite above). As a result, soldiers, tanks and armoured cars patrolled the streets, threatening a level of violence few could ignore, the LNER tried to present a picture of calmness with the slogan 'business as usual'. This is reflected in these heavily romanticised, wholly misleading pictures of volunteers manning the trains (opposite below left and right). (BS)

close to his heart. But he wasn't blind to the possibilities and in April ordered two more A1s, No. 2549, *Persimmon*, and No. 4480, *Enterprise*, to be fitted with 'Spencer's' valve gear. And in July they appeared and quickly confirmed the favourable impression established by *Centenary*, though Gresley is reported as still being a doubting witness to this accomplishment. However, it seems that his views softened somewhat in May 1927 when he rode on 2555's footplate, from Doncaster to London. Clearly impressed, he quickly moved to

implement the ideas Spencer had been championing for so long.

It hadn't been a quick process, but by 1927 the long lap valve had been successfully tested, opening the way for other developments, including the next phase of Gresley's Pacific programme. But in the background, the LNER, and much of British industry, faced a growing problem that would finally explode in 1926 with dramatic consequences.

The spark for the most extreme civil unrest was generated by the mine owners, who, in the face of reducing profits, forced severe wage

cuts and longer working hours on their employees. Lives that were already blighted by poor living and working conditions became even harder and widespread protests broke out. When the miners refused to accept these new and extremely poor terms of employment, the owners simply locked out 1.2million men and women and suspended their pay. Faced with such intransigence, the General Council of the Trades Union Congress called for strike action as a means of demonstrating how profound was the need for change. In May 1926, an estimated 1.7million workers

Engine No. 2565 *Merry Hampton*, which had been pulling the 10.00am service from Edinburgh, lies on her side awaiting salvage in May 1926 having been derailed by striking workers. More by luck than judgment there were no fatalities and after three months in the works at Doncaster, the engine re-emerged. (BS)

across many industries joined the miners in what became known as the General Strike. The disruption this caused was extreme over a nine-day period and the railways virtually came to a halt.

In London, soldiers and tanks were on the streets and violence occasionally erupted, especially when some workers or agitators tried to break picket lines. The atmosphere was tinderbox dry and was only one spark away from rioting and mass arrests to begin. These were black days indeed and even when the strike ended the

level of anger and resistance didn't abate.

Apart from a mass walk out by staff on the railways, the most serious incident involving the LNER occurred on 11 May when an A1 Pacific was deliberately de-railed near Cramlington, as Bert Spencer recalled:

Things came to a head, as far as the LNER was concerned, when an express train from Edinburgh to King's Cross [the 10am service pulled by Pacific No. 2565, *Merry*

Hampton] was derailed north of Newcastle by, we were told at the time, striking miners intent on stopping a coal train, but miscalculated. No one was killed, but this was more by luck than judgement. Due to the seriousness of this incident I was sent by Gresley to Newcastle that afternoon to assess the damage and report back to him that day on how quickly the locomotive might be moved.

When I arrived at Cramlington Edward

Thompson was there not only in his capacity as Carriage and Wagon Manager at Darlington, but also because he had extensive experience of accident investigation. Together we looked over the locomotive which still had not be righted at the time. We noted the damage, the position of the controls in the cab and observed the likely cause, which we concluded was by malicious intent, occasioned by the removal of fishplates, coach screws and a length of track. That evening we were joined by Colonel J.W. Pringle from the Ministry of Transport who was a well-known and respected figure in railway circles and who we assisted on this occasion. Thompson phoned through a report to the CME and my written report was in his hands the following afternoon. I believe a group of miners were later arrested for the crime, faced prosecution and were jailed.

In the aftermath of the derailment, eight miners were indeed arrested and prosecuted for their part in the incident, with some of them being imprisoned while No.2565 was repaired and then returned to duty. Sadly, industrial relations could not be fixed so easily and remained a constant concern for leaders, including Gresley, until Britain was again engaged in another world war, when other priorities rose to the surface.

In the meantime, business went on as usual and for the LNER this meant the achievement of a long held ambition to begin long distance, non-stop passenger

STRIKE AND POST-STRIKE INCIDENTS, INCLUDING TRAIN-WRECKING.

As might be expected, the incident at Cramlington hit the headlines in this country and overseas and did serious damage to the strikers' cause. To say the press had a field day would be an understatement, which did nothing to help in meeting the genuine and the pressing concerns of those living in poverty and want in many areas of Britain. (THG)

services from London northwards, where the A1s' potential would be tested fully, aided by Spencer's work on the long lap valve issue.

Even with a fleet of 52 Pacifics to play with, traffic demands were increasing sufficiently to justify building more. Whilst many people in Britain were still profoundly affected by austerity in the 1920s, there were some in the middle and upper classes able to enjoy a high

Against a background of strikes and high levels of poverty in the 1920s, it must have been difficult for Gresley and his team to focus on the development of new, high speed services that only a minority of the population could afford. But you have to plan for the future and hope, in the meantime, that such serious issues can be resolved. With a fleet of fifty-two Pacifics the LNER could at least take the company on to the next stage of its development, with *4472 Flying Scotsman* (seen in full flight in this photo) leading the programme in a high profile way. (BS)

standard of living. And this meant that long distant passenger services on the railways for work and pleasure were still drawing a large number of customer. In addition, the military, which still held many hundreds of thousands of men in establishments strung out along the main lines, continued to have a pressing and increasing requirement for the railways. One of their primary needs was to ensure the effective movement of these forces and their equipment, whether on duty or on leave, and the railways were still seen as the best way of ensuring this would happen. So for various reasons, the LNER believed that building more A1s was fully justified.

By this stage, they had proven their value but the design was undergoing change and refinement in an effort to improve their performance. As we have seen, long lap valves had been tried, tested and introduced as standard equipment. The original boilers, with superheaters containing 32 elements, produced a pressure of 180lb sq in, but this was now deemed insufficient for the long distance work the company planned. The development of a boiler producing 220lb sq in of pressure, with an enlarged superheater containing 43 elements, seemed to offer the level of performance and endurance now

needed. So, in 1927 Gresley was given permission to modify five A1s with this new boiler to test these theories and in July the first of them, A1, No. 4480, *Enterprise*, emerged from the workshops, nearly four tons heavier, to begin a series of comparative trials that would measure the benefits of each boiler/superheater combination. Shortly afterwards 4480 was joined in these trials by the second A1 to be modified, engine No. 2544 *Lemberg*. Here Spencer takes up the story:

'The only differences between the new and original boilers were an increase in the thickness of the barrel plates, a closer pitching of the firebox stays and an increase in the number of superheater elements from 32 to 43. The cylinders of No. 4480 were not altered, but those of No. 2544 were reduced to 18¼ in. diameter (to give the high-pressure boiler a tractive effort approximately equal to that of the standard 180lb. Pacifics), the tractive efforts being 36,465 lb. and 30,362lb. respectively as compared with 29,835 lb. on the standard A1 Class.

Engine No. 4480 proved highly successful in service, the increased power due to the use of the higher pressure with 20in. diameter cylinders enabling the engine to be worked at relatively early cut-offs on the heaviest trains.

Comparative trials were carried out between A1 class No. 4473, *Solario*, with 180lb pressure and No. 2544 with 220lb pressure (during February 1928, over a two-week period on the hardest duty of the time – the 1051 am from Doncaster to King's Cross and return at 1600 hrs). Both engines had long lap valve gear. Engine No. 4473 made six return journeys on consecutive days (312 miles per day) and engine No. 2544 made five return journeys the following week.

Whilst the coal consumption per mile and per ton-mile showed a substantial economy in favour of 2544, there was little to choose between the two engines when comparing coal and water consumption on a horsepower basis. Engine

No. 4473 did more work during the trials owing to greater wind resistance which adversely affected its coal and water consumption per mile and per ton-mile, these comparisons giving no credit for the extra effort due to weather conditions.

Many years later, Spencer touched on another issue Gresley and his team considered at the time when judging whether to proceed with a boiler producing 220lb per sq inch pressure:

There were concerns over the comparative maintenance costs between boilers operating with different pressures – higher pressures costing more or having shorter lives. Thom had presented a short paper on the subject to the A.R.L.E (Association of Railway Locomotive Engineers) when Gresley was President between 1926 and '27. He compared 180 and 200 lb. psi boilers and this led to a great deal of discussion by members each describing their own experiences. With the likes of Gresley, Thom, Stanier, Fowler, Beames and Bulleid in attendance there couldn't have been a more expert group of people, but even so no final

COMPARATIVE TESTS BETWEEN " PACIFIC " ENGINES WITH 180 AND 220 lb. per sq. inch BOILER PRESSURE

Made between King's Cross and Doncaster: February 1928.

Particulars	Engine 4473	Engine 2544
Boiler pressure lb./sq.in.	180	220
Cylinder diameter x stroke	20" x 26"	18¼" x 26"
Tractive effort at 85% B.P.	29,835 lb.	30,362 lb.
Average coal consumption :		
Lb. per D.B.H.P. hour	3.07	3.11
Lb. per mile	38.83	35.37
Percentage reduction on 220 lb. engine	—	8.9
Lb. per ton mile (excluding engine)	.092	.083
Lb. per sq. ft. of grate per hour	49.62	46.8
Average water consumption :		
Lb. per D.B.H.P. hour	25.17	25.45
Lb. per mile	317.5	288.8
Lb. per ton mile (excluding engine)	.752	.675
Average evaporation :		
Lb. of water per lb. of coal	8.18	8.17
Average speed in M.P.H. :		
Doncaster to King's Cross	54.93	56.84
King's Cross to Doncaster	50.73	52.54
Average weight of train behind tender :		
Doncaster to King's Cross	435 tons	428 tons
King's Cross to Peterborough	491 ,,	506 ,,
Peterborough to Doncaster	331 ,,	348 ,,
Average work done in H.P. hours per single journey	1970	1770

Left and overleaf: **When deciding** to increase the power of his Pacifics, Gresley chose to up the boiler pressure from 180 to 220lb, at the same time as increasing the number of superheater elements from thirty-two to forty-three. In February 1928, once new boilers had been fitted to five A1s, comparative trials were held the results of which were later published (left – the summary page). The picture on page 98 identifies the changes made to the engine's design because of this and how this work led to the construction of the A3, the first of which appeared in August the same year (the picture on page 99 shows the A3's engine diagram produced at Doncaster). (BS/RH)

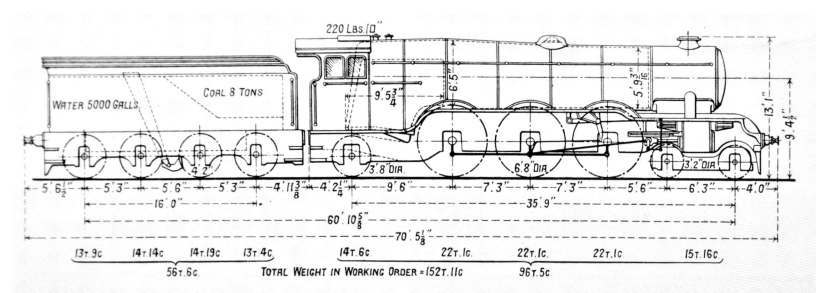

Diagram and Leading Dimensions of 4-6-2 Locomotive fitted with New High-Pressure Boiler.

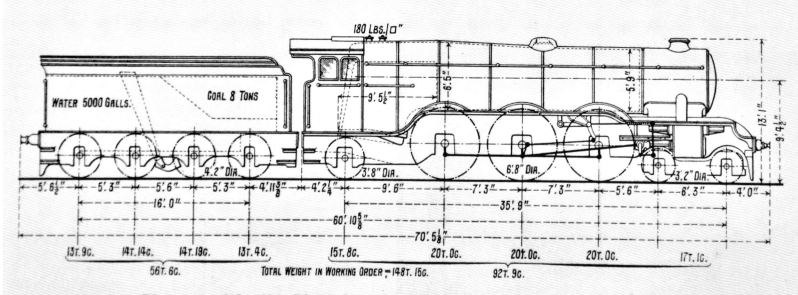

Diagram and Leading Dimensions of 4-6-2 Locomotive as previously in Service.

conclusion could be reached. However, the consensus, led by Stanier, seemed to be that there would be no appreciable difference in maintenance costs and the benefits of running with a boiler with higher pressure would outweigh any small difference, if it existed at all. With that assurance Gresley felt able to argue the benefits of conversion.

Armed with this limited information, Gresley sought authority to modify the rest of the class and apply these changes to a new batch of Pacifics which had been authorised in late 1927 by the Locomotive Committee. But lack of data also reinforced his view of another subject that

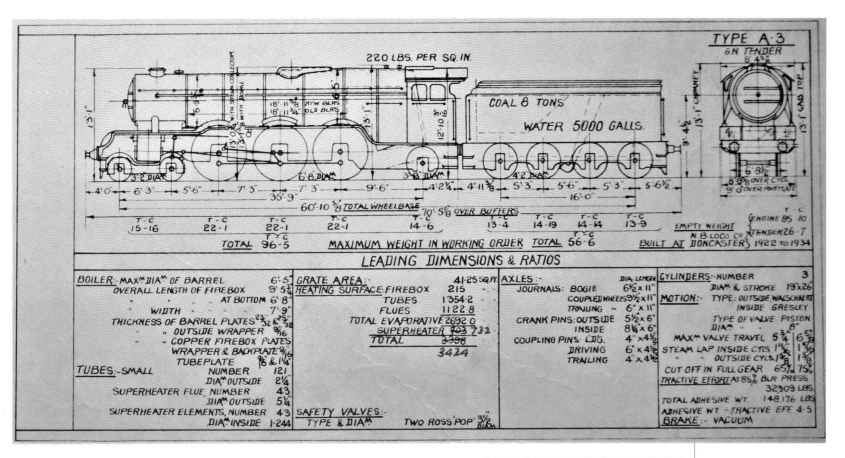

LEADING DIMENSIONS & RATIOS

TYPE A·3

220 LBS. PER SQ. IN.

COAL 8 TONS
WATER 5000 GALLS.

MAXIMUM WEIGHT IN WORKING ORDER

BUILT AT DONCASTER 1922 to 1934

The first A3 enters service. The Doncaster built engine No. 2743 *Felstead* began her operational life in August 1928 and lasted in service until October 1963. Here she is captured early in life doing exactly what she was designed for – pulling a premier express service. (RH)

was increasingly taxing him – the absence of adequate test facilities available to the LNER. As a scientist of note, he was only too aware of the need to test any new idea rigorously 'on the road' and in the laboratory, so that its merits, both short and long term, could be assessed and compared.

With this, the Pacific project moved into its next phase with the development of a 'Super Pacific', as some called it, though in reality it was designated the A3, with all but one of the remaining A1s eventually being upgraded to this new specification. The first of these engines, No. 2743, *Felstead*, was soon under construction and was quickly followed by nine more all

entering service between July 1928 and April 1929.

The arrival of these engines is now seen as a landmark in railway history, yet in his 1947 paper to the ILocoE, Spencer described their development in a most cursory way as though he, and possibly Gresley, did not see this stage of the Pacific programme as being that significant or important. True or not, his assessment is still interesting because it reveals how a design engineer of great skill views his work. There are no really clear definable steps, only a gradually evolving process without an end or beginning, just a continuous cycle of research leading to new developments. Of the A3s he wrote:

These engines had the identical design of 220lb per sq inch 6ft 5in diameter boilers fitted to the trials engines, but the diameter of the cylinders was increased to 19in, thus raising the tractive effort to 32,909lb.

Later engines of this class, commencing with engine No. 2500, *Windsor Lad*, had boilers fitted with a steam collector in the form of a steel pressing, integral with the dome, fed by a series of slots ½in wide in the top of the barrel plate. The collector is located on the tapered portion of the barrel and provides a steam supply at the maximum height above water level both for the

The eighth of the A3s, No. 2750 *Papyrus*, made her first appearance in February 1929 and was then based at King's Cross where she apparently gained a good reputation for fast running. (BS)

regulator and, from the rear end, for the steam manifold in the cab. All subsequent 6ft 5in diameter tapered boilers, including those for the streamlined Pacifics, were built with this type of steam collector.

Spencer's mention of the steam collector is a particularly interesting one especially when he said so little about the A3 programme in general. Later in life he went a little further by adding that that 'the true value of the 'banjo' dome is often overlooked, yet it was as significant a development as the many other ideas that found their way into the design of the Pacifics'. Sadly, he did not give his reasons for reaching this conclusion, so his train of thought is difficult to follow. Nevertheless, he clearly felt that this form of dome represented an important advance and improved the performance of these engines, presumably by its effectiveness in

preventing priming and stopping water being carried into the cylinders when an engine was working hard.

As work on the A3s gradually advanced, the long-held ambition of senior LNER managers to introduce long distance, non-stop services

from London to Edinburgh was coming to fruition, encouraged by the success of the A1s. To assess the capacity of engine and crew to undertake such a demanding task, a test run between London to Newcastle was arranged for 11 July 1927 with Bert Spencer on

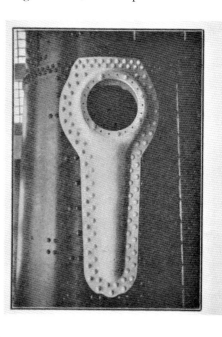 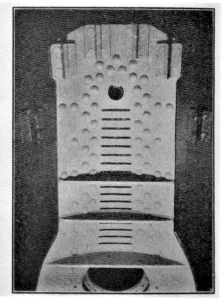

Spencer's photographs of the steam collector fitted to engine No. 2500, *Windsor Lad*, when built in 1934 (left – exterior view, right – interior view). This collector, which was given the nickname 'Banjo' Dome, proved so successful that it became a standard feature on all 6ft 5in diameter boilers, including the A4s. This distinctively shaped dome can easily be seen in the photograph of A3 No. 2506 *Salmon Trout* below. (BS)

A1 No. 4475 *Flying Fox* leaves King's Cross for Newcastle, on a rather misty 11 July 1927 morning. The aim was to prove that it was viable for these engines and crew to manage long, non-stop high speed passenger services to the north, with Edinburgh the eventual aim. While just about managing Newcastle, doubts were expressed by some, including Bert Spencer who rode on the train, that if Scotland were to be safely reached required more coal to be carried and a change of crew. The answer to these problems lay in building bigger tenders with a corridor (BS)

board representing Gresley. He later wrote:

'The CME instructed me to accompany the train northwards on the 11th to observe how the engine and its crew (Driver A. Tibworth and Fireman H. Mutton) performed. At this stage there were no A1s with 220lb boilers available and there was some concern that the lower capacity boilers might not cope well with such a demanding schedule. This proved not to be the case, but, I think, this was more to do with the skill of Alf Pibworth and Harry Mutton, who were known to perform wonders on the footplate of Pacifics, and, in Pibworth's case, the Atlantics.

During the 1925 exchange trials he had been on the footplate of 4474 when the engine turned in a quite exemplary performance on the mainline to Exeter. So it surprised no one when his name appeared on the roster for the run to Newcastle. By this stage he had become an old friend, but try as I might I could not get him drop the 'Sir' which ended each part of our conversations.

Engine No.4475, *Flying Fox*, which was thought to be one of the best A1s, left promptly at 9.50am and was scheduled to cover the 268 miles to Newcastle in 5½ hours. She was not long out of General Repair at Doncaster, during which her valve gear had been modified, if my memory serves me well. I do not believe that the other four engines selected to work

these trains [4474 *Victor Wild*, 2552 *Sansovino*, 2569 *Gladiateur* and 2575 *Galopin*] had been similarly modified at that stage, although each spent a few days in the Works being prepared for the service. So it was interesting to compare how 4475 performed with the others.

The journey was uneventful and we arrived at Newcastle on time to be greeted by a large crowd, including the Lord Mayor of Newcastle. Later in the day I spoke to the crew and could clearly see how much the run had taken out of them. Alf, who was pushing on a bit by then and not far from retirement, was kept on light duties for a week or so afterwards, such had been the strain. I reported to Gresley by phone and next day we, with Bulleid, discussed these events, with particular emphasis on coal consumption and the way the crew had handled their duties. While 8 tons of coal was sufficient for Newcastle, and provided a good reserve, the additional stage to Edinburgh would cut this to the bone. By some means an extra ton or so of coal had to be squeezed on to the tender. With regard to the crew it was clear that they had been tested to the limit. It was a point Gresley accepted without question, as did Bulleid.

So the main issue arising from this trial run was the question of capacity – the amount of coal carried was deemed insufficient to reach Edinburgh with a reasonable safety margin and the pressure on a single crew would be too much.

The answer, as it turned out, was a simple and practical one – design and construct an eight wheeled corridor tender capable of holding 9 tons of coal with a corridor to allow a crew change whilst the train was in motion. Work was quickly put in hand and the new tenders were built and ready for use in the spring the following year.

Another issue to be resolved before the King's Cross to Waverley non-stop service could be contemplated was the state of the line between York and Edinburgh. It was thought that it might present problems for the engine and crew in the last stage of a long, tiring journey. According to a short note written by Ralph Wedgwood to 'Mr Ballam' in early February, its suitability was to be assessed by running a trial to 'test the efficacy of this difficult section of track and make sure engines can pick up sufficient water when passing over the troughs at Wiske Moor and Lucker for their needs without causing delays. Please report to me and the CME the results of these tests'. Ballam, who appears to have worked directly for Wedgwood, did as he was instructed and sent a handwritten note to the General Manager, after a run behind the 1924 built, Gateshead based A1 Pacific No. 2568, *Sceptre,* on 10 February. This seems to have confirmed that all was well and elicited the simple response 'thank you' from the chief. With this task successfully completed, Wedgwood, in consultation with Gresley, could set a date for the inaugural Flying Scotsman non-stop service and harness the skills of the PR Department in ensuring it received maximum publicity.

Memorably engine No. 4472, *Flying Scotsman*, one of five locomotives prepared for the task, was selected to head the inaugural service on 1 May 1928. The engine and the train were showered with publicity in the days and weeks leading up to the great day. However, less was made of the reciprocal service that headed south to London that day pulled by engine No. 2580, *Shotover*, although its performance seems to have equalled 4472's.

However, praise for the new service wasn't universal, as some internal LNER correspondence makes clear. In a memo (produced in full in Appendix 5) to the General Manager, Mr. Ballam, who travelled to Edinburgh with Gresley that day, wrote a less than flattering summary. 'On the present working [set at 8¼ hours] the 'Flying Scotsman' hardly justifies its name I think, that we shall have to face pretty caustic criticism from the public, and the various remarks I overheard on the train only

The LNER's solution to the problem of crew fatigue and insufficient coal was a simple one – construct corridor tenders (above, thought to be in 1928 when attached to 4472 *Flying Scotsman*) that could carry 9 tons of coal and allow the crew to change mid-journey, thus ending the need for stopping. An order for ten new tenders was soon approved and by spring 1928 seven were ready for service with A1s. The last three were allocated to the first three A3s built – Nos. 2743, 2744 and 2745 – and appeared in August that year. It seems that attempts were made to keep their introduction a secret – the publicity value of the new non-stop service to Scotland being deemed too good not to exploit to the full. (below) A corridor tender (thought to be No. 5326) attached to the recently converted A1 to A3 No. 2580, *Shotover*, for her run from Edinburgh to London on 1 May 1928. (BS)

Before the non-stop service between London and Edinburgh commenced it was necessary to consider many issues, one being the state of the network north of York to the Scottish capital. A test run over this section of track was carried by A1 Pacific No.2568, *Sceptre* (top photo, which was taken when the engine was nearing completion at the North British Loco Co's works in Glasgow in August/September 1924) on 10 February 1928 from York to Waverley. The results, as recorded in the two charts above, prepared by Mr Ballam, suggest all was well. (RH)

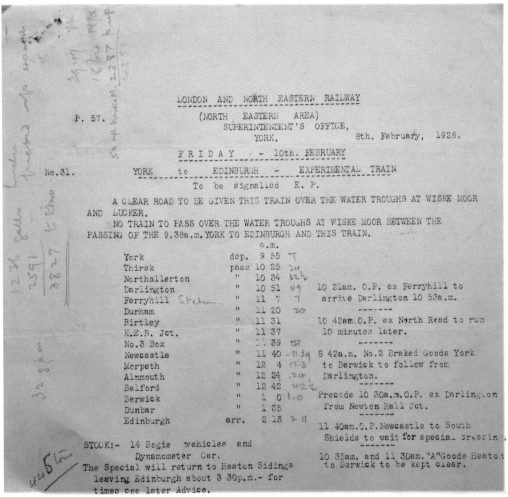

LONDON AND NORTH EASTERN RAILWAY

(NORTH EASTERN AREA)
SUPERINTENDENT'S OFFICE,
YORK.   8th. February, 1928.

P. 57.

F R I D A Y - 10th. FEBRUARY

No.31.   YORK   to   EDINBURGH - EXPERIMENTAL TRAIN

To be signalled E. P.

A CLEAR ROAD TO BE GIVEN THIS TRAIN OVER THE WATER TROUGHS AT WISKE MOOR AND LUCKER.
NO TRAIN TO PASS OVER THE WATER TROUGHS AT WISKE MOOR BETWEEN THE PASSING OF THE 9.38a.m. YORK TO EDINBURGH AND THIS TRAIN.

a.m.

York	dep.	9 55	
Thirsk	pass	10 25	
Northallerton	"	10 34	
Darlington	"	10 51	10 21am. O.P. ex Ferryhill to
Ferryhill	"	11 7	arrive Darlington 10 53a.m.
Durham	"	11 20	
Birtley	"	11 31	10 42am. O.P. ex North Road to run
K.E.B. Jct.	"	11 37	10 minutes later.
No.3 Box	"	11 39	
Newcastle	"	11 40	8 42a.m. No.2 Braked Goods York
Morpeth	"	12 4	to Berwick to follow from
Alnmouth	"	12 24	Darlington.
Belford	"	12 42	
Berwick	"	1 0	Precede 10 30a.m. O.P. ex Darlington
Dunbar	"	1 35	from Newton Hall Jct.
Edinburgh	arr.	2 13	

11 40am.O.P. Newcastle to South
Shields to wait for special crossing.

STOCK:- 14 Bogie vehicles and
Dynamometer Car.

10 35am. and 11 30am. "A"Goods Heaton
to Berwick to be kept clear.

The Special will return to Heaton Sidings leaving Edinburgh about 3 30p.m.- for times see later Advice.

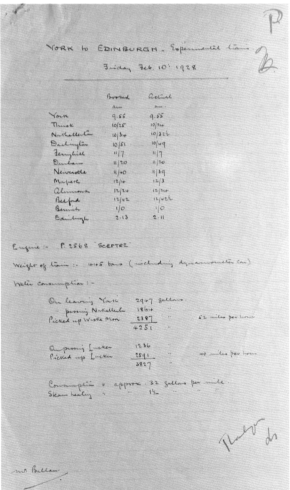

YORK to EDINBURGH. Experimental train

Friday Feb 10: 1928

	Booked	Actual
	a.m.	a.m.
York	9.55	9.55
Thirsk	10/25	10/24
Northallerton	10/34	10/32½
Darlington	10/51	10/49
Ferryhill	11/7	11/7
Durham	11/20	11/20
Newcastle	11/40	11/39
Morpeth	12/4	12/3
Alnmouth	12/24	12/20
Belford	12/42	12/42
Berwick	1/0	1/0
Edinburgh	2.13	2.11

Engine :- P. 2568 "SCEPTRE"

Weight of train :- 445 tons (including dynamometer car)

Water Consumption :-

On leaving York   2947 gallons
passing Northallerton 1864
Picked up Wiske Moor   2387   52 miles per hour
                        4251

On passing Lucker   1236
Picked up Lucker   2591   40 miles per hour
                        3827

Consumption = approx. 32 gallons per mile
Steam leakage   1½

Mr Ballam.

confirms my belief'. Nevertheless, he was generally satisfied with the train which, he reported as providing, 'maximum comfort on their day.'

In terms of timing, the point was well made. However, it would not be until May 1932 that the timings were accelerated to 7 hours and 50 minutes, suggesting that others did not agree with Ballam's assessment.

Bert Spencer, who was also present on the northbound train that day offered a slightly different, more pleasing description of the day. As an engineer, not an operations manager from Wedgwood's HQ team, he would have been assessing the ability of the locomotive and crew to meet such a demanding schedule, leaving timings for others to consider. He wrote:

There [was] a sizeable number of journalists on board as well as Sir Nigel, some of his family and many representatives from the railway. The journey passed without incident though at one stage it was suspected that a tender axle box might be overheating. But, if so, it didn't slow progress or delay the train in any way. Gresley and I took a number of parties up to the cab through the tender much to the CME's great pleasure, especially when taking the controls for short periods. By this stage he was becoming increasingly concerned about his wife's health and the first non-stop run to Edinburgh provided some distraction.

Having proved the viability of the non-stop service to and from

Scotland and seen it become well-established, Gresley and his team could move on to the production of the A3s. However, for the most part they slipped into service with

only minimal press attention, unlike No. 4472, which after her high profile run on 1 May simply garnered more publicity. Such was the allure of her name that in 1929 a

Left, below and overleaf: **Tuesday 1 May** 1928 and 4472 begins to pull away from Euston. For nearly two months before the inaugural run, she had been in the works under 'general repair' making sure she was on the 'top line' as Bert Spencer reported. It was an occasion for Gresley and the Company Chairman, William Whitelaw, to show their faces and enjoy the fruits of their labours. (Left) Gresley travelled with the train heading northwards, here posing with Driver Albert Pibworth, while Whitelaw (lower photo on page 106) greeted the southbound express at King's Cross and is seen congratulating both sets of crew. (DN)

feature film was made that exploited this appeal with great alacrity.

The plot was a simple case of heroes pursuing a villain intent on doing harm, made more interesting because it had a soundtrack. Here the climax of the film sees the 'bady' being pursued along the outside of the *Flying Scotsman* to the footplate of the locomotive as it hurtles northwards. With actors, not stunt men or women, risking their lives without safety equipment of any sort, the action is both dangerous and dramatic. With such a spectacle being enacted on screen, plus this famous engine as star, the film's success was guaranteed, only adding more lustre to 4472's ever growing reputation. This was a trick the LNER would repeat in 1935 when allowing the first A4, *Silver Link*, to appear in Will Hay's film *Oh, Mr Porter*, though on this occasion with no dangerous stunts and fewer risks to life and limb involved.

As this film gradually slipped from public view the more mundane business of life on the railways absorbed 4472 and her sisters. Yet, as this happened, the world was plunged into economic and social chaos by events in the USA. In a scene only too familiar to us today the urge to get something for nothing, through stock trading, overtook any thought of measured and sensible investment, so releasing a beast on New York's Wall Street. Shares rose, great profits were made and this attracted even unwary investors eager for an easy bonus. And like the South Seas Bubble of 1720, reality finally overtook the stock market followed by the inevitable crash with fortunes so rapidly made being lost.

Above and overleaf: **The 1929** thriller *Flying Scotsman* added new lustre to 4472's ever growing reputation in the public eye. Whether the LNER truly understood the nature of the film, and the very dangerous stunts by 'amateurs' that decorated its final scenes, is unclear. These were different times of course, but even so, senior LNER executives probably blanched at the risks being taken with their train and the damage to their reputation that would have followed if an actor had fallen to their death. Luckily all came safely through and 4472 found an even wider audience. These photos were taken during 'the shoot', with the most noteworthy showing Pauline Johnson, then aged 30, risking life and limb without training or safety equipment. This stunning picture then dominated the posters seen around Britain as crowds poured in to see the film. (BS)

It was a panic that quickly spread to Europe, infecting the economies of many countries including Britain.

The Great War was a catastrophe of massive proportions, inflicting huge emotional, physical, social and economic strain on a weary nation for a decade, now this crash threw recovery backwards again. Unemployment rates that had hovered around the 1.25million mark since the war rose rapidly to 3million plus during the early 1930s and most families 'felt the pinch', as it was graphically described at the time. The next few years required a great deal of effort if this recession was to be reversed and much would depend on actions taken by other nations as much as those by Britain itself.

Unfortunately, the revival was painfully slow and by the mid-1930s had barely begun to take effect, many industries still with some way to go before achieving their pre-1929 production levels. This was none more so than on the railways where revenue reduced, to be followed by a drawing in of belts making progress on many fronts difficult. Gresley would have his experimental four-cylinder compound high pressure W1 locomotive and a continuation of his existing A3, D49 4-4-0, J39 0-6-0 and B17 4-6-0 projects to engage him, but other development were held up through lack of funds. Nevertheless, he could still test and experiment where he could and in this way explore ways of improving his engines' performances.

Earlier in this book I briefly described Gresley's experiments with feed water heaters that began in the mid-1920s and focussed on the ACFI designed system. It seems that sufficient benefits were achieved for the CME to extend his experiments into the 1930's with the production of the first P2 2-8-2 No. 2001. In the long term, these experiments came to nothing and these heaters did not find wider favour in Britain. However, along the way two Pacifics were included in this programme – No. 2576 *White Knight* and No. 2580 *Shotover* – and were fitted with the ACFI equipment in 1929; the second engine a year after being converted into an A3. Why they should have

been adapted in this way isn't clear. It may simply have been a way of extending the experiment in preparation for more widespread use of heaters on his biggest engines. If so, the P2 proved to be the last occasion on which it was used and this only until rebuilt as a streamlined engine in 1937/38. 2576 and 2580 retained the heaters until 1938 and '39 respectively when removed during periods of general repair at Doncaster.

In Gresley's hands, the process of testing and evaluating was a continuous one, as he sought to wring the few last drops of potential from each of his engines.

A1 Pacific No. 2576, *White Knight* (left), was equipped with an ACFI feed-water heater during 1929, as was sister engine No. 2580 *Shotover* (below). Both would carry this modification for nine and ten years respectively, suggesting that Gresley was loth to give up these experiments and continued to study the data produced. (BS)

The files held by the National Railway Museum bear witness to all this work and a report compiled in 1930 provides us with one good example of all that he was pursuing at the time. Two new A3s, Nos. 2595, *Trigo*, and 2596, *Manna*, entered service on 22 February but with one notable difference between them. No. 2595 had been built with a slightly modified superheater, in this case a 'long loop version, which agrees with the standard type with the exception that the return is 8–10ft longer, giving approximately 30 per cent increased superheating surface'. As a means of establishing the benefits of this modification, a series of comparative tests were carried out between York and Newcastle during March and April

COMPARATIVE TESTS ON SUPERHEATERS FITTED TO A3 TYPE PACIFIC LOCOMOTIVES. SHEET 1

MADE BETWEEN NEWCASTLE & YORK. MARCH – APRIL 1930.

		ENGINE Nº2595 LONG LOOP ELEMENTS						ENGINE Nº2596 STANDARD ELEMENTS							
DATE		25·3·30		26·3·30		27·3·30		1·4·30		2·4·30		10·4·30		11·4·30	
ROUTE		NEWCASTLE TO YORK	YORK TO NEWCASTLE	NEWCASTLE TO YORK	YORK TO NEWCASTLE	NEWCASTLE TO YORK	YORK TO NEWCASTLE	NEWCASTLE TO YORK	YORK TO NEWCASTLE	NEWCASTLE TO YORK	YORK TO NEWCASTLE	NEWCASTLE TO YORK	YORK TO NEWCASTLE	NEWCASTLE TO YORK	YORK TO NEWCASTLE
LOAD BEHIND ENGINE	TONS	387·75	416·0	390·25	412·5	406·25	409·5	380·0	444·5	388·25		⊕ 438·5	443·25	384·75	480·5
NUMBER OF AXLES		50	48	50	48	54	48	50	52	48		56	52	50	56
NUMBER OF VEHICLES		12	13	12	13	13	13	12	15	12		14	14	12	15
NUMBER OF EXTRA STOPS		-	-	-	-	-	-	-	-	-		-	1	1	-
NUMBER OF SIGNAL & P.W. CHECKS		1	2	2	4	1	2	1	5	2		1	5	3	3
WEATHER		FINE		FINE		FINE		FINE		FINE	LOCOMOTIVE FAILED	FINE		FINE	
WIND - DIRECTION		S.W.		S.W.		S.W.		S		S.W.		-		W	
WIND - VELOCITY	M.P.H	7		6·6		4		10·2		3		NIL		4·5	
DISTANCE	MILES	80·33	80·3	80·33	80·3	80·36	80·3	80·33	80·3	80·33		80·3	80·33	80·31	80·54
TOTAL TIME START TO STOP	MINUTES	106·8	109	106·3	109·1	104·4	103·4	106·6	118·3	104·3		106·7	105·8	104·8	109·3
RUNNING TIME	MINUTES	100·5	104·7	99·1	105·0	97·7	98·1	99·6	114·3	97·3		98·2	102·0	97·9	103·8
AVERAGE SPEED	M.P.H	48·0	46·0	48·6	45·8	49·3	49·1	48·4	42·1	49·5		49·1	47·3	49·2	46·4
MAXIMUM STEAM TEMPERATURE	DEGREES FAH	635	655	645	640	635	640	665	665	660		672	670	662	665
AVERAGE STEAM TEMPERATURE	DEGREES FAH	600	606	588	597	604	606	633	609	618		621	632	616	630
AVERAGE BOILER PRESSURE	lb per □"	190	188	201	201	202	202	200	205	202		201	207	205	196
AVERAGE STEAM CHEST PRESSURE	lb per □"	179	180	181	184	194	189	136	139	149		182	189	186	185
AVERAGE CUT OFF	%	23	25	18	23	17	25	32	32	25		18	20	17	20
AVERAGE DRAWBAR PULL	TONS	2·21	2·46	1·71	2·07	1·98	2·15	1·92	2·09	1·81		2·23	2·52	1·98	2·54
AVERAGE DRAWBAR HORSEPOWER		632	677	496	566	585	630	555	527	536		655	712	581	710

⊕ LOAD INCREASED AT DARLINGTON TO 470·5 TONS.

In early 1930, in an effort to improve their superheating, two new A3s (Nos. 2595 and 2596) were tested, one of them in 'standard' condition the other with a 'long loop' superheater fitted, which increased the heating surface. The results confirmed an anomaly first spotted in the USA some years earlier which had shown that the extra heat generated 'may be lost whilst travelling along the distance in the cooler parts of the tubes'. From this it was concluded that there was no appreciable gain in fitting a 'long loop' superheater. (BS)

when both engines had barely been run in.

To a certain extent, the unnamed trials manager who compiled the report believed the results were affected by variables over which they had no control – principally the skill of each footplate crew, the weather and the varying state of each locomotive as small problems developed affecting performance. In so doing he was consciously, or unconsciously, supporting Gresley's long pursued case for building a dedicated test centre where any variables could be better controlled. Until one was available, making do was all they could do and, as the report makes clear the 'figures were averaged as it is impossible to keep running conditions perfectly uniform throughout a trip'.

In this case, the author concluded that sufficient could be gleaned from the tests to reach some conclusions about the benefits of fitting more 'long loop' superheaters:

(From the figures contained in the chart reproduced above) it may appear odd that the increased superheating surface has resulted in no temperature gain, but when it is considered that this additional surface is towards the smokebox, where the temperature is much lower, it will be seen that it is possible that the heat picked up near the firebox may be lost again whilst travelling along the distance in the cooler parts of the tubes.

Some years ago experiments were carried out in America with different lengths of return bend, and it was found that there was an economical limit

A3 No. 2751 *Humorist* in two of the many smoke lifting experiments carried out between 1932 and 1938. (Above) Here she is seen with a cut out in her smokebox and below with stovepipe chimney, a cut down smokebox plus small deflectors. These were well intentioned experiments but which seem to have been accompanied by little success. Full streamlining of the A4 Pacifics in 1935, plus all six P2s, was deemed to be a far better way of reducing the problem of drifting smoke. (BS)

In developing its record-breaking 'extra high speed' diesel electric railcar service with SVT 877, otherwise known as the Flying Hamburger (here shown at Hamburg Station with the new fast, steam powered railcar on the adjoining platform soon to depart for Lubeck), the DRG threw down a gauntlet that the LNER picked up. Rather than go down a similar route, Wedgwood and Gresley believed they could achieve the same, and better, with their Pacifics and peoceeded to do so with 4472 in November 1934 and even better with A3 No. 2750 *Papyrus* in March the following year. The arrival of the A4 that year cemented the company's ascendency. (THG)

of length, and when this was exceeded there was a fall in temperature which substantiated the results obtained during these current trials.

It is interesting that the author has been careful to explain his reasons for these conclusions and then thrown in a brief reference to research in the USA that underpins his point that there was little to gain from this modification to the superheaters. He was clearly writing for someone, possibly Gresley or Bulleid, who, having set the idea in motion, was more likely to question the findings very closely. Such is the nature of any talented design engineer seeking to push back the boundaries of what was possible, and this appears to have happened here.

It was also at this time that Gresley's developing interest in streamlining, which I described in Chapter 1, was applied to the A1/A3s. Having rehearsed the results of Frederick Johansen's research at the NPL with W1 in 1929, he wished to see if some of these lessons might aid smoke lifting with his Pacifics.

This was a perennial problem for locomotive crew, with poor visibility caused by drifting smoke believed to have been a contributory factor in a number of accidents. With the assistance of Johansen, who had use of the wind tunnel at Teddington, a number of simple modifications were developed and then tested using a scale model of No. 4472. Some of the better ideas emanating from his research, including cut outs in the smokebox, small deflectors

on top of the smokebox and a rimless chimney, were then tried on the real thing, though with little real success. In 1932, A3 No. 2751 *Humorist* was assigned to this trial, which ran on into the late 1930s, then post war were superseded by more successful experiments with larger deflectors of various types on her and other engines. However, the development of completely streamlined engines, though not eradicating the problem of smoke drifting entirely, was thought by many in this country and overseas to present a far better solution to the problem.

In 1932, as *Humorist* began this long period of testing, Gresley and his draughtsmen had begun to consider the merits of full streamlining more actively, partly encouraged by events in Germany.

And as they did so the next stage of the Pacific programme was set in motion and the A1 and A3s began to their slip into comparative obscurity. But before they did so there were two special events to savour. The build up to these is best described by Gresley himself in his 1936 Presidential Address to the IMechE:

In 1932 a new stage in the development of railway operations was initiated by the introduction of extra high-speed railcar service, particularly in Germany. The diesel engine had reached a high state of development and railway engineers produced diesel-electric railcars capable of maintaining much higher average speeds than those of steam trains.

Whether Germany or the USA was first in the field of this new development is immaterial. Engineers in both countries were working simultaneously on the idea and their products appeared in 1932.

After prolonged trials (in Germany) the Flying Hamburger was put into regular service in May 1933; its average speed is 77.4mph. It consists of two coaches only, articulated, and carried on three bogies. The motive power is two Maybach 410hp diesel engines mounted on the outer bogies and directly coupled to electric generators. Since then many new services with two and three coaches have been inaugurated in Germany.

The success and popularity which has followed the introduction of the various extra-high speed trains is such that their running has become firmly established and is bound to be extended.

The demand for trains of greater carrying capacity has led to the development of steam locomotives capable of hauling much heavier trains; such locomotives have been built in Germany and America.

In Germany new streamlined high-speed locomotives were built and in May 1936 a steam operated service started between Berlin and Hamburg making an average speed of over 74mph, which is the fastest steam operated train in the world.

I visited Germany in the latter part of 1934 and travelled in the Flying Hamburger from Berlin to Hamburg and back. I was much impressed with the smooth running of the train at a speed of 100mph, which was maintained for long distances, that I thought it advisable to explore the possibilities of extra high speeds travel by having such a train for experimental purposes.

I approached the makers of the train and furnished them with particulars as to the gradients, curves and speed restrictions on the line between King's Cross and Newcastle. With the thoroughness characteristic of German engineers, they made an exhaustive investigation and prepared a complete schedule showing the shortest possible running times under favourable conditions. They then added 10

per cent, which they regarded as adequate to meet varying weather conditions and to have sufficient time in reserve to make up for such decelerations or delays as might normally be expected.

When he returned to Britain, it seems likely that he and Wedgwood would have discussed the implications of what SVT 877 was achieving with the result that 'My Chief General Manager suggested that with an ordinary Pacific engine faster overall speed could be maintained with a train of much greater weight, capacity, and comfort (than the German railcars).'

The meaning is clear. Wedgwood wanted to consider other options before exploring a diesel railcar solution, if this is what his CME wished to do. Bearing in mind the cost of developing such a service, this represented the most pragmatic approach to the problem. There was also the issue of electrification to consider, which by 1934 was back on the table as a viable option with great impetus provided by central government eager to make full use of the ever-expanding national grid. There would be little point in investing heavily in a diesel solution if electric express trains could soon be developed reasonably quickly. But for the coming of war this would undoubtedly have been the case.

So the die was cast and a plan was outlined that would determine whether steam could do the job as well or better than the DRG's railcar. Inevitably this involved a great deal of testing and analysis. Gresley approached this with some caution and proposed that a

(Right) To Driver William Sparshatt fell the honour of taking 4472 on the trial high speed run from London to Newcastle on 30 November 1934 during which they officially topped 100mph for a steam locomotive for the first time (notwithstanding the GWR's earlier, unofficial claim for this record). (Below) The official log of 4472's record that day. (BS)

trial run be undertaken on Friday 30 November over a shorter distance – King's Cross to Leeds and back the same day – with a train weighing only 147 tons and including restaurant and dynamometer cars. For such a special run, 4472 *Flying Scotsman* was, unsurprisingly chosen.

It seems that a degree of secrecy surrounded this trial. As a result, the engine's departure wasn't attended by the usual clutch of photographers, newsreel cameramen or onlookers. It would be different that evening when the

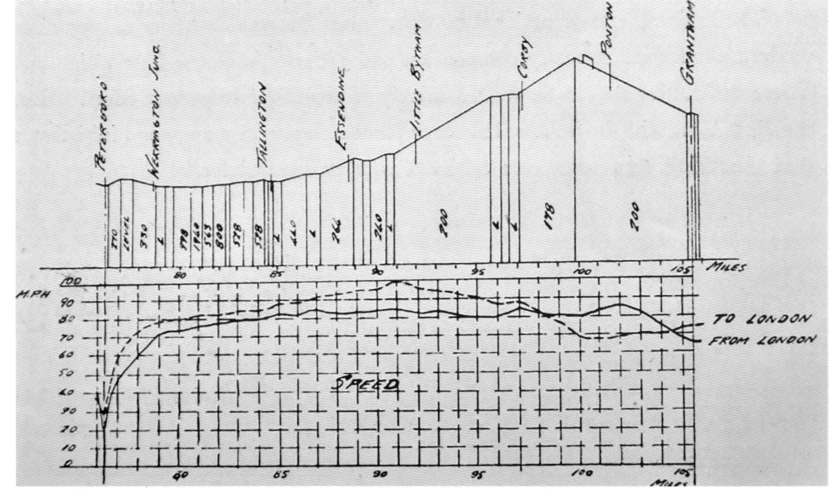

press got wind of the day's events and reporters, including some from the BBC, clamoured for more information. So, the departure went largely unheralded, but had Bulleid on the footplate to assess the engine's performance.

With William Sparshatt and Fireman Robert Webster in charge 'a fast run was expected', as Spencer later wrote. So it proved to be with the driver accelerating the lightly loaded train so quickly away from platform No.11 at King's Cross that he almost derailed the engine on the sharp curve leading to the mainline. After this speedy start he didn't let up for the rest of the day, exhausting his fireman in the process, as a rather breathless report in the LNER's *Journal* made clear:

The outstanding features of the outward trip were the 94.7mph at Three Counties and the most wonderful uphill climb from Tallington to Stoke tunnel at an average of 82½mph, the overall timing from King's Cross to Leeds being 151 min 56 sec., 13 min .04 sec. under schedule.

In view of the more satisfactory results achieved, it was decided to add two extra vehicles to the train, bringing the load up to 208 tons. The return journey was not uneventful and the outstanding excitement was the run between Stoke tunnel and Essendine. It was quite obvious to those on board that history was being rapidly made, and mile posts of 97½mph and 100mph were reported – the dynamometer car reading subsequently confirming the latter. The sensation of timing these speeds

was even more exciting than watching a closely run race, and the thrill as the quarter-mile posts were passed at an ever reducing number of fifths of seconds is indescribable. King's Cross was reached in 157 min 17 sec., again under schedule despite a serious permanent way slack near Sandy, and the second run was over.

Hearty congratulations to Driver Sparshatt for his courage, skill and determination, whilst Fireman Webster put up an equally fine performance of skill and endurance. Inspector Holder, who rode with them, also played his part on the footplate.

It is interesting to note that at all speeds the riding was excellent and gave no cause for unease at any time.'

When later recalling the day's event, in his speech to the IMechE, Gresley made no mention of the speeds achieved, but simply stated:

'A trial with a train of seven bogies demonstrated that the run could be accomplished with reliability in less than four hours under normal conditions. I felt that to secure a sufficient margin of power it would be essential to streamline the engine and train as effectively as possible, and at the same time to make sundry alterations to the design of cylinders and boiler which could conduce to freer running and to securing an ample reserve of power for fast uphill running.

While the research was in progress the opportunity was taken to measure the

A rare picture of 4472 *Flying Scotsman* on 30 November as she thundered to Newcastle and back that day breaking a significant record in the process. (BS)

air resistance, at zero yaw, of one-twelfth scale models of the LNE locomotives *Flying Scotsman* No. 4472 and No. 10000 (4-6-4) (the latter already having been wind tunnel tested at Teddington when under development to ascertain the most effective streamline shape to fit around its unique boiler arrangement).

We discovered that with a total air resistance of 38.4% the horse-power absorbed by the unstreamlined Pacific with six coaches would amount to 111 at 60mph, 262 at 80mph, 512 at 100mph and 885 at 120mph. When we later compared this to LMS's six-hour runs between London and Glasgow we estimated that the horse-power absorbed by air resistance amounted to about 380 hp over the course of the journey (and about 43 % of the drawbar horse-power). In both cases, it was concluded that a streamlined locomotive and train would have been considerably more effective.

However, before we grappled more fully with the general principles of streamlining we sought answers to the perennial question of drifting smoke, the dangers this caused and the best way to eradicate or reduce the problem.

According to Spencer:

Gresley was loth to apply the sort of smoke deflectors then coming into use, particularly on the LMS's Royal Scots, to his Pacifics believing that they destroyed their classic lines.

Instead we were committed to a number of experiments and began modifying two A3s to test different theories. On one, engine No. 2747 Coronach, the smokebox was cut away or had small deflectors added after a Kylchap exhaust and then a double chimney were fitted.

The NPL played a key role in this work, but were too hard pressed with other wind tunnel testing tasks, relating to aircraft and ship development, to do all we required and so agreement was reached with the City and Guilds Engineering College to undertake some of the testing work in their laboratories. This ensured that any proposal that might help steam and smoke to be thrown clear of the cab, particularly when working at early cut-off, might prove effective when matched to a full scale locomotive. To assist in this direction and to provide an improved lookout the cab front was made wedge-shaped – a practice followed in the subsequent A4 programme, the P2s, when engine No. 10000 was rebuilt, the two streamlined B17s and the conventionally shaped V2 2-6-2 tender engines.

The trial was deemed a great success and supported the development of this type of service and new trains to haul them. As a result, Wedgwood presented a memo to the board in early January summarising the results of the test and seeking approval to design and build a new locomotive and rolling stock to take the proposed service to a new level of speed and comfort.

With time pressing, he was given outline permission to proceed with this remarkably ambitious plan, one that would very soon become linked to celebrations surrounding King George V's Silver Jubilee.

As planning proceeded, so a second high-speed trial was held on 5 March, this time between London and Newcastle, with A3, No. 2750, *Papyrus* in charge. One of the many reports written at the time recorded that:

The LNER beat the world's record for speed by a steam train by running from London to Newcastle in under four hours. The train consisting of a dynamometer car, restaurant car, three first-class corridor coaches, and a brake van, had a weight of 213 tons, with a seating capacity of 204 passengers, and was hauled by a 'Super Pacific' type engine, built at Doncaster in 1929.

The train left King's Cross at 9.8 am and reached Newcastle at 1.4½ pm., nearly four minutes ahead of schedule. As far as Doncaster timings were inside schedule, but owing to the derailment of some wagons at Arksey, it was necessary to slow down and finally to stop, because of single line working ahead. By Darlington the lost time had been regained and the average speed for the whole journey was 67½mph. The highest speed recorded was 88mph just north of Hitchin. The driver of the outward run was H. Gutteridge and his fireman A. Wightman.

At Gateshead sheds 'Papyrus' was found to be in excellent

condition and was used for the
return journey with W. Sparshatt
as driver and R. Webster as
fireman. At 3.47 pm the return
journey was begun. As far as
Grantham schedule times only
were kept as long slack was
necessary north of Doncaster
at the scene of the derailed
coal train, but after this driver
Sparshatt took the opportunity
of showing what his engine
could do. For over 12 miles from
Corby and down the long drop
from Stoke Box to Tallington, the
average speed was over 100mph
and just south of Little Bytham
105.5mph was registered for 30
seconds, and for 10 seconds it
reached 108mph. This it may
be confidently asserted marks a
world's record for speed.

The whole journey from
Newcastle to King's Cross was
completed in 3 hrs 51mins at an
average speed of 69.6mph. The
train had thus covered 536.4
miles in 7 hrs 47½ mins.

At the AGM meeting of
the LNER, held on the 8th, in
London, Mr William Whitelaw,
the chairman, said the trial
run was so encouraging that
they would give immediate
consideration to the question of
putting on a record speed train,
to be called the 'Silver Jubilee,
between King's Cross and
Newcastle in the autumn.

This was a great triumph, but it
was one that contained a note of
finality for the A1/A3 programme.
They could still lead the way,
when it came to pulling many
of the LNER's express passenger
services, but the streamlined A4
Pacifics, which began to appear in

A3 No. 2750 *Papyrus*
gets underway from
King's Cross on its record
breaking return trip to
Newcastle on 5 March
1935. (BS/RH)

With the dawn of 1935 the A1/A3s dominated the East Coast Mainline and, with 4472 at their head, continued to attract press interest. No. 2750 *Papyrus'* record run on 5 March that year only served to cement their reputation in the public's eye. But a new wind was blowing at Doncaster and in September that year would be unleashed with the streamlined A4s quickly usurping the older Pacifics, which continued to ply their trade for the next 30 years or so, but out of the limelight. Here No. 2566 *Ladas*, the 1924 built A1, does just that at an unrecorded location. In 1939, she will be rebuilt as an A3 in which state will remain in service until 1962. (RH)

September 1935, would soon eclipse them in the public eye and take over many of the most glamourous duties. Only time would tell if they could recapture some of this star quality, and here 4472 would always lead the way. Then came the war and all locomotives, whatever their purpose or status, simply became anonymous, utilitarian machines in a much deadlier contest, this time for survival.

Chapter 4

FOLLOW THEM TO THE END OF THEIR DAYS

When the sleek, ultra-modern A4s first appeared, the casual observer might have been forgiven for thinking that they represented a major step forward in steam locomotive design. The reality may have been rather different, as my late uncle, Ronald Hillier, who witnessed the first running of the A4 pulled Silver Link service in 1935, later observed:

[There was] speculation about its design. Such an advanced shape must have had something special inside, especially when news of its high-speed runs appeared. It was easy to forget that it was just another steam locomotive and its modern form may not have reflected the aging and soon to be obsolescent state of its engineering.

The contrast in looks and style between the A4s and A1/A3s (here represented by No. 4467 *Wild Swan* and 4480 *Enterprise*, photographed near King's Cross Station) is only too apparent, leading some casual observers to believe that the new engines contained many new, cutting edge features. In reality the only significant difference lay in the level of streamlining employed, other elements, sometimes enlarged, were simply carried over from one class to the other as part of an evolutionary process. (RH)

This may well have been so, but they were important nonetheless because, as Bert Spencer recorded:

They were the final step in a process begun before the Great War. Their impact on the railway world was huge; far far greater than his A1 and A3 Pacifics, the P2s or any other of his designs. Some later wrote them off as a publicity stunt because of their streamlining, but this does them a great dis-service. They were much more than that and, I believe, benefitted greatly from research into aerodynamics carried out over many decades. It was these ideas mixed with Gresley's own well established design principles that produced these exceptional locomotives.

From this it may be safe to assume that the 'streaks' represented a major step forward, but their creation probably signified that steam had reached the peak of its development and its decline had begun. However, no one could have foreseen in 1935 that steam locomotion would enjoy an Indian Summer brought on by the trauma of another world war and its consequences. But for these tragic events, Gresley's plans for electrification would surely have taken root more quickly and provided a more efficient successor to steam, so foreshortening the lives of the Pacifics and much else besides.

So the A4's arrived and, in due course, their number would increase to thirty-five, adding substantially to an already large fleet of Pacifics. Comparisons between each class were inevitable,

but, of course they had much in common because of the evolutionary nature of Gresley's work. He was by nature a scientist who advanced by measured steps, at each stage analysing performance and testing alternative solutions, when they presented themselves. Spencer again caught a flavour of this when describing how lessons learnt when operating the A1/A3s had been absorbed by designers into the A4 programme:

The cab layout was very similar to the A3s. The wheel diameters and wheelbase divisions were the same and the axle loading remained at 22 tons. Gresley's standard three-cylinder and 2 in 1 conjugated valve gear was also used without modification. He also perpetuated the use of ball and roller bearings in the reversing shaft, the eccentric crank bearing vacuum operated clutch and the conjugating levers.

He then moved on to describe where modifications had been applied to enhance the A4's performance:

Several modifications were made in the basic three-cylinder Pacific design to ensure freer running and an ample reserve of power for fast uphill working. The boiler pressure was increased from 220lb to 250lb per sq in and the distance between the tubeplates was reduced from 19ft to 17ft 11⅞in, the combustion chamber length being increased accordingly.

The three 18½in x 26in cylinders [as opposed to

cylinders measuring 19in x 26in on the A3s] were provided with piston valves increased from 8in to 9in diameter and particular attention was paid to the size and shape of the steam and exhaust passages. In the actual casting the passages were carefully examined and all roughness removed. Standard Pacific valve gear, with full cut-off restricted to 65 per cent, was fitted.

To this would be added another modification that Gresley had been toying with for a time. Over a four-year period, he had been conducting trials with the Kyosti Kylala and Andre Chapelon Kylchap designed double blastpipe and chimney, beginning with P2 No. 2001 *Cock of the North*. In due course, the other five members of this class would be similarly fitted. He then modified his W1, No, 10000, in 1935 with the same system in an attempt to rescue this experimental locomotive from the ignominy of failure. It didn't help sufficiently and in 1937 the engine was rebuilt in conventional, but streamlined form, retaining the Kylchap system in the process.

Determined to explore this concept further, Gresley then applied the Kylchap system to the 1929 built A3 No. 2751 *Humorist* to see if the Pacifics might benefit from this modification. To do this, he applied the version he had used on the W1 in 1935, but with the diameter of the choke increased to 1ft 3in, to match the space available in the Pacific. This led to the chimney orifice being increased to 1ft 5⅜in, while the liner's bottom opening was set at 1ft 4 13/16 in.

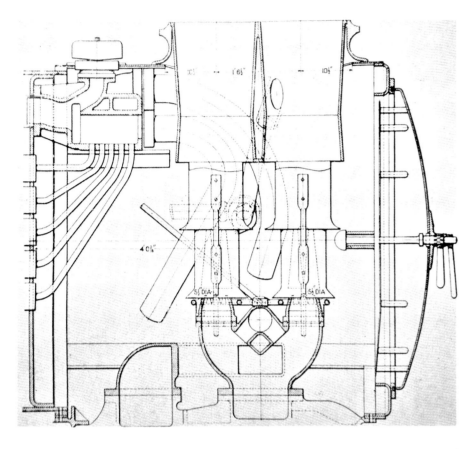

locomotives, including the early Pacifics would benefit from Kylala and Chapelon's work, though it wouldn't be a quickly moving programme.

Although the A4s took over many of the duties the A1/A3s had once dominated, they weren't eclipsed as front-line engines. The same could not be said of Raven's five A2 Pacifics, which had laboured in comparative obscurity since first appearing in 1922. Surprisingly, no real effort was made to modify these engines and bring them closer to the Gresley model. However, there were two significant exceptions.

In September 1929, No. 2404 was fitted with a spare A1 boiler, because it was cheaper to do so when a replacement was needed than build a new boiler to match those produced by the NER for these engines years earlier. To do this, No. 2404's firebox had

(Left) How the Kylchap exhaust and the double blastpipe system were adapted for use on an A3. Before this happened, the system had been tried on the P2s and W1 then A3 No. 2751, pictured below with these modifications added. During Gresley's time as CME, very few engines were so fitted and there is no clear indication that he wished to convert all his high-performance engines in this way. However, it was a solution that BR continued to explore post war with Bert Spencer as a very keen advocate, suggesting he may have been gently pushed by Gresley to experiment with the concept in the first place. (BS)

At the same time, the diameter of the blastpipe orifice was fixed at 5¼ in. and taper blocks fitted to restrict the nozzle area of both pipes set to 33.92 sq in.

During July 1937, *Humorist* was returned to traffic, with small deflectors fitted on either side of the new chimney, for evaluation. Together these modifications were deemed a success and so it was decided to extend the experiment to the A4 programme. In 1938, four new engines – 4468 *Mallard*, as a prototype, then 4901 *Capercaillie*, 4902 *Sea Gull* and 4903 *Peregrine* – were fitted with this exhaust system, with 4468 employing the concept to good effect in July 1938 when breaking the speed record for steam. In due course, other

Vincent Raven's fifth and final Pacific – A2 No. 2404 *City of Ripon* – after being modified in 1929 with a spare A1 boiler, making it look like a hybrid NER/GNR engine. It was an unrepeated experiment and by 1937 all the A1s 1922 competitors had, rightly or wrongly, been withdrawn from service and scrapped. (BS)

Below left and below right: **The arrival** of the A4s in 1935 saw the streamliners begin to grab the headlines that had once the province of the A1/A3s. They continued to ply their trade, as these two pictures of No. 4472 demonstrate, but never again, in LNER or BR service, would they enjoy the iconic status that had once been their due. Only in preservation would *Flying Scotsman* get this back, and more. (BS)

to be increased in length and the footplate had to be widened, all of which gave the locomotive a distinctively Gresley look. This was further enhanced in 1934 when the original NER 6-wheeled tender was replaced by Gresley 8-wheeled non-corridor tenders.

Nevertheless, these modifications could not save 2404, or her sisters for that matter, and limited route accessibility was cited as the reason for their withdrawal from service in 1936/37. The existence of so many other Pacifics and the arrival of the

V2 2-6-2s would also have weighed heavily in this debate. Ex-members of the North Eastern Railway might have been saddened by the loss of the A1s' 1922 rival, after only 13 or 14 years of service, but Gresley was unlikely to have viewed them with any great enthusiasm. So they were consigned to the scrapyard, allowing him to fill their place with more A4s in the LNER's inventory.

The years up to the outbreak of war in September 1939 saw some revival in Britain's finances and while huge social and economic

pressures still existed, leaving a trail of poverty in its wake, many saw these years as a period of recovery. The LNER, and the other big railway companies, saw trade pick up, with its express passenger services attracting ever increasing numbers of travellers. However, the network's infrastructure was badly in need of extensive modification and repair, and this tended to absorb much of the income that was being generated. And then came the Second World War and a further period of decline

in the railway's condition. So, it is, perhaps, unsurprising that the number of accidents increased, some of these involving the A1/A3s. The most serious of them, in the pre-war years, took place on a snowy afternoon, later described as a 'white out', in Scotland during December 1937.

At 16.37 hrs on the 10th, the afternoon express train from Edinburgh to Glasgow, which had left the capital only minutes earlier pulled by A3 No. 2744 *Grand Parade,* was in collision with the late-running 2:00 pm express train from Dundee to Glasgow at Castlecary Station, killing 35 people with 179 injured.

The Edinburgh train hit the rear of the standing Dundee train at an estimated speed of 70mph. Due to the confined nature of the crash site, the rear four coaches of the Dundee train disintegrated completely. The engine of the Dundee train, LNER Class D29 No. 9896 *Dandie Dinmont,* was pushed forward by nearly 100yds with the brakes on. The Edinburgh train's locomotive, which had been buried under some of its own over-riding carriages, was damaged and later towed to the works for assessment.

It seems that in the rush to clear the damaged trains and before all the facts were known, responsibility for the accident was deemed to fall on the shoulders of the driver of the Edinburgh train. As a result, he was committed to court on a charge of culpable homicide for allegedly driving too fast in very poor weather conditions, but, after further investigation, the charge was dropped. Instead, the Accident Inspecting Officer, in his official report, concluded that

the signalman was primarily at fault. Bearing in mind the terrible weather conditions prevailing at the time, this judgement may seem harsh, especially as the Dundee train had also run past a signal set to danger due to poor visibility, only managing to stop just beyond

Left, below and overleaf: **The dreadful** aftermath of the accident at Castlecary on 10 December 1937 when the driver of A3 No. 2744 *Grand Parade,* which was pulling an Edinburgh to Glasgow express, failed to see danger signals and ploughed into the back of another passenger train, which itself had overrun signals but had been brought to a rapid halt by a more alert crew. As a result, 35 people died and 179 were injured. The 1928 built Pacific, though appearing to be lightly damaged, was written-off and days later the next A3 in the production line received her name. (BS)

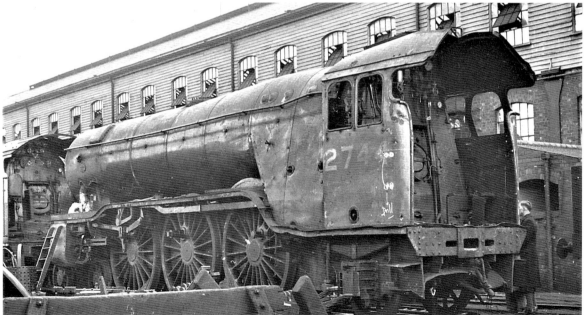

it. Then the Edinburgh train did the same but didn't pull up in time. Despite this, it was still thought that the Castlecary signalman had, in those few very difficult minutes, failed to check the first train's whereabouts and then allowed the following train into the section. With so many dead and injured, someone had to be held responsible, but, in the circumstances, the 'guilty party' seems to have been more a victim of circumstances than deliberate error.

Even though Britain had enjoyed peace for twenty years, events in Europe, led by the rise of Nazism and Fascism, were taking Europe inexorably towards another war. While Gresley's Pacifics went about their business, all around them was about to change as a shaky peace gave way to appeasement and, finally, the outbreak of the bloodiest conflict imaginable. Yet, when it came, many were still surprised and shocked that it had come to this and went on as though the trouble might pass. It didn't and Britain had to hastily make good years of letting its defences make do with limited investment. All this rapidly changed, but it takes a long time and much money to turn round years of neglect and so it proved to be in the early years of the war.

As happened in 1914, the government virtually nationalised the whole railway network overnight and pressed it into war service. But kneejerk reactions are invariably accompanied by poorly thought-out solutions. For the LNER's Pacifics, this meant that some bright soul thought them too glamorous to survive the rigours of war and mothballing for the duration was the only viable course of action to take. Some in fact were withdrawn from service until Gresley, as Spencer recalled later, pointed out that 'the Pacifics were just locomotives and were capable of pulling huge loads of any type'. Spencer then added that the CME's arguments 'prevailed … and throughout the war they did sterling service with minimal maintenance and attention'.

The size of the additional work that fell on the shoulders of the LNER's workforce in 1939 was enormous. Ronald Matthews, who had become Chairman in 1938, later tried to quantify the size of the task and the effort needed to guarantee success:

During those years, special trains with troops, stores, ammunition and other Government traffic numbered 127,000 apart from the vast tonnage of traffic and innumerable passenger journeys by ordinary services on Government account. There was also the part played by the LNER in connection with the Bomber Offensive. With more than three quarters of the Nation's bomber aerodromes on its system, the LNER bore the brunt of the vast movement necessary to build them, staff them and service them. The building of the aerodromes in East Anglia alone involved 1,700 special trains in the transport of 750,000 tons of slag and tarmac: the movement of aerodrome personnel called for 460 special trains and every raid of 1,000 bombers meant the running of 28 trains of petrol and 8 trains of bombs over our

In the years immediately before the Second World War, Gresley's health was noticeably in decline as arteriosclerosis slowly took hold. Although only 60 when this photo was taken, he looks much older and the effects of this advancing illness seem only too obvious. On 5 March 1936, he is pictured alongside B17 4-6-0 the day it was named *Arsenal* at King's Cross Station. (BS)

system. Without efficient rail transport the Bomber Offensive as planned would have been impossible.

Luckily, all this work did not fall in the first two years of the war; if it had, no company, no matter how well run, could have coped. In reality there was a slow build up that gradually absorbed more and more effort to match an ever growing world wide commitment by Britain's armed forces. But it was a war of attrition which soon began to drain the reserves of both men and machines, none more so than on the railways. In the hands of someone like Gresley, who had always displayed such skill and energy in managing his department, the impossible could become the possible. However, illness had

stripped him of much of his vitality and by 1940 he was unable to contribute as much as he had once done. So it fell to his senior officers, led by Edward Thompson and Arthur Peppercorn, to shoulder this ever increasing burden. When Gresley died on 5 April 1941, and in recognition of the great skills he had displayed throughout his career, Thompson stepped up to become CME.

In the first two years of his tenure, defeat was a strong possibility and every effort was being made to produce a workable fleet of engines to match the heavy demands placed on them. But, as staff left to join the forces, there was a lowering of maintenance standards which effected engine availability. This was none more so than with Gresley's three-cylinder

As the war progressed, Gresley's Pacifics found themselves becoming mixed traffic engines. In this case No. 2597 *Cicero*, in a very clean state, appears to be making light work of a very long line of wagons. (BS)

engines. Statistics collected by the CME's own staff soon confirmed this to be so, particularly with the Pacifics and the increased maintenance they required to keep them going in the face of such heavy demand.

In confirmation of this, we have an account written by E.S. Beavor, a pre-war Doncaster apprentice who would rise to become a Locomotive Shed Master, who hinted at significant and unquantified problems in the running department with Gresley's valve gear:

After the first year of the chaotically deteriorated maintenance following the outbreak of war, Gresley's 2-to-1 conjugated valve was running

about on many locomotives with so much wear that steam distribution was seriously inefficient. This condition had led to so many over-loaded middle big ends that even Gresley in his later days was significantly worried about it. To a notable degree it was due to his own gross lack of concern for repair facilities in the running sheds [over which he had no day to day control] ; King's Cross 'Top Shed' in particular was a disgrace of a place …

None of the sheds were provided with even the simplest equipment which would have enabled local staff to overhaul a 2-to-1 gear. Instead, the parts had to be sent away by

stores van to the main works, and the engine itself was then immobilized for a week or longer before the material came back again.

With direct government control to contend with, this wasn't solely a matter for the LNER to sort out. In 1941, the Minister of Transport set up a committee, under the chairmanship of Sir Alan Mount, the Chief Inspecting Officer of Railways, to oversee the use being made of all the workshops. He had, as his main target, the need to sort out 'the extreme unevenness of work being undertaken in support of the war' and identify any significant problems. All the CMEs were members as were representatives of various government ministries and the Admiralty. At the same time, the Mechanical and Electrical Sub-Committee of the Railway Executive, formed early in the war, came under the chairmanship of William Stanier. Its brief was similar to the Mount Committee and in this role could wield considerable power and influence over individual railway companies.

Ernest Cox, observed the workings of both committees and the extreme pressure they brought to bear on the CMEs of each company. He wrote:

The Mount Committee waged a ceaseless war of nerves on the CMEs and Sir Alan used techniques of his former enquiries into train accidents to conduct inquisitions into everything which prevented or delayed increase in Government work in railway shops (both committees gathered fortnightly for meetings throughout the war).

By March 1942 the first rumbles were heard of shortages of locomotives to cope with the enormously increasing war traffic and the REC had to report that it was 500 locomotives short to deal even with the traffic in hand, to say nothing of what was to come. Now all our activities were thrown into reverse and within a month or two Mount and committee were exerting as much pressure to get all war work out of the workshops which could in any way impede production of locomotives and wagons. The companies were only permitted to build mixed traffic or freight engine.'
In such a critical environment, any significant maintenance

and availability issue would be scrutinised closely. So the growing problem of the Gresley engines was finally brought to their attention. We do not know who sponsored this or why and there has been speculation over the years that it was Thompson himself, desperate to get the matter sorted out. Either way, he decided to engage Stanier, as chairman of the M & E Sub-committee, in the debate and sought his advice and opinion on the subject.

Cox left behind a brief, but interesting account of what happened next:

This association led to an intensely interesting diversion in 1942 when Thompson arranged with Stanier for me to visit and prepare a report on the 2 to 1 valve gear … It was an unassailable fact that unit play at each of the eight pin joints

was multiplied by eleven by the time it reached the middle valve, and in fully rundown condition the lost motion could amount to ⅜th. This resulted in reduced power at low speeds due to insufficient port opening,

Left and above: **The effort** to meet the requirements of war took an ever increasing toll on the locomotives, rolling stock and the railway's infrastructure. This was especially so when the Blitz began in 1940. Bombing raids hit most parts of Britain, with the railways becoming primary objectives for the Luftwaffe. Engine sheds and stations were easy targets in daylight, much less so at night in the black-out, and many were hit as these two photos demonstrate very graphically. In the right hand picture, an unidentified A1/A3 just seems to have avoided destruction, other engines being far less lucky. (BS)

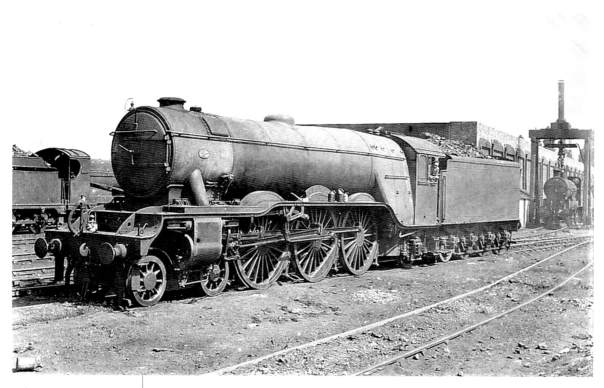

As the war progressed, lower cleaning standards would often make the engines virtually anonymous, as this picture quickly confirms. Sadly, Bert Spencer kept no notes with this photograph except for the year '1943'. However, the nameplate, although covered in dirt suggests she may be 2543 *Melton* which didn't become an A3 until 1947. (BS)

while at high speeds the combined effect of overtravel of the valve, plus whip in the combining levers, could produce up to 50% more power in the middle cylinder than in either of the outside. There was also a spate of hot inside big-ends, ten times as many in the inside position as at the outside, six times as many as the LM experienced with the inside big-ends on a comparable number of its own three-cylinder engines. The high speed engines of the 4-6-2 class suffered the highest proportion of failures, the 2-6-2 and 2-8-2 types also being high. A certain lack of stiffness in the marine big-end arrangement also appeared to contribute to this result.

The '2 to 1' valve gear although theoretically correct is,

in practice, incapable of being made into a sound mechanical job, and rapid wear of the pins, and incorrect steam distribution, are the inevitable results of its use. In view of its inherent defects and the discontinuance of its use throughout the world, a good case can be made for not perpetuating it in any future design.

It is certain that with this arrangement of valve gear it will be necessary to give the engines a frequent overhaul in the Shops and even then it is not possible to eliminate the effect of lost motion due to running clearance required in the pin joints and the effect of expansion of the outside valve spindle on the inside valve.

It is a matter of consideration, therefore, as to whether certain

of the classes should not be fitted with an independent inside valve gear.

The excessive inside big end trouble experienced is, in my opinion, due mainly to the design of the big end. The alternative designs already developed by the LNER should alone bring about considerable improvements. The use of higher grade white metal and the elimination of the brass strip across the bearing are also, in my view, worthy of consideration in view of extensive experience with three-cylinder engines on the LMS.'

Thompson accepted this report in its entirety, but before implementing its recommendations, he debated the issues raised with his General Manager and, presumably, sought the opinion of Peppercorn and Windle. Later he wrote that:

'After considerable discussion we agreed that an independent report should be submitted on the working of all engines on the LNER with this motion. The resulting report led to a fundamental change of direction of LNER locomotive policy'.

On the cover of his copy of the report, Charles Newton, who had become General Manager in 1939, has written 'Standardisation of locomotives and rolling stock is essential if we are to make this work ...' And earlier, he sent a memo to Thompson encouraging him to 'press ahead with this work in all haste, but with due regard given to other priorities'. So sanctioned, the CME could begin

to tackle the growing problem of the three-cylinder engines and, at the same time, set down his thoughts on standardisation and begin the process of narrowing down the number and types of engines to be included in an all-encompassing plan. But wartime need still took priority and he must have realised that such a programme would only come to fruition when the conflict had been brought to a successful conclusion. In tackling this task, Thompson began by setting down a number of guidelines for Newton's agreement:

Standardisation is not intended to lay down hard and fast rules from which

there can be no departure. It is only necessary to see where the bulk of the traffic can be dealt with by a limited number of locomotive classes, keeping in mind the necessity for continuous study and testing to judge whether improvements or modifications are required from time to time.

By this means the advantages of standardisation can be secured without involving the stagnation so far as research and development are concerned. If improvements were considered desirable in one of the standard types, one or two locomotives would be selected for experimental purposes. These

after modification to incorporate the new devices and new ideas, would be tested against unaltered engines, and if they proved satisfactory would form the basis for a change in the standard.

From this point we need to consider a more comprehensive policy, the first step being to divide locomotive types, totalling 166, into three Groups:

The new standard types will be constructed when it has been established that a demand cannot be met by one of the existing types.

The second group includes existing locomotive types which are considered worth maintaining until the end of their useful lives – new

Something of a mystery surrounds this photo. The notes attached to this negative by Bert Spencer simply record '2567 about to be lifted – 1944'. There is nothing more specific regarding location, date or reason for the 'lift'. If it were a maintenance task the operation would surely have been carried out in a workshop with their overhead travelling cranes. So, it seems more likely that the cranes are lifting her back on to the track after a derailment. (BS)

No. 4470 *Great Northern* had by the time war came slipped down the pecking order of Gresley's Pacifics and was described as being 'an average old tub with nothing much to write home about – a low pressure A1 rarely used on the heaviest jobs'. In this state, she could have been turned out as an A3 or, as happened, become a candidate for rebuilding as a new type of Pacific. So, in September 1945, she emerged as a prototype Class A1/1, in the process setting-off a controversy, over Thompson's perceived motives in authorising this conversion, that has lasted to this day. (BS)

boilers will be built for them as required and they will not be broken up until they become obsolete (there are eleven types in this group - the A1, A3, A4, B17, D49, B16, K3, V2, O4, V1 and V3s).

The third group includes all the remaining locomotive types, all considerably older types which are no longer satisfactory or whose work could, with advantage, be transferred to one of the new types in group one. Nevertheless, this is only a general policy, and not an invariable rule.

It would seem from this paper that, although he had serious concerns about the condition of engines with Gresley's 2 to 1 valve gear, Thompson still saw them playing an active role for many years to come. Nevertheless, he had no intention of building more and when considering his new standard designs decided to focus on alternative solutions. With the war

coming to an end, he could begin to experiment and did so with engines deemed increasingly unfit for their duties for one reason or another, or simply to try out new ideas on any locomotive entering the workshops for a period of major maintenance.

By 1944, the A1s were all approaching 20 years of age or more. Like most locomotives of the time, they had become the worse for wear due to the heavy demands placed on them by war. So, it was inevitable that high performance engines such as this should suffer more than other types because they tended to be worked to their maximum capacity over prolonged periods. Some of them had been modified to become A3s in a project that crawled along at a snail's pace until 1948 but did not tackle the central issue of correcting the declining state of Gresley's 2 to 1 valve gear. For some reason, No. 4470 *Great Northern* wasn't included in this programme and by 1944 was described by Richard Hardy, then working as a

draughtsman at Donacster, as being 'an average old tub with nothing much to write home about at that time – a low pressure A1 rarely used on the heaviest jobs.'

So, despite being the first of Gresley's Pacifics she had become little more than another engine that had slipped down the pecking order. In this guise, she became a candidate for rebuilding, as Thompson considered the next generation of standard Pacifics and wished to experiment with some alternative ideas, particularly the removal of the conjugated valve gear. So, in May 1945 she entered the workshops to re-appear four months later still as a Pacific, but in an entirely new guise.

The rights or wrongs of this conversion have since set off a long running controversy, with some claiming that Thompson, for some reason, acted out of spite by deliberately destroying Gresley's magnificent prototype. The truth of the matter seems to be that Thompson, aided by his Chief Draughtsman Edward Windle, was simply making plans for the future, as he was tasked to do by his Chairman and General Manager. To do this, and with limited resources at his disposal, he decided to follow a course Gresley often took and experimented with an existing locomotive to see what might be achieved. *Great Northern* was next in line for repair and became his prototype for the next generation of standard Pacifics. Was there malice in his actions? Probably not, but in Appendix 4 I have analysed in detail the whys and wherefores of the case and how the modifications of 4470 were seen at the time.

However, 4470 proved to be the only A1 converted in this way and Thompson, having tested his theories on new designs, allowed the remaining seventeen members of the class to be rebuilt as A3s instead. In reaching this decision, he may have been helped by information he and Windle gleaned from the construction of four A2/1 Pacifics, in place of four new V2 2-6-2s, and the rebuilding of the six 2-8-2 P2s as Class A2/2 Pacifics during 1944/45. From all this work emerge the Class 2/3s in 1946/47 and then the new Class A1s (which meant the remaining Gresley A1s were all redesigated A10s) and A2s in 1947/49 under Peppercorn's guiding hand.

For those who like to speculate on railway matters, the LNER's Pacific programme over 27 years has left a rich legacy of design work and controversy to explore with the inevitable comparison between Gresley's Pacifics and their successors at its core. However, one inevitable conclusion the impartial might reach is that the A1/A3s stood up well against the types that followed. This was specially so in their modified state and despite any limitations placed on them by having to run with the 2 to 1 valve gear. Would they have been better if this had been replaced by a third set of independent valve gear? Possibly, but Thompson wasn't prepared to sanction this change, preferring instead to allow staff in workshops and sheds to cope with any problems the conjugated valve gear caused.

In doing this, he may have provided an answer to those who later questioned his motives in rebuilding *Great Northern*. If he

The streamlined P2s become Pacifics. During 1944, long running problems with these engines, including incidents of fractured crank axles, were highlighted by the Regional Manager responsible for them, and prompted Thompson and Windle to consider how these difficulties might be overcome. Their solution was to rebuild them as Class A2/2 Pacifics. These two pictures capture No. 2006/60506 *Wolf of Badenoch* before and after conversion. (BS/RH)

In 1946, the LNER introduced two new numbering system for its locomotives. Here we see No. 66, previously 2565, *Merry Hampton*, which, very briefly, had been No. 534. Finally, in BR colours she became No. 60066. When this photograph was taken the engine had just been converted from an A1 to A3. (BS)

was acting out of malice, surely he would have delighted in 'destroying' other parts of Gresley's legacy, even rebuilding the A4s. He didn't, so one is left to assume that he recognised their many virtues, took what he could from their design and sought to produce the next generation of Pacifics using the Gresley engines as a template. He may not have been entirely successful in this, but I believe his motives were honest ones and were actively encouraged and supported by those around him. Either way, as war came to an end, the A1/A3/A4s were given a new lease of life as nationalisation plans for Britain's rail and coal industries formed in the minds of the new Labour government that came to power in July 1945. However, it would take nearly 2½ years for British Railways to be created and the Big Four disappear. In that time, each company struggled on as best it

could trying to reverse the ill-effects of war on their locomotives, rolling stock and infrastructure.

Even though the axe was about to fall, few, if any, knew what the future held or the way the new organisatiion might be run. Some may have hoped that things would continue as before, while others worried that they might be absorbed into a single mass with little or no freedom of movement to enjoy or exploit. While these debates raged Peppercorn, who was promoted to CME in 1946, continued with the long established Pacific programme and began the process of bringing all the fleet back to a pre-war standard of maintenance. And added to this was one key project – the revival of pre-war plans for electrification and the completion of the Sheffield to Manchester and Liverpool Street Station to Shenfield lines. So, until BR was formed, much was going

on, and so they were hardly wasted years. However, it was a period coloured by a number of serious accidents in which the tired state of the network may have played a part. Two of these incidents involved A3s.

The first of these occurred on 9 August 1947, when a twelve carriage passenger express from King's Cross to Leeds, pulled by V2 No. 936, entered an occupied section of track near Balby Junction, Doncaster. As a result, it ran into the back of the earlier running 1.10 pm from King's Cross to Leeds, at approximately 40mph. This train, which was made up of fourteen coaches and was hauled by A3 No. 50 *Persimmon*, had been stopped by the Home signal at the junction and was just moving forward when the collision occurred.

In the Ministry of Transport Report, written by Lt Colonel A. Mount, the outcome of the accident was carefully précised and then, having sifted a considerable amount of evidence, the author moved to confirm the likely cause:

Each train was heavily loaded and carried approximately 700 passengers, a number standing in the corridors. It is regretted that 18 passengers lost their lives, including a Railway Servant and three who died after admission to hospital. Altogether 118 passengers were injured or subsequently complained of shock, 51 of whom were detained in hospital. In addition, the Driver and train attendant of the 1.25 p.m. train suffered injuries. Medical attention was forthcoming at once.

The accident would not have occurred had the modernisation of the signalling at Doncaster, postponed on account of the war, been completed, or even if Balby Junction Down Main Home lever No. 2 had been controlled by the block instrument at 'Line Clear'.

The second crash occurred on 26 October 1947 near the village of Goswick in Northumberland. The *Flying Scotsman*, consisting of fifteen carriages pulled by A3 No. 66 *Merry Hampton*, carrying about 420 passengers travelling from Edinburgh to London King's Cross, became derailed killing twenty-eight people and injuring another sixty-five.

The train was scheduled to be diverted on to a goods loop at Goswick to avoid some essential engineering work. To do this safely, the driver had to slow his locomotive down but failed to do so in response to a cautionary signal near the diversion. As a result, the train entered a 15mph section at

The scene of devastation near Balby Junction when a Leeds express pulled by a V2 running at about 40mph, ran into the back of an earlier express from London to Leeds hauled by A3 No. 50 *Persimmon*. The Pacific seems to have suffered only minor impact damage and according to her Record Cards did not require repair in the nearby workshops. The lower picture shows *Persimmon* at King's Cross shortly after the accident, apparently showing no ill-effects from the disaster. (BS)

approximately 60mph, forcing the engine and most of the carriages off the track and then on to their sides.

At the inquiry that followed it was shown that the driver, fireman and guard had all failed to read the notice concerning the diversion posted at Haymarket depot, so failed to appreciate the problem that lay ahead.. The driver was deemed to be principally at fault and sought to excuse himself by claiming that he had missed the distant signal because of drifting smoke from the engine's chimney. This may have been so, but the accident investigators, Colonel A. Trench and Lt Colonel G. Wilson, gave little credence to this claim and laid the blame for the accident entirely at the driver's feet. In his summary, Trench wrote:

For simply missing a notice posted for crew at Waverley regarding a diversion at Goswick, 28 people paid with their lives and many more were injured on 26 October 1947. Here we see the scene of devastation that greeted emergency services. The engine, No. 66 *Merry Hampton*, wasn't too severely damaged and returned to traffic on 2 January 1948. (BS)

In brief, having failed to see the Distant, Driver Begbie did not exercise reasonable and proper caution by a substantial reduction of speed until such time as he was in a position to be certain that all the Goswick signals, viz the Home, Main Starter and Advanced Starter, were Clear for him. The main responsibility for this accident must therefore rest on Driver Begbie. Although there is no definite evidence to confirm it, we cannot but feel that his grave breach of discipline in taking an unauthorised passenger on the footplate [in this case Leading Stoker T Redden RN who had just applied for a post in the Locomotive Department have persuaded Begbie to let him ride on the footplate for experience] may well have had some bearing on his failure to exercise proper caution in the operation of his train. He is 59 years of age, and his record during his 28 years' service as driver has been fairly good; it has been clear for the last 4 years.

A contributory cause of a lesser degree was the failure of Driver Begbie, Fireman Baird and Guard Blaikie to see the notices of diversion before leaving Edinburgh. It is clear that the warning notices were posted there on the preceding day, and all three of the train crew should have seen the notices.

After being lifted back on to the track, *Merry Hampton* was transported to Doncaster for repair, entering the workshops on

13 November and re-appearing a few weeks later on 2 January 1948. As Bert Spencer later wrote:

After this accident, following the one at Cramlington in 1926 during the General Strike, this engine was thought to be something of a Jonah amongst the crew at her home shed of Haymarket. I was told that every effort was made to have her transferred south, which eventually she was a few years later. Some footplate crew were very superstitious.

The engine's return to traffic coincided with the creation of the nationalised BR. Within weeks the first visible signs of the change became apparent as each locomotive lost its old company logo to be replaced by 'British Railways' hand painted on their tenders. The re-badging was a simple process, less so the tricky business of bringing these strongly independent companies together to create a single corporate identity that would act as one. For a year or so, the old teams, led by their CMEs, carried on as new structures and working practices were established. So, Peppercorn at Doncaster, Oliver Bulleid on the Southern, Frederick Hawksworth on the Western and George Ivatt at Derby watched and waited until they were replaced and did what they could with locomotive programmes already in being.

For Peppercorn this meant bringing the LNER's long running Pacific programme to an end and making sure the restoration of his fleet after the war's great strain was brought to a successful

How Gresley's ideas on Pacific's were developed by his successors Edward Thompson and Arthur Peppercorn. (Top) Thompson's 1947 built A2/3 No. 523 Sun Castle captured at Potter's Bar during April 1948. (Below) Peppercorn's aptly named 1947 built A2 No. 525 at King's Cross when brand new and just before BR came into existence. Both classes were built with three cylinders, but neither used Gresley's 2 to 1 valve gear arrangement, instead the LNER's Chief Draughtsman, Edward Windle, introduced three independent sets of valve gear. Although they were visually different strong family traits still existed. (BS)

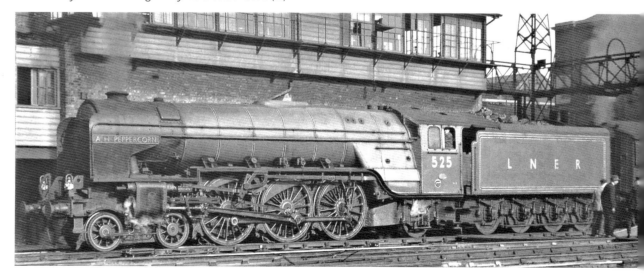

The birth of BR in 1948 seems to have caught managers on the hop with little or no thought being given to the new logos to be carried by locomotives. The answer proved to be a simple one; paint 'British Railways' on the tenders while a longer term solution was considered. In due course the lion on a wheel logo appeared, followed later by a lion holding a wheel sitting on a crown. The two photos above capture No. 60106 *Flying Fox* and an unidentified Pacific running at speed shortly after nationalisation. (BS/RH)

conclusion. When Peppercorn retired in 1949, he was replaced by his deputy, John Harrison, now with the title of Mechanical and Electrical Engineer for the region. He carried on with this work, but at the same time became actively involved in producing BR's new standard classes of steam engines. This he did until 1951 when posted to Derby to succeed Ivatt, who had retired. In his place at Doncaster came Kenneth Cook from Swindon, who is recorded as being something of a reluctant appointee to the old LNER. True or not, he didn't let any disappointment cloud his professional judgment and set to with great vigour to tackle the multitude of problems he faced at Doncaster, with the performance of the Gresley Pacifics high in his priorities.

Both Thompson and Peppercorn had coped with the deteriorating condition of the high performance three-cylinder engines with 2 to 1 valve gear by upping the maintenance schedules and routines, plus carrying more spares at sheds to reduce their time out of service. Cook, being a specialist in high precision engineering techniques preferred to tackle the problem in a different way.

When becoming President of the ILocoE in 1955, he described in great detail how he had harnessed these techniques to improve locomotive performance. In his speech, entitled 'The Steam Locomotive – A Machine of Precision', he set out his thoughts on the key issues involved and the potential benefits. For the future of Gresley Pacifics, Cook's work proved crucial and may have ensured that they carried on until

BR decided to end steam across its network. For this reason, it is important to understand the methodology and techniques he used. His key messages were:

The technique of constructing and maintaining steam locomotives is now at the summit of accuracy and if and when they fade away in this country it will not be on account of any decline in the excellence of its mechanism.

The basic mechanism of an orthodox locomotive is unique in its power and is transmitted equally through two, three or four axes whose centres are partly fixed but are subject to considerable movement relative to their locations and to each other. Concentrated power is transmitted between the axes by rigid couplings subject to rotating and alternating tensional and compressive forces. These movements, caused from within the locomotive by its direct or induced forces and from without by irregularities of the track, have an effect upon the dimensions between axis centres and argument may develop as to whether extreme basic accuracy is necessary.

It is true that if there are errors in original setting, the movement of the axles during motion and power transmission may tend to cancel them out, but they may equally add to the error and also to the stresses set up. It is therefore fairly clear that the greater the original accuracy the lower will be the maximum stresses set up in components and it also enables initial tolerances of working parts to be reduced to a minimum, which itself reduces hammering effects in bearings and the rate at which wear and slackness develop.

I would like to emphasize that these remarks may only apply to certain parts of the locomotive and not necessarily to each and every part. In general, it is probably correct to say that the more accurately centres of holes are maintained the better, but there are some components in which very close tolerances are detrimental and therefore a proper balance is necessary. But on the other basic components of power transmission in a locomotive, and in many other parts, a high degree of accuracy is highly desirable and economical.

We should probably all agree that the economical criterion of locomotive performance is cost per mile in similar conditions of operation and one of the greatest factors in producing low cost per mileage obtained between heavy repairs. In

No. **60066** *Merry Hampton* on duty with an unidentified Pullman train with late BR markings, but not yet fitted with trough deflectors. This will happen in late 1961, nearly two years before withdrawal from service. (RH)

carrying out a heavy repair, the dismantling and erecting costs are fairly constant whatever the mileage and a higher mileage enables these to be spread and to produce a lower overall figure. High precision in basic details of a locomotive can make a big contribution to economy.

There are two ingredients in the production of accuracy in a locomotive mechanism – measurement and working to measurement. Measurement has to cater for three-dimensional requirements over an extensive area and many years have been needed to arrive at the present possibilities. Each Works has to cater for a number of combinations of these dimensions within the overall maxima and hence any system must be flexible enough to cater for these at reasonable cost and facility.

With good craftsmen working under favourable conditions fairly good results were still obtainable and high-speed locomotives were repaired and maintained, although at the expense of slack initial fits of some wearing parts. But when things did not proceed according to schedule, poor light, blunt pops and a short-sighted erector, considerable inaccuracies did occur and many engineers spent much time endeavouring to develop better systems. And [he added later] attempting to overcome the maintenance problems that arose from the additional wear created by these inaccuracies and slack fit.

Overcoming these problems proved extremely difficult with the equipment then at their disposal and engineers spent much time trying to find a better way of working 'with little progress being made until optical methods became available and opened the way for advances in direct measurement, which introduced the concept of frame alignment'. Here Cook described the evolution of such apparatus:

The first major step was due to a well-known optical instrument maker who in the 1920s produced a telescope in conjunction with a collimator. The telescope enabled a line of sight to be taken free of all deflection and the function of the collimator was to pick this sight up in absolute parallelism. The cross lines of the infinite scale of the collimator will only register zero from the telescope if the former is correctly located parallel in the line of sight. Hence if this be suitably and accurately mounted at right angles to a straight edge or the tube supported horizontally in the driving horns, at the designed distance from the locating point on the cylinder, an axis has been set-up co-incident with the desired centre of the driving axle. By this means, an accurate survey of all guide faces relative to cylinders at the commencement of repair can be made and decisions taken as to the most economical directions for correction.

At the Machine Tool Exhibition in 1952 a British optical exhibit was noticed that appeared capable of development although at that time it had no reference to locomotives. The makers became very anxious to co-operate and quite quickly a method, utilising instead of a collimator a reflecting mirror fixed parallel to and in line with a straight edge method much simpler than the German, and capable of proceeding very much further in the quest for accuracy, was adopted. It became known as the Auto-Reflexion.

This apparatus proved fully usable in the construction of locomotives to ensure initial accuracy and during general repairs when it can ensure and maintain accuracy over a long working life.

With such precision measuring tools becoming available, Cook was one of the first in the railway industry to exploit their potential and in 1953 purchased examples for use in the workshops at Doncaster and Darlington. Their arrival proved a godsend for the LNER's Pacifics, which soon showed the benefit of having such a tool to help improve performance and reliability. Bert Spencer later wrote of the impact Cook's work had in arresting the deteriorating condition of the three-cylinder locomotives and the way he improved staff morale at the same time by enhancing skill levels, which some felt had been allowed to deteriorate in the years since the war:

By his actions alone, which included the introduction of precision engineering, Cook managed to reverse this trend

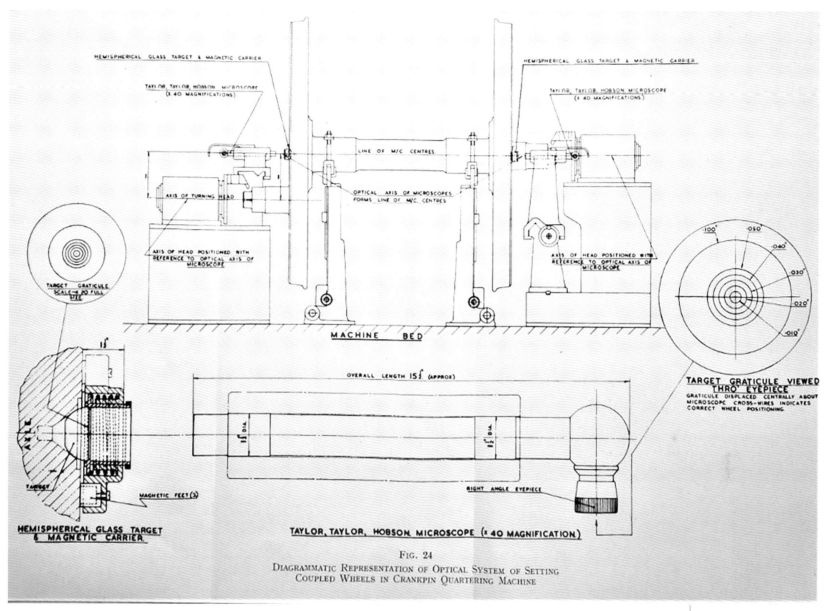

FIG. 24
DIAGRAMMATIC REPRESENTATION OF OPTICAL SYSTEM OF SETTING
COUPLED WHEELS IN CRANKPIN QUARTERING MACHINE

The key to the introduction of precision engineering through optical measurement in Britain was probably through the work of Moller-Wedel, but it did not become a reality until Taylor, Taylor and Hobson's developed a good working model in the post war years that British companies could acquire. Taylors, Hobson had, by this stage, a long history of producing high quality lenses which had helped develop the film industry in the early twentieth century. The reliability, accuracy and reputation of their products was deemed second to none and led them into the world of component inspection and optical equipment where they soon became specialists. Success in this field soon led to a wide range of metrology instruments becoming widely available. However, it was a link up with the J Arthur Rank Organisation in 1947 that broadened their research on lenses, precision photographic shutters and optical instruments. This included the Talyrond 1 – the world's first roundness measuring instrument – and two years later the Micro Alignment Telescope, which was given wide publicity during the 1952 Machine Tool Exhibition. It was this instrument that was then taken up by the railway industry, most notably Kenneth Cook at Doncaster. Such was its importance to his work that he included this diagram in his presentation to the ILocoE, which shows it being applied to the setting of coupled wheels. (KN).

The problems caused by drifting smoke were never entirely resolved and until the end of steam the LNER/BR Pacifics continued to be fitted with deflectors of varying shapes and sizes. Here we see (above) No.60112 *St Simon* running at speed with small deflectors fitted either side of her double chimney. In October 1962 these would be replaced by trough deflectors. (Below) No. 60107 *Royal Lancer* was fitted with trough deflectors in 1962 only to be withdrawn from service in September the following year. This photo is thought to have been taken in 1963 when the engine was laid up as an active reserve, possibly at Grantham where she was consigned in June that year, being scrapped that November. (THG)

and bring back some much needed pride in what we were doing. He also fought to bring as much work as possible to the workshops, which encouraged many to view the future more optimistically. But his impact on locomotive performance, and his desire to see Gresley's Pacifics give of their best while steam lasted, was without doubt something of which he should have been justifiably proud.

Cook remained at Doncaster until retirement beckoned in 1959 and, as Spencer confirmed, his time there proved of the greatest importance, though he made light of his achievements. By the time he departed, the writing was on the wall for steam traction, with some thinking that the eventual construction of 999 new standard class steam engines to be so much wasted effort. They argued that electrification and dieselisation should have been pursued with greater vigour from the beginning of nationalisation to allow true modernisation to take place. They were undoubtedly right, but the parlous state of Britain's finances in the years following the war and the super-abundance of domestically produced coal dictated a steam based policy.

However, by the late 1950s a new reality had dawned and the 1954 Modernisation Plan, when enacted, finally sounded the death knell for steam. At its core lay a massive programme of investment in alternative forms of motive power. It may have been overly ambitious, considering the slow progress made by then, but better that way than repeat earlier mistakes. As things turned out, the last steam locomotives didn't finally disappear until 1968 so enthusiasts had many more years to enjoy seeing them in all their smoky glory. And in these final years, the A3s, all the A1s having been converted in one way or another, made their presence felt, aided by Kenneth Cook and the efforts of his many engineers.

As the end of steam approached, accidents still occurred with gloomy regularity, one of the most serious of these involved another A3, thought to be Heaton based No. 60072 *Sunstar*. It occured on 15 December 1961 when pulling thirty-four empty wagons from King's Cross to Newcastle. The official report of the accident recorded:

A Class C (fully fitted) goods train, pulled by a V2 2-6-2, had been signalled into the Up Goods line at Connington South. There was thick fog and the train was travelling at about

10 m.p.h. and was following a Class H (unfitted) goods train when, at 1 mile plus beyond Connington South, an Up empty coaching stock train hauled by a Deltic diesel engine [thought to be No, D.9012 *Crepello*], which had also been signalled into the Goods line and was travelling at about 30 m.p.h., ran into its rear end. As a result of the collision the brake van of the Class C train, the two wagons next to it and the leading wagon were derailed, and the brake van was thrown on to its side on the Up Main line, in which position it also lay foul of the Down Main line. Some 3-4 minutes later another Class C train, pulled by an A3, which was travelling at about 50 m.p.h. on the Down Main line, struck the brake van a glancing blow. The engine was turned on to its side and 32 wagons were derailed and

were spread over the Up and Down Main and Down Goods lines. Some 3-4 minutes later still, yet another Class C train, which was travelling at about 35 m.p.h. on the Up Main line, ran into the wreckage. Its engine also came to rest on its side and the first 15 wagons were

Left and above: **Perhaps one** of the most usual accidents involving an A3 occurred at York on 5 August 1958. The driver of the 1934 built engine No. 60036 *Colombo*, named after the 2000 Guineas winner of that year, appeared, as Bert Spencer wrote on these two prints, to be 'trying to take a fence with a flat trained racing horse'. In fact, the engine had been allowed to enter a bay platform too quickly and, as a result, climbed over the buffers and ran into one of the station's kiosks with dramatic, but luckily no lethal consequences. The engine spent 2½ months in the works at Doncaster before returning to traffic on 14 November. (BS)

This photo, according to notes on the back of the print, is thought to show A3 No. 60072 on her side and about to be lifted following the crash at Connington on 15 December 1947. At this stage, the engine hadn't been fitted with trough deflectors, though had received a double chimney, which this engine appears to carry. *Sunstar* was taken to Doncaster for repair and then withdrawn in April 1962, presumably because her condition was thought too poor and, with diesels coming on stream in ever increasing numbers, was no longer needed. (RH)

piled on top of one another and on top of the derailed wagons of the Down train to form a large heap of wreckage. which blocked all the four tracks.

During this period there was still sufficient interest in steam locomotion for them to be thought worth modifying, most notably by adding the Kylchap exhaust and double blastpipe, plus a variety of smoke deflectors, so continuing the search for solutions to the perennial problem of drifting smoke. With so little time to go before steam disappeared, the effort and funds expended on these refinements

might be thought unnecessary with hindsight but go ahead they did. Perhaps, with the Pacifics still putting up rousing performances along the East Coast Mainline as the 1960s approached, some thought they might go on for many more years yet to come; certainly with suitable diesel replacements only slowly coming forward – the Deltics would only arrive in 1961/62, the first twenty Class 47s in 1962, whilst the Class 40s failed to impress – this wasn't an unreasonable conclusion. But slowly and surely their number increased and, after some teething problems, began to give BR managers a viable alternative,

allowing the number of A3s and A4s to be reduced year by year. So, during 1961 six were withdrawn, although one, No. 60104 *Solario,* had already preceded them by nearly two years. In December 1959 she had been assessed as being in such a poor condition when entering the workshops at Doncaster that the cost of a General Repair was deemed a waste, so she was scrapped instead.

1962 saw another twelve taken out of service, plus the sole A1/1 *Great Northern.* Then the cull reached its height with thirty being withdrawn in 1963, including No. 60096 *Papyrus,* the one-time speed record holder, and *Flying Scotsman.* No. 4472/60103 could so easily have been cut up like her sisters, BR's preservation policy being described at the time as 'a little hit and miss' by a charitable journalist. However, a wiser mind prevailed and Alan Pegler rescued the engine, allowing her to continue her beguiling life in preservation. Sadly, the last twenty-six of the class were not so lucky with twenty-three being scrapped in 1964, two in 1965 and the final one, No. 60052, *Prince Palatine,* in January 1966. This locomotive ended her days at St Margaret's in Scotland having been a well-travelled engine since built in 1924, and finding herself based at nine different sheds, some on numerous occasions, since becoming an A3 in 1941.

The end of steam was long drawn-out affair, but by the mid-1960s you would be hard-pressed to have seen a Gresley Pacifics running south of the Scottish Border. But time and tide wait for no man and the age of the diesel soon banished many memories of all those engines that had dominated life in Britain

I was lucky enough to witness the last years of Gresley's Pacifics first hand and can vouch for the fact that more often than not they were in poor external condition. But, just occasionally, one would show up in a sparkling state, ever reducing numbers of shed staff having made a big effort to produce a shiny engine when rostered to a fast express. (Top left) No.60052 *Prince Palatine* slowly ambles by during 1962, in a mucky condition, just before being fitted with deflectors. (Top right) No. 60048 *Doncaster*, still with small deflectors either side of her double chimney, which she will soon lose, 'running light' in 1960. (Bottom left) An A3 that was too dirty to identify passing through Doncaster. (Bottom right) No. 60052 again but this time in pristine condition towards the end of her life as she became the last A3 in service. She appears to have been cleaned up for an enthusiasts' special and will, in January 1966, be condemned then sold for scrap to P.W. McLellan of Langloan, West Lothian. (THG)

for so long. However, nostalgia for the past seems unavoidable and, these engines, which when running had been responsible for covering travellers and the general public alike with dirt, grime and heavily polluting fumes, became objects recalled with great affection and wistful stares when a preserved example passed by. *Flying Scotsman*, more than any other steam locomotive, has become a live, highly sought after personification of this lost world and is followed by large crowds wherever she goes because of it.

Yet it might have been so different if BR's bureaucrats had succeeded in removing every last vestige of steam in Britain during the 1960s. Being aware that the cull of engines was ruthlessly and very quickly gathering pace, Alan Pegler, businessman and entrepreneur,

As steam came to an end withdrawn engines could be seen in various stages of decay around sheds awaiting the cutters' torch. (Top left) No.60046 *Diamond Jubilee* at Doncaster in 1963 apparently in the process of being dismantled. (Top right) No. 60083 *Sir Hugo* which was condemned in 1964 and sold to Hughes Bolckow of North Blyth. (Bottom left) A note with this negative suggests the engine is No. 60100 *Spearmint* but neither the number or nameplate confirm this. If it is *Spearmint* then the location may be Darlington where the engine was consigned for scrapping in 1965 after spending most of her career based in Scotland. (Bottom right) No. 60069 *Sceptre* still apparently in working condition, but withdrawn from service. (THG)

stepped in and saved the most famous engine of her age. He then drew on her undoubted fame, so carefully nurtured by the LNER in the 1920s and '30s, to make her a great attraction again. In truth, the advent of the A4s had largely eclipsed the deeds of all the A1/A3s, but in preservation 4472/60103 recaptured her glamour and has probably become even more famous in the process. There is little to stop her continuing in the same way for a long time to come, even when her operating days have come to an end. But metal components can be replaced so she may just carry on working her magic, although the outcome of any debate concerning originality as opposed to creating a replica might make this less desirable. So, in the end, she may simply become a static exhibit at York, still to be admired but not seen working on the mainline where her power and beauty only really become apparent.

For myself, though, the locomotives are only part of the story. Without all the men and women who played a part in their design, construction, maintenance and running, the engines would not have existed or have had such appeal. The past, though familiar to us today through films and books, is 'a foreign country: they do things differently there'. In truth, we cannot fully understand their world simply by catching sight of a gleaming preserved A3 or viewing the occasional documentary on TV that uses the same pieces of old black and white film accompanied by often repeated clichés. To do otherwise, it is necessary to view life through their eyes, appreciate the problems they faced when at work or at home, because, in the 1920s, '30s and '40s, they faced many extreme challenges that few today can know or have experienced.

Theirs was a much tougher world where success was achieved in the face of the most extreme social, economic and international pressures, at a time when deference and acceptance were demanded and expected. And yet, the men and women on the railways still took great pride in what they did even though the burden placed on them was a very heavy one indeed. This was nowhere more apparent than on the footplate of Gresley's Pacifics where men, often in poor health, working in very trying conditions and struggling to survive on meagre wages, often performed miracles with their demanding, avaricious engines. To read contemporary accounts of their day to day work is one of the few ways we have to get a true sense of the lives they lived, its pressures and its joys.

My last photo of 60103 *Flying Scotsman* taken when she came thundering past in the early 1960s (near Hadley Wood I think). (THG)

From very early in its existence, the editors of the *Meccano Magazine* had a fascination with life on steam engines. In due course, they employed a writer, operating under the nom de plume 'a Railway Engineer', to travel the country on various locomotives and record what he saw and experienced. By this means, he has left us a rich legacy of material describing the lives and skills of the footplate men, particularly those working the A1/A3s. One example of his work, written following a journey south on the 'Leeds Breakfast Flyer' provides us with a very fitting end to this book:

Boasting the second fastest schedule on the LNER and the seventh fastest in Great Britain, the 7.50 am express from Leeds to King's Cross is deservedly a great favourite with travellers. This train, after some smart running between its early stops, makes a tremendous sprint from Grantham to London, 105½ miles in 100 minutes – an average of 63½mph.

Engines are changed at Doncaster, and in the yard here I joined Driver Duddington and Fireman Atkins on a standard Pacific No. 2559 *Tetrarch*. On this occasion traffic was so heavy that a relief train was necessary. With a load of only six coaches the Pacific got away in great style and we had no trouble with signal checks.

When seeing or reading about steam engines it is often easy to forget the men who made them what they were, day in and day out. By any standard they had tough lives, suffering from all sorts of work related ailments, with few living long beyond retirement as a result. So in remembering 4472, and all the other steam locomotives, we have to honour the memory of these, largely forgotten and anonymous, men. Here we have just a small selection of the LNER's 'Top Link' drivers who made all this possible. (Top row left to right) Driver Sparshatt, Driver Bayne and Driver Carmen. (Middle row) Driver Lake, Driver Rayment and Driver Duddington. (Opposite above row) Driver Davidson with his unnamed Fireman and Driver Allen with his Fireman Hazeldene. (THG)

The express proper arrived from Leeds in the charge of a big three-cylinder K3 Mogul. This was quickly detached and we backed gently down on to the train, which was loaded to eleven corridor coaches – 400 tons with passengers and their luggage.

This train has an intermediate stop at Retford. The short run of 17½ miles from Doncaster, booked in 20 minutes start to stop, was smartly run with a maximum speed of 70mph. For the next stage, to Grantham, the 33 miles are booked to be run in 35 minutes, a very sharp timing because there is considerably more uphill than down on this stretch. Right at the start comes 5 miles up at 1 in 200 to Markham summit. Full regulator was used almost immediately and as we picked up speed, the cut-off was gradually reduced from 65 per cent to 28 per cent at

Gamston signal box, 3 miles out. Speed had then risen to 46mph and steadily continued to rise until we passed the summit at 49mph. The five miles from Retford had been covered in the fast time of 7¾ minutes.

Now cut-off was brought right back to 18 per cent, but the regulator remained fully open. We touched 78mph at Crow Park, kept up a fine pace across the Trent Valley and reached Grantham almost exactly on time.

The main interest in the journey is centred in the flying run from Grantham to London, and for such a schedule our load of 400 tons behind the tender was a stiff proposition. The first 5½ miles are rising at 1 in 200. Driver Duddington started off with 60 cut-off and full regulator, The Tetrarch accelerated rapidly, and the cut-off was reduced step by step until, only 2½ miles from the start, it was down to 30 per cent, so it remained until

Stoke summit. The speed rose to 47mph, and the summit was passed in 8½ minutes from Grantham.

The stretch of line from Stoke down to Peterborough is to quote another Pacific driver 'a grand place if you are in a hurry,' and rarely fails to provide thrilling running [as it would do a few years later when Duddington broke the speed record for steam on this section of line with Mallard]. On this trip of mine the tradition of Pacific speed was nobly upheld. Throughout the descent the regulator was kept fully open, but cut-off was no more than 18 per cent. The speed rose rapidly on passing Stoke. Corby was passed at 75, Little Bytham at 83, and near Essendine we got up to 86mph. Being on the footplate at such a speed is an extraordinary experience. In big modern engines, the bumping and hard riding that

The allure of steam, and particularly Gresley's Pacifics is, to my mind the perfect way of ending this book. (Below) Both these photos were taken in the last few years of steam on the East Coast Mainline when there were no adoring crowds around just two locomotives doing their duty. (Below left) An A3 made anonymous by many weeks of dirt. (Below right) A3 No. 60107 *Royal Lancer* in, for the time, a clean condition. In this form she will be condemned in 1963. (THG)

are so noticeable at 50 or 60mph gradually seem to lessen as the speed rises, and the engines develop an almost uncanny smoothness when they get into the eighties. The Tetrarch was no exception and the motion was extremely steady. Another notable feature of this headlong dash was that never once was there a tendency for the steam to beat down and obscure the view from the cab.

This great 'spurt' took us over the 19.3 miles from Corby to New England North Junction at an average speed of 79mph. So we came through Peterborough in 28 minutes – exactly a minute early. Speed was brought down to 20mph for the awkward curves through the station and then the driver opened up to full regulator and roared over the Nene Viaduct, getting a beautiful view of Peterborough Cathedral as we crossed.

On the dead level from Yaxley onwards Driver Duddington

used 25 per cent cut-off and full regulator and yet the speed did not rise above 62½mph, due to the effect of the very strong west wind… I calculated that this wind was equal to over 120 tons extra on the train and in calm weather we should have attained a speed little if anything under 75mph.

Right on to Hitchin we received severe buffeting, the 27 miles from Huntingdon to this point taking 25½ minutes instead of the very fast 22 minutes allowed. On the last 30 miles into London, however, the line is much more sheltered and we made a truly thrilling finish and the Tetrarch simply raced away… At Barnet the speed was up to 80mph, 86 at New Southgate and finally 87½mph through Wood Green. In and out of tunnels at an ever-quickening pace, culminating in the breath taking sweep over the junctions at Wood Green, was

an experience never to be forgotten.

The signals were momentarily against us at Holloway and about a mile outside King's Cross we had a slow-up to 10mph for permanent way repairs so we reached the terminus in 104¾ minutes from Grantham. It is difficult to estimate exactly how much time we lost through the wind, but I think we could have completed the journey in 99 minutes in calm weather. With a 400 ton load this was a fine piece of work and a magnificent all-round display of Pacific ability, especially of sustained steaming power.'

It is the images conjured up by this article that will stay in my mind, plus memories of the times I was privileged to ride behind these magnificent engines and meet the men who made their deeds possible. To all of them this book is dedicated.

KEY BIOGRAPHIES OF THOSE HAVING SOME INVOLVEMENT IN THE LIVES OF THE A1/A3s

Banbury, Frederick Sir (1st Baronet)

He was born in 1850 and attended Winchester College before entering business and, in 1872, joined the Stock Exchange. He was elected to parliament in 1892 where he remained until 1924. In 1917, he became chairman of the Great Northern Railway, on the death of William Jackson. In his role with the GNR he actively encouraged Gresley in developing his first Pacifics and then approved the finances to make them a practical reality. In honour of his contribution to the company, the second A1, No. 1471, was given his name. He died in 1936.

Bannister, Eric

He was born on 8 September 1908 in Ewecross, in the West Riding of Yorkshire. His parents moved to Doncaster where Eric was educated at Doncaster Grammar School then became a premium apprentice at Doncaster Works. On successfully qualifying in the early 1930s, he found a post in the Drawing Office at Doncaster, before transferring to King's Cross in 1935 as assistant to Oliver Bulleid and Bert Spencer in the Headquarters there. In these two posts he was directly involved in the development of all the Gresley Pacifics. In December 1940, he transferred to Dukinfield and, in the following year, was promoted to Assistant Works Manager at Gorton. He retired due to ill-health but lived on until 1989, when he passed away in a nursing home in Settle.

Bulleid, Oliver V S

He was born in 1882 in New Zealand to British émigré parents, then returned to Britain following the death of his father in 1889. From an early age, engineering and science had fascinated him and he attended Accrington's Municipal Technical School for four years before becoming an apprentice under Ivatt at Doncaster in January 1901. He also attended local evening classes and then more advanced courses at Sheffield, Leeds and London Universities. Clearly imbued with great ambition and talent, he quickly rose through the ranks. In 1906, he was appointed to be Assistant to Frank Webster, the Loco Running Superintendent at Doncaster and took charge of 'experiments with petrol motor driven coaches'. This was quickly followed by Assistant to the Works Manager (Wintour) where he managed 'Shop Costs'.

As time passed, he decided to broaden his horizons and seek work beyond the confines of the GNR and took a post in Paris with the French Westinghouse Company as a test engineer. This was quickly followed, in 1910, by a period as Mechanical Engineer for exhibitions with the Board of Trade in London. But this job came to a premature end a year later and he returned to the GNR and was appointed Personal Assistant to the newly promoted Gresley so beginning a long and mutually beneficial relationship, only broken, temporarily, by Bulleid's military service in the Great War.

In 1937, he was appointed Chief Mechanical Engineer of the Southern Railway where his remarkable Pacifics both astounded and frustrated in equal measure. In 1949, he joined Coras Iompair Eireann Railway in Ireland, remaining with them until retirement at the age of 76. He died in April 1970 when living in Malta.

Broughton, Harry

He was a schoolmaster's son born at Monks Coppenhall in Cheshire on 23 April 1870. He became an apprentice under Francis Webb at Crewe in the late 1880s and then a fitter when qualified. Being a near contemporary of Gresley on the LNWR may have influenced the CME in selecting Broughton to be CD, in succession to William Elwess in 1927. Broughton remained in post until 1935 when he retired and during his time at Doncaster was closely involved in the development of many locomotives including the A1s, A3s and P2s.

Chapelon, Andre

He was born in Saint-Paul-en-Cornillon in October 1892 and was educated at the renowned Ecole Centrale Paris, but his time there was interrupted by the Great War, in which he served with distinction in the front line as an Artillery Officer with the 106th Regiment. Returning to civilian life in 1919, he completed his course at the Ecole Central and graduated in 1921,

finding work with the PLM Railway in their Rolling Stock and Motive Power section.

In many ways, this period of his life was an apprenticeship in which he learnt the more practical elements of design. This he did in the capable hands of Etienne Tribolet, a senior mechanical inspector at Lyon. It was during this period that he began delving into the area of thermo-dynamics in some depth, developing theories that would underpin much of his later work. By the mid-1920s, when he first came to Gresley's attention, he was formulating ideas, based on the work of Kyosti Kylala, a Finnish engineer, on locomotive exhaust systems. This would result in the Kylchap model being developed, which would seriously impact on Gresley's work and that of many other steam locomotive designers in the future. He died in July 1978.

Churchward, George Jackson

He was born in Stoke Gabriel in Devon on 31 January 1857 and died in Swindon in December 1933. In 1873, he became a pupil at the South Devon, Cornwall and West Cornwall Railway's Locomotive, Carriage and Wagon Works at Newton Abbot, a short distance from his home. When the Great Western Railway absorbed this company three years later, Churchward transferred to Swindon to complete the last year of his education.

He remained in Wiltshire for the rest of his life, progressing through the ranks to become the GWR's CME in 1902 (retiring in 1922). Like his keen admirers, Nigel Gresley and William Stanier, Churchward was considered an outstanding

engineer, but not a great innovator. He understood that all variations on steam locomotive design had probably been discovered and tested by others and that this wealth of experience could inform his own design work, including his first and only Pacific, the Great Bear.

His aim was always to establish best practice and absorb what he observed to improve engine design and take steam development as far as it could possibly go. He also understood the need for standardisation, the complexities of engine testing and the streamlining of workshop facilities.

Churchward's impact on railway history is undeniable, as was his influence on the great engineers who followed in his footsteps, including Gresley.

Cook, Kenneth

He was born in Bath in August 1896 the third child of Walter, a wholesale clothing manufacturer, and his wife Kate. Coming from a relatively wealthy background, his parents chose to have him educated at King Edward VI's School in the city. At 16, he became a Premium Apprentice at the GWR's Swindon Works. Here he quickly he came under the influence of George Churchward, for whom he developed a deep and lasting respect. However, he found his training temporarily halted by the coming of war. Although he could have claimed reserved status, he chose to volunteer for active service as a private with the Royal Army Service Corps in 1915. He finally left the Army in 1921 having served on the Western Front and in Salonika

After this enforced six-year absence Churchward readily

accepted him back into the fold to continue his training. Initially this involved evening classes at Swindon Technical College, then attendance on a three-year course on a day release basis. His performance was such that he was rated top of his class in all subjects each year and at the end of the course was awarded the coveted Chairman's Prize.

As his training came to an end, he was assigned to the CME's Drawing Office to study locomotive design for twelve months and following this he was posted to the Experimental Section where he could closely observe engines being run through their paces on the rolling road in the company's test facility. Having studied design and performance in such detail, and presumably proved himself an adept pupil in the process, Churchward appointed him Technical Inspector to the Locomotive Works. Further promotions followed as he moved, inexorably, to the top. Assistant to Works Manager, then Assistant Works Manager in 1932, Works Manager in 1937, Works Assistant to the CME in May 1947, Principal Assistant a year later and finally Mechanical and Electrical Engineer at Swindon in January 1950.

In 1951 he was appointed Mechanical and Electrical Engineer at Doncaster, succeeding John Harrison. Until his retirement in 1959 he successfully led his large team and by introducing precision measuring techniques ensured that the Gresley Pacifics, in particular, operated to a high level of efficiency and avoided rebuilding or an early demise. He died in July 1981.

Cox, Ernest Stanley

He was born in Lanarkshire on 17 June 1900 and died on 19 September 1992. His father was a Principal Clerk with the Customs and Excise Department and so the family often moved. Ernest's younger brother was born in Yorkshire and they both attended Merchant Taylors School in Crosby, Lancashire. In 1917, he began an apprenticeship at the Horwich Works of the Lancashire and Yorkshire Railway, under George Hughes. A gifted engineer, once qualified he was soon promoted and by 1934 was Assistant Works Superintendent at Derby, quickly moving on to become Personal and Technical Assistant to the CME at Euston. During the war, he was seconded to the Railway Executive and postwar his star kept rising until he became Assistant CME to British Rail.

He held a number of unique positions within the LMS and BR and was one of only a few chief officers to record his memories of those days. Many historians have questioned the veracity of his recollections, but they still contain many revealing eyewitness accounts and critical assessments of Stanier and Gresley and their way of working. In 1944, he and Stanier were commissioned by the LNER to review the performance of Gresley's three-cylinder locomotives with the 2 in 1 valve gear, particularly when fitted to the Pacifics and P2s. The report is highly critical and invaluable for that reason, coming as it did from a wholly impartial and knowledgeable source.

Dalby, W.E.

He was born on 21 December 1862 and entered the GER's Stratford Works in 1876 under William Adams. Eight years later, he had risen to become Chief Assistant in the Permanent Way Department at Crewe. On the way, he was awarded a Whitworth Scholarship, which allowed him to study for an external BSc at London University. As his studies deepened, he became attracted to academia and, in 1891, became assistant to Professor Ewing, who was then in the process of setting up the Engineering Department at Cambridge University. This led, two years later, to the award of an MA for the work he had undertaken during this challenging phase. More appointments and honours followed and by the 1920s he had become Professor of Engineering at London University, worked on various government commissions, seen war service as a consulting engineer to the War Office and Admiralty, and been elected as a Fellow of the Royal Society. Yet throughout this time, his fascination with steam locomotives remained a constant in his life, with his 1902 book *The Balancing of Engines* becoming a key reference source in the industry. Throughout his career, he acted as mentor to many leading figures in the railway industry, including Gresley, whose Pacifics, in particular, benefitted from his advice.

He was Vice-President of both the Institute of Mechanical Engineers and the Institution of Civil Engineers. In 1913 he was elected a Fellow of the Royal Society. He died at his home in Ealing, London, on 25 June 1936

Edge, Douglas Ross

He was born on 19 April 1885 in Altringham and in 1902 became an apprenticeship fitter at the Gorton Works of the Great Central Railway. On qualifying, he rose quickly through the ranks becoming a specialist in carriage and wagon work in the process. On amalgamation in 1923, he was the C & W Works Manager at Dukinfield, where he remained until 1934 when transferred by Gresley to Doncaster to take on a similar task there. When Bulleid left the LNER to become the Southern Railway's CME, Edge replaced him at King's Cross.

In his role as Gresley's Principal Assistant he was closely involved in all matters relating to the Pacifics, though is likely to have deferred to Bert Spencer as the deep expert on all locomotive matters. He retired in the late 1940s and died in April 1970 when living in Essex.

Elwess, William

A farmer's son, he was born near Doncaster Works in 1867 where he appears to have served his apprenticeship before becoming a fitter. A move to the drawing office followed and he rose to become Chief Draughtsman, relinquishing the post on retirement in 1927, being replaced by Harry Broughton. He died in 1946 having taken a leading role in developing the A1s and A3s

Gresley, Sir Herbert Nigel

He was born in June 1976 in Edinburgh. His father, Nigel, was the rector of Netherseal in Leicestershire where he and his wife Joanna raised their five children, a daughter and four sons. He attended Barham House Preparatory School in St Leonards-on-Sea, Sussex, before moving to Marlborough College during September 1890.

As a child, he often expressed a 'wish to become an engine driver' and it was a fascination that remained with him into adulthood, fostered by his father who was a keen amateur scientist. From this, Herbert discovered the world of engineering and found a calling that fascinated him, encouraged in his studies by his family and teachers at Marlborough. As a result, and when the opportunity arose, he began an apprenticeship with the London and North Western Railway's Locomotive Department at Crewe, then under the control of Francis William Webb, the Locomotive Superintendent, who guided his career from 1893 until 1898. On qualifying, he found a post with John Aspinall, then CME of the Lancashire and Yorkshire Railway, based at Horwich, where, over the next five years, Gresley quickly rose through ranks.

In 1900 he was the Loco Shed Foreman at Blackpool, then from 1900 to 1901 Outdoor Assistant of the Carriage and Wagon Department. Then for a year he was Assistant Works Manager at Newton Heath, with another year as the Works Manager there before promotion, in 1904, to Assistant Superintendent. Such success will always spark interest from other employers within such a competitive industry and this proved to be the case here. The Great Northern Railway were seeking a new Carriage and Wagon Superintendent in late 1904, the current incumbent, Frank Howden, having decided to retire. Henry Ivatt, the GNR's Locomotive Superintendent, had arranged for the post to be advertised, but none of the six candidates were found to be suitable, which led Ivatt,

to approach Gresley. A private interview followed and from this Ivatt and William Jackson, the company Chairman, felt sufficiently confident to offer him the post with a start date of 20 February 1905. So began the most important period in Gresley's career, success followed success and when Ivatt retired in 1911, Gresley replaced him as Locomotive Engineer. In due course, when the LNER was formed in 1923, he was chosen to be its first Chief Mechanical Engineer and his path to greatness and the Pacifics was set fair. He died in April 1941 when still in post.

Harrison, John 'Freddie'

He was born in Yorkshire in February 1904 and educated at Malvern Wells Primary School in Worcestershire, then Wellington College, in Berkshire. From early in his career, as a premium apprentice at Doncaster, he was identified as rising star by the Works Manager. As a result, he found himself cultivated and promoted by Gresley, Thompson and Peppercorn in turn. In 1926, as a sign of the esteem in which he was held, he was put in charge of the engine sheds at Wigan and St Helens. Then in 1930 he was promoted to be Assistant to the Works Manager at Gorton and seven years later he was posted to Doncaster, becoming Robert Thom's assistant in the process. After only twelve months in this prestigious post, he was promoted again as the Locomotive Works Manager at Gorton. Here he remained until Gresley's death when the new CME, eager to harness Harrison's undoubted skills, promoted him to be Mechanical Engineer of the

Great Central Section. He held this post until in 1945 when Thompson transferred him to Cowlairs, in the northern suburbs of Glasgow.

Here he remained until 1947 when, a year into Peppercorn's reign as CME, he transferred to Doncaster, with James Blair moving northwards to take his place. According to the few records that remain, Harrison was initially appointed Assistant to the CME, replacing Roy Hart-Davies, who became Mechanical Engineer Scotland (Outdoors), and soon afterwards was promoted to Assistant CME, a post he occupied until 1948 when appointed by BR as Mechanical and Electrical Engineer for the region, absorbing many of Peppercorn and Henry Richards' duties in the process. Following the CME's retirement in 1949, Harrison took sole charge at Doncaster and held the post there until 1951 when appointed to Derby in a similar capacity. Seven years later his rise to the top of his profession was complete when promoted to be BR's Chief Officer for Mechanical Engineering, its CME in all but name. He retired in 1966 and died in Cambridge on 22 May 1996.

Holcroft, Harold
He was born in Wolverhampton on 12 February 1882 and undertook a premium apprenticeship at the Wolverhampton works of the GWR and subsequently found permanent employment under the directing hand of George Churchward, the CME. At Swindon he assisted in the design the 4300 class 2-6-0 Moguls, before moving on to the South Eastern and Chatham Railway, where he worked as Assistant to

Maunsell. In due course he was directly involved in the design of the company's Moguls, and in 1923 transferred to the Southern Railway when it was created as part of amalgamation. After Maunsell's retirement in 1937, Holcroft continued to work for the Southern Railway under Bulleid until his retirement in 1946. He died in February 1973.

He was an inventor by nature and took out his first patent when only 18. He continued on this creative path throughout his life, during which he developed an early version of a conjugated valve gear to drive the valves of three-cylinder engine from only two sets of valve gear. In due course this brought him into direct contact with Gresley as he developed his own version of the 2 to 1 valve gear which then led to concerns being raised over possible plagiarism. These issues seem to have been resolved and, in due course, Holcroft collaborated with Nigel Gresley to develop the Gresley conjugated valve gear for his three-cylinder engines; the Pacifics being the highest profile locomotives to benefit from their combined efforts.

Jackson, William 1st Baron Allerton
He was born in Otley, near Leeds, on 16 February 1840 and was a noted businessman and Conservative politician who became Chairman of the Great Northern Railway. In this role he was responsible for recruiting Nigel Gresley and, when the opportunity arose agreed his promotion to Locomotive Engineer. It was Jackson who set him on the path to greatness and gave him the freedom to experiment and so the Pacifics were born. Sadly, Jackson

did not live to see the result of all these labours dying on 4 April 1917.

Matthews, Sir Ronald Wilfred
Matthews was born on 25 June 1885 in Sheffield and died there on 1 July 1959. He was educated at Eton and entered business with the steel industry and became Chairman of the Sheffield firm of Turton Brothers and Master Cutler along the way. In 1929 he was invited to join the LNER's Board of Directors and became Chairman in September 1938 when William Whitelaw retired. Throughout his time with the LNER he was a strong supporter of Gresley's plans and helped carry through his proposals for new engines, including the Pacifics. He remained in post until the LNER was absorbed by British Railways, where, as Geoffrey Hughes wrote in his book *LNER*, 'he continued to purvey the atmosphere of friendliness which characterised the LNER hierarchy'. In 1941, he had the unenviable task of finding a successor to Gresley in time of war and chose Edward Thompson, a choice that some later criticised. Nevertheless, he successfully led the company through a very difficult period, with Matthews a commendably staunch ally.

Quite separately Matthews was Chairman of the Railway Companies' Association, during the Second World War and helped in exploring postwar reconstruction needs. He was also Deputy Chairman of the Independent Television Authority.

Peppercorn, Arthur
He was born on the 29 January 1889 to Alfred, a clergyman serving at

St Luke's Church in Stoke Prior, and his wife Agnes, from Queensland; the ninth of their ten children. He is recorded as receiving private education before attending Hereford Cathedral School between 1901 and 1905 following which he elected to become a premium apprenticeship at Doncaster under Henry Ivatt.

In 1912, when applying for membership of the IMechE Peppercorn simply recorded that his five years apprenticeship saw him:'… passing through the machine, erecting shops, &c., also drawing office.' In addition, he described attending Doncaster Technical School between 1906 and 1908 where he undertook evening classes in Machinery Drawing, Mathematics, Applied Mechanics, steam and more to round out his education. By now this was fairly traditional fare for the budding engineer and his work and dedication clearly drew the attention of Gresley, in particular, who seems to have taken the young man under his wing.

When his training was complete he was assigned to Colwick Loco Depot in Nottingham where he did a variety of duties, including assisting the foreman, shed fitting and loco firing for nearly 2½ years. This proved to be an excellent grounding and prepared him for his next post of any importance, Assistant to the District Locomotive Supt at Ardsley, then at Peterborough from 1914. But the Great War intervened and his undoubted skills and willingness to volunteer saw him commissioned into the Royal Engineers.

In the postwar years, his career continued to blossom under Gresley's guiding hand, with moves to Retford as District Locomotive Superintendent, then Doncaster before becoming the Carriage and Wagon Works Manager at York, where he remained for six years. Two senior appointments followed, the first to Stratford, as Loco Running Superintendent, then Darlington, as Mechanical Engineer. But everything changed when Gresley died and he returned to Doncaster to be both Assistant CME to Thompson and Mechanical Engineer in charge of the works. In 1946, he succeeded Thompson as CME, retiring in 1949; he died in 1951.

Spencer, Bert

He was born on 6 May 1898, the fifth child and fourth son of Abel Spencer, a 'journeyman' cabinet maker who became a carriage fitter with the GNR, and his wife Sarah. He proved to be a gifted child and successfully passed through Doncaster's Grammar School, then the Mechanical Engineering faculty of the Technical College before beginning an apprenticeship at the railway works in July 1914.

Undoubtedly he was a clever student and one who shone throughout his time as an apprentice. Whilst at Doncaster, he was tutored by John Bazin, the Assistant Works Manager, who actively encouraged him in his studies. With Bazin's backing he spent a year at Horwich in the drawing office, which helped broaden his knowledge of locomotive design.

On returning to the Drawing Office at Doncaster, he became directly involved in the design of the A1s and very quickly established himself in the hierarchy of the organisation there. His skills were now well honed and the advice he gave on many issues, including ways of improving the Pacific, brought him to Gresley's notice and in due course the young man was transferred to the CME's HQ team at King's Cross and promoted to be Gresley's Technical Assistant on locomotive matters. In this crucial role he became the CME's right-hand man and remained in this role until Gresley died in 1941. During this period, he contributed greatly to the design of the A3s, P2s and A4s and much else besides.

Following Gresley's death he transferred to Doncaster where he became involved in production management. Then, with an end to the war in sight, he assisted Thompson in formulating future locomotive strategy, a role he continued under Peppercorn as Mechanical Engineer, then with British Railways. He retired in 1958 after a long and distinguished career and died in 1968, in Devon.

Street, Thomas Archibald

He was born during 1883 in West Derby, Lancashire, and served his apprenticeship at Horwich, where he emerged as a millwright before training to become a draughtsman. He moved to Doncaster in 1911 as a draughtsman. During his career with the GNR and then the LNER, he served Gresley in a variety of posts, specialising in locomotive design, before being appointed Chief Draughtsman in early 1935 when Harry Broughton retired. During these years, he was directly involved in the development of all the Gresley's Pacifics. Following the CME's death in 1941, he transferred to the electrification side of business as CD to Henry Richards, being replaced by Edward Windle. He remained at Doncaster until retirement and died in 1953.

Thom, Robert Absalom

He was born in Old Machar in Aberdeenshire on 14 June 1873. After attending the Causewayend School he began an apprenticeship, in 1888, with the Great North of Scotland Railway, qualifying five years later. He chose to remain in Scotland to gain experience then applied to become Works Foreman for the Metropolitan Railway Company at Neasden in North West London. There seems little doubt that he was an ambitious man and pursued promotion whenever he could. During 1902 he was appointed as the Locomotive, Carriage and Wagon Superintendent of the Lancashire, Derbyshire and East Coast Railway Here he remained until this company was taken over by the Great Central in 1906, when he became Deputy Locomotive Works Manager at Gorton in Manchester. This appointment lasted until amalgamation, during which time he rose to become Assistant to the CME, John Robinson.

In 1923, he became District Mechanical Engineer at Gorton. A move to Cowlairs Works near Glasgow as Scottish Area Mechanical Engineer followed, before he became Mechanical Engineer and Works Manager at Doncaster in 1927. It was here that his career reached its peak and he became a pivotal figure in the production of the A3s, P2s and A4s amongst others. He also

oversaw some of the early A1 to A3 conversions. He retired in 1938 and died in the early 1950s.

Thompson, Edward

He was born on 25 June 1881 and grew up in Marlborough, his father, Francis, being an assistant master at the public school there. In fact, his and Gresley's paths probably crossed between 1890 and '93, when Herbert was a pupil there and possibly under Thompson senior's care. Unusually for the time Thompson, though interested in engineering, didn't follow the apprenticeship route into this profession, but read Mechanical Sciences at Pembroke College, Cambridge, instead. He was awarded a BA in 1902 and soon after became a premium pupil with Beyer Peacock to learn about the more practical elements of engineering. Soon afterwards, he found employment with the Running Department of Midland Railway as an 'Improver'.

Ever conscious of the need to gain experience, he left Derby in 1905 to become a supervisor at the Royal Ordnance Factory at Woolwich. And so his climb upwards began and a move to the NER, with postings to Hull, Darlington and Gateshead followed in quick succession. He was then recruited by Gresley to be his Carriage and Wagon Superintendent at Doncaster, where he remained until the Great War intervened, in which he served with distinction rising to the rank of Lt Col in the process.

He returned to the GNR in 1919, but soon sought a return to the NER to become the Works Manager

in the Carriage and Wagon Department at York. Amalgamation three years later meant a move to Darlington where he became Area Carriage and Wagon Works Manager under Gresley once more.

In 1927 he was posted to Stratford in East London as Assistant Mechanical Engineer, and moved again in 1933 when he was chosen to replace Stamer at Darlington. And here he remained until 1938, managing the continuing production of the B17s, J39s and the second batch of V2 2-6-2 tender engines then being introduced into service.

In 1938, he became the Works Manager and Mechanical Engineer at Doncaster. By then the premier status of this works was beginning to fade. The glamorous days of the Pacific construction programme were over and the work Thompson inherited focussed on maintenance tasks and the construction of the V3 2-6-2T and the V2. This was the situation he found himself in when Gresley died suddenly in 1941 and he was thrust into the limelight as CME. From this point on, his career and the future of Gresley's Pacifics were closely entwined, some might say, with controversial results. He remained in this post until 1946 and died in 1954, while on holiday in Wales.

Wedgwood, Sir Ralph Lewis, 1st Baronet

He was born at Barlaston Lea, Stoke-on-Trent, the son of Clement Wedgwood and his wife Emily, daughter of the engineer James Meadows Rendel on 2 March 1874. He was educated at Clifton College and Trinity College, Cambridge. After graduating, Wedgwood was recruited by Sir George Gibb to the North Eastern Railway. After a period of general training, he was appointed Assistant Dock Superintendent at West Hartlepool from 1 May 1900. Two years later, he became District Superintendent at Middlesbrough, then was promoted to be Divisional Goods & Mineral Manager, Newcastle, in 1905. When Eric Geddes became Deputy General Manager in 1912, Wedgwood succeeded him as Chief Goods Manager. After war service with the Ministry of Munitions (when he held the rank of Brigadier-General) he returned to the North Eastern Railway in 1919 as Deputy General Manager. When Sir Alexander Kaye Butterworth retired, Wedgwood succeeded him as General Manager for the last year of the NER's existence and was selected as Chief General Manager of the London & North Eastern Railway from its formation on 1 January 1923. He was chairman of the wartime Railway Executive Committee from September 1939 to August 1941. He was knighted on 10 July 1924 and created a baronet on 20th January 1942.

From the beginning of the LNER's existence he established the closest possible working relationship with Gresley and gave the CME great latitude in developing locomotives and rolling stock. As such he played a leading role in the creation of the LNER Pacifics, in particular. He died on 5 September 1956.

Whitelaw, William

He was born on 15 March 1868 and attended Harrow and then Trinity College, Cambridge. He was elected MP for Perth in 1892 but lost his seat three years later. In 1898, he was made a director of the Highland Railway, then Chairman from 1902

to 1912, and again from 1916. He was later Chairman of the North British Railway, then at Grouping moved to the LNER. This, of course, coincided with the most dynamic period of Gresley's career when locomotive development moved forward in leaps and bounds. It is true to say that without Whitelaw's support and patronage, the Gresley legend might have been significantly less noteworthy. Whitelaw resigned from this post in September 1938 and died on the 19th January 1946.

Windle, Edward

He was born in 1893 in Doncaster. His father John, a railway clerk, died in the West Yorkshire Asylum in March 1903, leaving a widow a daughter and three sons. In straitened circumstances, employment became essential for the boys and each joined the GNR Works at Doncaster when their time came. In the 1911 Census, Edward is listed as being a fitter's apprentice and, according to Spencer, 'quickly showed his worth caught Gresley's eye and made rapid progress, becoming essential to the CME in the process'. This patronage, coupled to Windle's developing skills as a design engineer, meant that he played an active role in the development of the A1s, A3 and A4s and much else beside.

In due course, he rose to become Chief Locomotive Draughtsmen and in 1941 succeeded Tom Street as Chief Draughtsman. He remained in this post throughout the difficult war years until BR was formed. In this organisation, his authority, as it was for all the Chief Draughtsmen, was reduced, but in his new role he played a leading part in establishing BR's requirement for a new group of standard engines and

the design work that followed. It seems he retired in 1953 and lived on in Doncaster until his death in November 1960.

Wintour, Francis

He was born in 1862 in Lincolnshire and became an engineering apprentice with Manning, Wardle & Co in 1888. He then worked for the Lancashire and Yorkshire Railway and was recruited by Henry Ivatt in 1905 to become the District Loco Superintendent at King's Cross. By the time Gresley was appointed to be the GNR's Locomotive Engineer in 1911, Wintour had been promoted to Works Manager at Doncaster. Under Ivatt, he had been successful in this post and might have expected to be considered for the top job in time. But this wasn't to be and though described by Bert Spencer, Gresley's trusted assistant, as a 'very skilful engineer, but a forthright and strong individual who tended to call a spade a spade', he continued to serve the CME very effectively until his retirement in 1927.

His knowledge of locomotive design and construction methods appears to have been good and his influence on the N1 and N2 designs has long been suggested. But his pivotal role as Works Manager, and the heavy demands this placed upon him, precluded greater involvement in design work. However, he had a degree of oversight of this work through the drawing office that sat beside him at Doncaster. In time he would be appointed Assistant Mechanical Engineer such was the faith Gresley had in him and ensured that the Pacifics built at Doncaster were produced on time and to the highest standard.

INDIVIDUAL HISTORIES OF THE A1/A3s

Name: *Great Northern*
Numbers: 1470, 1470n, 4470, 113 and 60113
Works Number: 1536 (built at Doncaster).
Date to traffic: 11 April 1922.
Rebuilt as A1/1: September 1945.
Withdrawn from service: Condemned in November 1962 and cut up at Doncaster in February 1963.
Total mileage: 2,078,000 (as A1 and A1/1 – 1,212,000 and 866,000 respectively). (All mileages in this appendix to nearest thousand).
Modifications: 1930 – Long Travel Valves fitted; 1937 – Blow-down Apparatus fitted; 1945 – rebuilt as A1/1 rather than to A3 standard with double chimney, Kylchap exhaust and small smoke deflectors then larger deflectors three months later.,
Boilers fitted: 7646 when new, 7783 in April 1927, 7646 in May 1933, 7774 in February 1937, 7767 in March 1940, 9487 in October 1945, 9031 in January 1950, 9031/29288 in May 1951, 29275 in August

1952, 29329 in May 1957, 29275 in June 1959 and 29332 in February 1961.
Tenders attached: 5211 when new, 5227 from June 1928 and 5582 from February 1937.
Colour schemes: April 1922 – GNR colour scheme applied - upper works of loco in green, with tender painted in two shades of green. The lower works of loco and tender painted light brown. LNER green scheme possibly applied in 1923, then black from February 1942, GER blue from September 1945, LNER green May 1947, BR blue from January 1950 and BR green from August 1952.
Sheds: Doncaster when new, Gorton from July 1944, King's Cross from October 1944, Doncaster from November 1945, King's Cross from October 1945, Gateshead from July 1947, Haymarket from September 1947, King's Cross from September 1947, New England from June 1950, Grantham from September 1951, King's Cross from September 1957 and Doncaster from October 1957.

Name: *Sir Frederick Banbury*
Numbers: 1471, 4471, 102 and 60102.
Works Number: 1539 (built at Doncaster).
Date to traffic: 10 July 1922.
Rebuilt as A3: October 1942.
Withdrawn from service: Condemned in November 1961 and cut up at Doncaster in November 1961.
Total mileage: 1,905,000.
Modifications: 1922 Indicator gear fitted; 1930 – long travel valves fitted; 1937 – Blow-down Apparatus fitted; 1942 – rebuilt as an A3; 1953 – right-hand to left-hand drive; 1956 - to 75% cut-off; 1959 – double chimney and Kylchap exhaust fitted.
Boilers fitted: 7693 when new, 7878 in April 1928, 7804 in April 1933, 7772 in May 1935, 7785 in November 1939, 8248 in October 1942, 9571 in May 1947, 27052 in August 1951, 27000 in June 1965, 27001 in June 1958 and 29285 in May 1960.
Tenders attached: 5223 when new, 5378 in April 1925, 5223 in November 1925, 5323 in April 1928, 5324 June 1929, 5290 in October 1936, 5292 in October 1942.
Colour schemes: July 1922 – GNR colour scheme applied - upper works of loco in green, with tender painted in two shades of green. The lower works of loco and tender painted light brown. LNER green scheme possibly applied in 1923, then black from October 1942, LNER green May 1947, BR blue May 1949 and BR green August 1951.
Sheds: Doncaster when new, Grantham from December 1932, Doncaster from May 1933, Grantham from July 1943, New England from April 1944, Grantham from October 1944, Leicester Central May 1949, Neasden from Jult 1954, Leicester Central from November 1954, King's Cross from September 1957, Doncaster October 1957, Grantham from June 1959 and King's Cross October 1960.

Name: *Flying Scotsman*
Numbers: 1472, 4472, 103 and 60103.
Works Number: 1564 (built at Doncaster).
Date to traffic: 24 February 1923.
Rebuilt as an A3: January 1947.
Withdrawn from service: January 1963 for preservation.
Total mileage: 2,075,000 in LNER/BR service.
Modifications: 1927 – Variable blast pipe on; 1928 – long travel valves fitted; 1939 – Blow-down apparatus fitted; 1947 – rebuilt as an A3; 1948 – to 75% cut-off; 1954 – right-hand to left-hand drive; 1959 – double chimney and Kylchap exhaust fitted; 1961 – trough deflectors fitted.
Boilers fitted: 7693 from new, 7878 in April 1928, 7804 in May 1935, 7772 in May 1935, 7785 in November 1939, 8078 in January 1947, 9119 in March 1948, 9448 in December 1949, 27015 in March 1952, 27074 in April 1954, 27007 in October 1955, 27011 in July 1957, 27044 in January 1959, 27047 in August 1960 and 27058 in June 1962.
Tenders attached: 5223 from new, 5378 in April 1925, 5223 in November 1925, 5323 in April 1928, 5324 in June 1929, 5290 in October 1936, 5640 in July 1938, 5640 in January 1963 and 5325 in preservation.
Colour schemes: LNER green from new, black April 1943, LNER green January 1947, BR blue in December 1949 and BR green in March 1952.
Sheds: Doncaster when new, King's Cross in April 1928, Doncaster in March 1939, New England in March 1944, Gorton in July 1944, King's Cross in October 1944, New England in November 1944, Doncaster in December 1944, Leicester Central in June 1950, Grantham in November 1953, King's Cross in June 1954, Grantham in August 1954, King's Cross in April 1957.

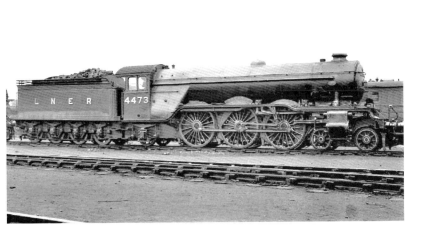

Name: *Solario*
Numbers: 1473, 4473, 104 and 60104.
Works Number: 1565 (built at Doncaster).
Date to traffic: 17 March 1923.
Rebuilt as an A3: October 1941
Withdrawn from service: Condemned in November 1959 and cut up at Doncaster in December 1959.
Total mileage: 1,874,000.
Modifications: 1927 – long travel valves fitted, 1937 – Blow-down Apparatus fitted, 1941 – rebuilt as an A3, 1950 – to 75% cut-off, 1953 – right-hand to left-hand drive, 1959 double chimney and Kylchap exhaust fitted.
Boilers fitted: 7694 from new, 7646 in December 1927, 7701 in October 1929, 7792 in June 1932, 7647 in November 1934, 7700 in April 1936, 9123 from October 1941, 9483 from January 1946, 27030 February 1951, 27010 from June 1953, 27052 fromJuly 1955, 27035 from December 1956 and 27040 from April 1958.
Tenders attached: 5224 from new, 5254 in March 1929.
Colour schemes: LNER green from new, black February 1943, LNER green January 1947, BR blue January 1950 and BR green June 1953.
Sheds: Doncaster from new, Copley Hill from September 1937, Doncaster from November 1937, Copley Hill from November 1937, Doncaster from January 1938, Gorton from May 1939, King's Cross from February 1943, Leicester Central June 1950, Neasden from July 1954, Leicester Central from December 1954, King's Cross from September 1957, Doncaster from October 1957, Grantham from June 1959 and King's Cross in November 1959.
Name: *Victor Wild*

Numbers: 1474, 1474n, 4474, 105 and 60105.
Works Number: 1566 (built at Doncaster).
Date to traffic: 24 March 1923.
Rebuilt as an A3: October 1942.
Withdrawn from service: Condemned in June 1963 and cut-up at Doncaster in August 1963.
Total mileage: 2,223,000.
Modifications: 1929 – long travel valves fitted, 1937 – Blow-down Apparatus fitted, 1942 – rebuilt as an A3, 1947 – to 75% cut-off, 1953 – right-hand to left-hand drive, 1959 – double chimney and Kylchap exhaust fitted, 1960 – trough deflectors fitted.
Boilers fitted: 7695 from new, 7700 from September 1929, 7804 from July 1935, 7646 from October 1937, 8076 from October 1942, 9572 from May 1947, 9212 from August 1948, 9216 from March 1950, 27050 from July 1951, 27051 from February 1953, 27056 from August 1954, 27048 from August 1957, 27017 from March 1959 and 27070 from December 1960.
Tenders attached: 5225 from new, 5327 from October 1933, 5225 from August 1934, 5329 from September 1934, 5225 from September 1934.
Colour schemes: LNER green from new, black from October 1942, LNER green from May 1947, BR blue from March 1950 and BR green from February 1953.
Sheds: King's Cross when new, Doncaster in January 1927, Gorton in February 1939, Leicester Central from August 1939, Gorton from December 1939, Gorton from October 1942, King's Cross from November 1942 and Grantham from September 1951.

Name: *Flying Fox*
Numbers: 1475, 4475,106 and 60106.
Works Number: 1567 (built at Doncaster).
Date to traffic: 28 April 1923.
Rebuilt as an A3: March 1947.
Withdrawn from service: Condemned December 1964 cut up at R.A. King's of Norwich during 1965.
Total mileage: 2,643,000.
Modifications: 1928 – long travel valves fitted, 1947 – rebuilt as an A3, 1947 – to 75% cut-off, 1953 – right-hand to left-hand drive, 1958 – double chimney and Kylchap exhaust fitted, 1961 – trough deflectors fitted.
Boilers fitted: 7696 from new 7699 from July 1928, 7878 from July 1933, 7768 from March 1937, 7779 from June 1940, 7767 from July 1945, 9569 from March 1947, 9208 from May 1950, 27000 from April 1952, 27030 from December 1953, 27002 from July 1955, 270063 from April 1960 and 27047 from June 1962.
Tenders attached: 5226 from new, 5228 from July 1928, 5329 from August 1928, 5225 from September 1934, 5329 from September 1934, 5323 from June 1935, 5483 from October 1936, 5279 from March 1937, 5278 from June 1940.
Colour schemes: LNER green from new, black from February 1942, LNER green from March 1947, BR blue from May 1950 and BR green from May 1952.
Sheds: King's Cross from new, New England from June 1940, Grantham from April 1944, King's Cross from April 1944, Gorton from July 1944, King's Cross from October 1944, Copley Hill from December 1944, New England from January 1945, Grantham from November 1947, King's Cross from February 1953, Grantham from October 1953, Copley Hill fromMay 1954, Leicester Central from August 1955, Grantham from September 1957, Doncaster from September 1963 and New England from October 1963.

Name: *Royal Lancer*
Numbers: 1476, 4476, 107 and 60107.
Works Number: 1568 (built at Doncaster).
Date to traffic: 26 May 1923.
Rebuilt as an A3: October 1946.
Withdrawn from service: Condemned in September 1963 and cut up at Doncaster during October 1963.
Total mileage: 2,252,000.
Modifications: 1928 – long travel valves fitted, 1946 – rebuilt as an A3, 1948 – to 75% cut-off, 1952 – right-hand to left-hand drive, 1959 – double chimney and Kylchap exhaust fitted, 1962 – trough deflectors fitted.
Boilers fitted: 7965 from new, 7700 from September 1929, 7804 from July 1935, 7646 from October 1937, 9515 from April 1951, 27083 from December 1952, 27047 from August 1956, 27039 from May 1958, 27035 from November 1959 and 27044 from February 1962.
Tenders attached: 5225 from new, 5327 from July 1933, 5225 from August 1934, 5329 from September 1934, 5225 from September 1934, 5267 from September 1963.
Colour schemes: LNER green from new, black from February 1943, LNER green from October 1946, BR blue from October 1949 and BR green from December 1952.
Sheds: King's Cross when new, Doncaster in January 1937, Gorton in February 1939, Leicester Central in August 1939, Gorton in December 1939, King's Cross in October 1946, Leicester Central in June 1950, Copley Hill in July 1952, Leicester Central in August 1952, Grantham September 1957, King's Cross in October 1960 and Grantham in June 1963.

Name: *Gay Crusader*
Numbers: 1477, 4477, 507, 108 and 60108.
Works Number: 1569 (built at Doncaster).
Date to traffic: 16 June 1923.
Rebuilt as an A3: January 1943.
Withdrawn from service: Condemned October 1963 and cut up at Darlington in November 1963.
Total mileage: 2,079,000.
Modifications: 1926 – valve gear modified, 1927 – 'Diamond' soot blower fitted, 1928 – long travel valves fitted, 1937 – Blow-down Apparatus fitted, 1942 – rebuilt as an A3, 1949 – to 75% cut-off, 1953 – right-hand to left-hand drive, 1959 – double chimney and Kylchap exhaust fitted, 1961 – trough deflectors fitted.
Boilers fitted: 7698 from new, 7704 from June 1928, 7703 from November 1929, 7765 from September 1933, 7697 from June 1937, 9213 from January 1943, 9124 from August 1947, 27077 from October 1953, 27010 from July 1955, 27064 from July 1957, 27077 from May 1959, 27083 from September 1960 and 27018 from April 1962.
Tenders attached: 5228 from new, 5211 from June 1928, 5266 from June 1937 and 5223 from April 1962.
Colour schemes: LNER green from new, black from January 1943, LNER green from August 1947, BR blue from September 1950 and BR green from February 1952.
Sheds: Doncaster from new, Grantham November 1934, Doncaster April 1935, Gorton December 1941, King's Cross January 1943, Doncaster January 1951, King's Cross June 1952, Neasden September 1952, King's Cross March 1953, Neasden November 1953, King's Cross July 1955, Neasden October 1955, King's Cross January 1957, Doncaster October 1958, King's Cross November 1958, New England September 1961, Grantham June 1963 and Doncaster September 1963.

Name: *Hermit*
Numbers: 1478, 1478n, 4478, 508, 109 and 60109.
Works Number: 1570 (built at Doncaster).
Date to traffic: 30 June 1923.
Rebuilt as an A3: November 1943.
Withdrawn from service: Condemned in December 1962 cut up at Doncaster in April 1963.
Total mileage: 2,076,000.
Modifications: 1930 – long travel valves fitted, 1943 – rebuilt as an A3, 1947 – to 75% cut-off, 1952 – right-hand to left-hand drive, 1959 – double chimney and Kylchap exhaust fitted, 1961 – trough deflectors fitted.
Boilers fitted: 7699 from new, 7765 from March 1928, 7701 from March 1933, 7791 from January 1938, 9445 from November 1943, 9116 from March 1947, 8080 from May 1948, 9451 from November 1949, 29322 from November 1954, 27052 from January 1957, 27029 in March 1959 and 29373 from January 1961.
Tenders attached: 5229 from new, 5259 from March 1932, 5289 from April 1940, 5271 from December 1953 and 5268 from January 1961.
Colour schemes: LNER green from new, black from March 1942, LNER green from March 1947, BR blue from November 1949 and BR green from November 1952.
Sheds: Doncaster when new, Grantham in September 1924, Doncaster in April 1938, Gorton in March 1939, King's Cross in November 1942, Copley Hill in February 1943, Doncaster in September 1943, Copley Hill in December 1943, New England in May 1944, King's Cross in September 1944, Grantham in September 1951, Doncaster in October 1953, King's Cross in June 1958, Doncaster in October 1958 and King's Cross in April 1959.

Name: *Robert the Devil*
Numbers: 1479, 4479, 110 and 60110.
Works Number: 1571 (built at Doncaster).
Date to traffic: 25 July 1923.
Rebuilt as an A3: August 1942.
Withdrawn from service: Condemned in May 1963 and cut up at Doncaster in June 1963.
Total mileage: 2,149,000.
Modifications: 1930 – long travel valves fitted, 1942 – rebuilt as an A3, 1949 – to 75% cut-off, 1953 – right-hand to left-hand drive, 1959 – double chimney and Kylchap exhaust fitted, July 1961 – trough deflectors fitted.
Boilers fitted: 7700 from new, 7697 from February 1929, 7647 from December 1931, 7697 from September 1936, 7695 from November 1936, 7776 from October 1940, 9211 from August 1942, 9566 from February 1947, 9215 from August 1950, 27056 from August 1951, 27070 from July 1954, 27025 from June 1957, 27020 from May 1959 and 27052 from March 1961.
Tenders attached: 5230 from new.
Colour schemes: LNER green from new, black from August 1942, LNER green from February 1947, BR blue from August 1950 and BR green from August 1951.
Sheds: Grantham from new, New England from 1 1942, Grantham from October 1942, King's Cross from October 1946, Grantham from September 1951 and King's Cross from June 1957.

Name: *Enterprise.*
Numbers: 1480, 1480n, 4480, 111 and 60111.
Works Number: 1572 (built at Doncaster).
Date to traffic: 17 August 1923.
Rebuilt as an A3: July 1927.
Withdrawn from service: Condemned in December 1962 and cut up at Doncaster in April 1963.
Total mileage: 1,937,000.
Modifications: 1927 – rebuilt as A3 and long travel valves fitted, 1949 – to 75% cut-off, 1953 – right-hand to left-hand drive, 1959 – double chimney and Kylchap exhaust fitted, 1961 – trough deflectors fitted.
Boilers fitted: 7701 when new, 8027 from July 1927, 8251 from July 1930, 8248 from August 1934, 8082 from February 1936, 8078 from April 1941, 9214 from February 1943, 9452 from October 1940, 27049 from June 1951, 27023 from December 1954 and 27025 from June 1959.
Tenders attached: 5231 when new, 5223 from April 1937, 5477 from May 1938 and 5569 from January 1945.
Colour schemes: LNER green from new, black from August 1942, LNER green from February 1947, BR blue from August 1950 and BR green from August 1951.
Sheds: Grantham when new, Doncaster in July 1927, Carlisle in December 1928, King's Cross in April 1929, Doncaster in April 1929, King's Cross in March 1939, Grantham in December 1941, Copley Hill October 1943, Grantham in October 1943, New England in May 1944, Doncaster in December 1948, Neasden in February 1949, Leicester Central in March 1955 and Grantham in September 1957.

Name: *St Simon*
Numbers: 1481, 1481n, 4481, E112 and 60112.
Works Number: 1573 (built at Doncaster).
Date to traffic: 8 September 1923.
Rebuilt as an A3: August 1946.
Withdrawn from service: Condemned in December 1964 and cut up by R A King's of Norwich in 1965.
Total mileage: 1,962,000.
Modifications: 1929 – long travel valves fitted, 1937 – Blow-down apparatus fitted, 1949 – to 75% cut-off, October 1952 – right-hand to left-hand drive, 1958 – double chimney and Kylchap exhaust fitted, 1959 – small deflectors fitted, 1962 – trough deflectors fitted.
Boilers fitted: 7702 from new, 7694 from June 1928, 7693 from January 1931, 7702 from June 1933, 7779 from December 1934, 7784 from September 1939, 8780 from August 1946, 8783 from January 1948, 9453 from March 1949, 27028 from February 1951, 27045 from October 1952, 27026 from July 1956, 27086 from July 1958, 27009 from February 1960 and 29295 from October 1962.
Tenders attached: 5232 from new, 5643 from May 1937, 5280 from April 1938, 5223 from May 1938, 5211 from January 1948 and 5289 from October 1962.
Colour schemes: LNER green from new, black from February 1943, LNER green from August 1946, BR blue from January 1951 and BR green from October 1952.
Sheds: Doncaster from new, Gateshead in November 1923, New England in November 1927, Doncaster in November 1927, Grantham in February 1931, Doncaster in February 1931, Copley Hill in December 1943, Doncaster in May 1944, Grantham in October 1945, King's Cross in May 1946, Copley Hill in June 1950, Doncaster in November 1950, Copley Hill in April 1951, Doncaster in September 1951, Grantham in October 1951, Doncaster in February 1953, Grantham in June 1959, Doncaster in September 1963 and New England in October 1963.

Name: *Melton*
Numbers: 2543, 512, 44 and 60044.
Works Number: 1598 (built at Doncaster).
Date to traffic: 28 June 1924.
Rebuilt as an A3: September 1947.
Withdrawn from service: Condemned June 1963 and cut up at Doncaster in November 1963.
Total mileage: 1,992,000.
Modifications: 1930 – long travel valves fitted, 1937 – Blow-down apparatus fitted, 1947 – rebuilt as A3, 1947 – to 75% cut-off, 1952 – right-hand to left-hand drive, 1959 – double chimney and Kylchap exhaust fitted, 1961 – trough deflectors fitted.
Boilers fitted: 7703 when new, 7693 from February 1929, 7783 from December 1930, 7789 from June 1933, 7766 from November 1935, 7879 from February 1941, 7797 from February 1946, 8226 from September 1947, 9984 from August 1949, 27033 from March 1951, 27039 from December 1956, 27035 from May 1958 and 27072 from October 1959.
Tenders attached: 5253 from new, 5269 from new, 5224 from June 1929, 5580 from August 1938, and 5274 from December 1952.
Colour schemes: LNER green from new, black from December 1942, , LNER green from September 1947, BR blue from August 1949 and BR green from December 1952.
Sheds: Grantham from new, Doncaster in August 1924, Gorton in September 1924, King's Cross in March 1927, Doncaster in March 1927, Grantham in January 1930, King's Cross March 1930, Doncaster June 1930, New England March 1944, King's Cross in September 1944, Copley Hill in December 1944, New England in January 1945, Grantham in November 1947, Copley Hill from April 1950, Doncaster from September 1951, Leicester Central from November 1953, Neasden from March 1955, King's Cross from March 1956, Grantham from September 1956 and King's Cross from April 1957.

Name: *Lemberg*
Numbers: 2544, 513, 45 and 60045.
Works Number: 1600 (built at Doncaster).
Date to traffic: 26 July 1924.
Rebuilt as an A3: December 1927.
Withdrawn from service: Condemned November 1964 and cut up at A. Draper of Hull in 1965.
Total mileage: 1,907,000.
Modifications: 1927 – rebuilt as an A3 and long travel valves fitted, 1953 – right-hand to left-hand drive, 1958 – to 75% cut-off, 1959 – double chimney and Kylchap exhaust fitted, 1962 – trough deflectors fitted.
Boilers fitted: 7704 from new, 9028 from December 1927, 8027 from January 1931, 8224 from May 1933, 8029 from May 1936, 8226 from May 1937, 8248 from March 1938, 8031 from May 1942, 8250 from June 1947, 9450 from February 1949, 27007 from November 1950, 27063 from October 1953, 27028 from January 1958, 27024 from June 1960 and 27021 fromNovember 1962.
Tenders attached: 5254 from new and 5228 from April 1929.
Colour schemes: LNER green from new, black from May 1942, LNER green from June 1947, BR purple from June 1948, BR blue from November 1950 and BR green fromMay 1952.
Sheds: Gorton from new, Doncaster in August 1924, Gateshead in January 1937, Heaton in May 1938, Gateshead from January 1940, Darlington in February 1954, Gateshead in March 1954, Darlington in March 1954, Gateshead in October 1954, Darlington in November 1955, Gateshead in May 1956, Darlington in May 1958, Gateshead in November 1958, Heaton in September 1962, Darlington in December 1962, Heaton in June 1963, Gateshead in June 1963 and Darlington in December 1963.

Name: *Diamond Jubilee*
Numbers: 2545, 514, 46 and 60046.
Works Number: 1601 (built at Doncaster).
Date to traffic: 9 August 1924.
Rebuilt as an A3: August 1941.
Withdrawn from service: Condemned in June 1963 and cut up at Doncaster in August 1963.
Total mileage: 2,039,000.
Modifications: 1931 – long travel valves fitted, 1939 – Blow-down Apparatus fitted and rubber fairing added, 1941 – rebuilt as an A3, 1947 – to 75% cut-off, 1952 – right-hand to left-hand drive, August 1958 – double chimney and Kylchap exhaust fitted, 1961 – trough deflectors fitted.
Boilers fitted: 7763 from new, 7778 from May 1931, 7795 from March 1933, 7703 from July 1936, 9122 from August 1941, 9510 from July 1946, 9983 from August 1949, 27047 from June 1951, 27051 from August 1954, 29306 from January 1960 and 27086 from December 1961.
Tenders attached: 5255 from new, 5266 from June 1928, 5644 from June 1937.
Colour schemes: LNER green from new, black from March 1943, LNER green from November 1947, BR blue from August 1949 and BR green from October 1952.
Sheds: Gorton from new, King's Cross in September 1924, Grantham in June 1928, Copley Hill in September 1943, King's Cross in December 1944, Copley Hill in May 1948, Doncaster September 1951, Grantham in June 1959, New England in September 1962 and Grantham in April 1963.

Name: *Donovan*
Numbers: 2546, 515, 47 and 60047.
Works Number: 1602 (built at Doncaster).
Date to traffic: 30 August 1924.
Rebuilt as an A3: January 1948
Withdrawn from service: Condemned in April 1963 and cut up at Doncaster in June 1963.
Total mileage: 2,089,000.
Modifications: 1927 – long travel valves fitted, 1947 – rebuilt as an A3, 1946 – to 75% cut-off, 1953 – right-hand to left-hand drive, 1959 – double chimney and Kylchap exhaust fitted, 1961 – trough deflectors fitted.
Boilers fitted: 7764 from new, 7704 from May 1930, 7776 from October 1934, 7804 from June 1939, 8778 from January 1948, 27015 from December 1950, 27069 from February 1952, 27043 from July 1953, 27-73 from December 1957 and 27042 from July 1959.
Tenders attached: 5256 from new, 5327 from May 1928, 5256 from May 1938, 5269 from June 1938, 5284 from July 1944 and 5280 from May 1948.
Colour schemes: LNER green from new, black from December 1942, LNER green from January 1948, BR blue from June 1949 and BR green from February 1952.
Sheds: King's Cross from new, Grantham in June 1928, King's Cross in June 1928, Neasden from June 1939, Gorton from February 1941, King's Cross in December 1942, Gorton in July 1944, King's Cross in October 1944, Copley Hill in December 1944, Doncaster in January 1945, Grantham in October 1945, King's Cross in May 1946, Doncaster in May 1950, King's Cross in January 1951, Grantham in September 1951, King's Cross June 1954, Grantham in October 1954 and New England in September 1962.

Name: *Doncaster*
Numbers: 2547, 516, 48 and 60048.
Works Number: 1603 (built at Doncaster).
Date to traffic: August 1924.
Rebuilt as an A3: May 1946.
Withdrawn from service: Condemned in September 1963 and cut up at Doncaster in September 1963.
Total mileage: 1,907,000.
Modifications: 1928 – corridor tender attached and long travel valves fitted, 1946 – rebuilt as an A3, 1952 – right-hand to left-hand drive, 1956 – to 75% cut-off, May 1959 – double chimney and Kylchap exhaust fitted, 1959 – small deflectors fitted, 1961 – trough deflectors fitted.
Boilers fitted: 7765 from new, 7784 from February 1928, 7794 from July 1932, 7793 from October 1935, 7796 from January 1937, 7789 from July 1939, 9123 from May 1946, 9573 from June 1947, 9211 from November 1948, 10542 from September 1950, 27018 from September 1952, 27047 from September 1954, 27061 from August 1956, 27039 from November 1959 and 27083 from April 1962.
Tenders attached: 5257 from new, 5327 from April 1928, 5256 from May 1928, 5327 from May 1928, 5273 from July 1933, 5566 from December 1941, 5283 from September 1952 and 5483 from April 1962.
Colour schemes: LNER green from new, black from September 1942, LNER green from June 1947, BR blue from September 1950 and BR green from September 1952.
Sheds: Grantham from new, King's Cross in March 1927, Grantham in March 1927, King's Cross in April 1928, Doncaster in October 1935, Leicester Central in February 1949, Doncaster in November 1953, King's Cross in June 1958, Doncaster in January 1959, Grantham in February 1959, New England in September 1962 and Grantham in April 1963.

Name: *Galtee More*
Numbers: 2548, 517, 49 and 60049.
Works Number: 1604 (built at Doncaster).
Date to traffic: September 1924.
Rebuilt as an A3: October 1945.
Withdrawn from service: Condemned in December 1962 and cut up at Doncaster in April 1963.
Total mileage: 2,005,000.
Modifications: 1928 – long travel valves fitted, 1945 – rebuilt as an A3, 1954 – right-hand to left-hand drive, 1955 – to 75% cut-off, 1959 – double chimney and Kylchap exhaust fitted, 1960 – trough deflectors fitted.
Boilers fitted: 7766 from new, 7775 from July 1930, 7694 from July 1931, 7879 from April 1932, 7771 from April 1935, 7789 from March 1938, 7770 from April 1939, 8224 from October 1945, 8782 from August 1950, 27025 fromJuly 1952, 27053 from May 1954, 27016 from December 1955, 27007 from March 1959 and 27005 from October 1960.
Tenders attached: 5258 from new, 5270 from September 1931, 5269 from June 1933, 5270 from April 1934, 5262 from December 1941 and 5232 from October 1962.
Colour schemes: LNER green from new, black from March 1942, LNER green from December 1946, BR blue from August 1950 and BR green from July 1952.
Sheds: Grantham from new, Doncaster in August 1930, Grantham in August 1930, New England in January 1942, Grantham in October 1942, New England in October 1942, Grantham in May 1943, Doncaster in October 1943, Grantham October 1944, Doncaster in December 1944, Leicester Central in February 1949, King's Cross in May 1955, Leicester Central in October 1955 and Grantham in September 1957.

Name: *Persimmon*
Numbers: 2549, 518, 50, E50 and 60050.
Works Number: 1605 (built at Doncaster).
Date to traffic: October 1924.
Rebuilt as an A3: December 1943.
Withdrawn from service: Condemned in June 1963 and cut up at Doncaster in August 1963.
Total mileage: 2,035,000.
Modifications: 1927 – long travel valves fitted, 1943 – rebuilt as an A3, 1949 – to 75% cut-off, 1952 – right-hand to left-hand drive, 1959 – double chimney and Kylchap exhaust fitted, 1961 – trough deflectors fitted.
Boilers fitted: 7767 from new, 7777 from October 1928, 7790 from February 1932, 7789 from May 1936, 7698 from May 1937, 9446 from 1943, 9115 from April 1947, 9447 from August 1948, 9122 from July 1949, 27045 from May 1951, 27081 from September 1952, 27078 from August 1954, 27084 from March 1956, 27013 from November 1957, 27013 from November 1957, 29272 from October 1959 and 29299 from October 1961.
Tenders attached: 5259 from new, 5264 from April 1934, 5289 from June 1934 and 5259 from February 1940.
Colour schemes: LNER green from new, black from March 1942, LNER green from April 1947, BR blue from July 1949 and BR green from September 1952.
Sheds: Doncaster from new, Grantham in July 1927, New England in January 1942, Grantham in July 1942, New England in October 1942, Grantham in May 1943, King's Cross in October 1946, Grantham in May 1948, King's Cross in June 1948, Neasden in February 1949, King's Cross inJuly 1955, Neasden in October 1955, King's Cross in June 1956, Grantham in September 1956 and New England in June 1962.

Name: *Blink Bonny*
Numbers: 2550, 519, 51 and 60051.
Works Number: 1606 (built at Doncaster).
Date to traffic: November 1924.
Rebuilt as an A3: November 1945.
Withdrawn from service: Condemned in November 1964 and cut up by Hughes Bolckow of North Blyth in 1965.
Total mileage: 1,993,000.
Modifications: 1927 – long travel valves fitted, 1945 – rebuilt as an A3, 1948 – to 75% cut-off, 1952 – right-hand to left-hand drive, 1959– double chimney and Kylchap exhaust fitted, 1962 – trough deflectors fitted.
Boilers fitted: 7768 from new, 7696 from January 1929, 7774 from March 1931, 7778 from May 1933, 7703 from May 1934, 7696 from May 1936, 7765 from May 1938, 8081 from November 1945, 27013 from November 1950, 27028 from December 1952, 27080 from July 1954, 27056 from February 1958 and 27033 from March 1960.
Tenders attached: 5260 from new and 5580 from December 1952.
Colour schemes: LNER green from new, black from March 1942, LNER green from May 1947, BR blue from November 1950 and BR green from December 1952.
Sheds: Gorton from new, Grantham in February 1925, New England in January 1942, Grantham in May 1943, New England in June 1944, Gorton in July 1944, King's Cross in October 1944, Grantham in November 1944, King's Cross in October 1946, Neasden in February 1949, Grantham in November 1953, Copley Hill in May 1954, Heaton in September 1957, Gateshead in January 1958, Darlington in June 1958, Gateshead in December 1958, Darlington in June 1960, Gateshead in December 1960, Heaton in September 1962, Darlington in June 1963 and Gateshead in December 1963.

Name: *Prince Palatine*
Numbers: 2551, 520, 52 and 60052.
Works Number: 1607 (built at Doncaster).
Date to traffic: November 1924.
Rebuilt as an A3: August 1941.
Withdrawn from service: Condemned in January 1966 and cut up by P W McLelian of Langloan in 1966.
Total mileage: 2,021,000.
Modifications: 1929 – long travel valves fitted, 1941 – rebuilt as an A3, 1953 – right-hand to left-hand drive, 1958 – to 75% cut-off, 1958 – double chimney and Kylchap exhaust fitted and 1962 – trough deflectors fitted.
Boilers fitted: 7769 from new, 7768 from November 1929, 7774 from July 1933, 7794 from November 1936, 8084 from August 1941, 9484 from April 1946, 10543 from July 1950, 27021 from April 1952, 27064 from September 1953, 27064 from September 1953, 27058 from April 1955, 27012 from November 1958, 27027 from March 1960 and 29294 from October 1962.
Tenders attached: 5261 from new, 5229 from August 1941 and 5288 from September 1953.
Colour schemes: LNER green from new, black fro April 1943, LNER green from June 1947, BR blue from May 1949 and BR green from April 1952.
Sheds: Gorton from new, Grantham in February 1925, Copley Hill in September 1943, New England in May 1944, Doncaster in December 1948, Leicester Central May 1949, Neasden in July 1954, Leicester Central in December 1954, Copley Hill in August 1955, Heaton in September 1957, Gateshead in January 1958, Darlington in June 1960, Gateshead in December 1960, Heaton in September 1962, Darlington in December 1962, Heaton in June 1963, Gateshead in June 1963 and St Margaret's in August 1963.

Name: *Sansovino*
Numbers: 2552, 521, 53 and 60053.
Works Number: 1608 (built at Doncaster).
Date to traffic: December 1924.
Rebuilt as an A3: September 1943.
Withdrawn from service: Condemned in May 1963 and cut up at Doncaster in 1963.
Total mileage: 1,993,000
Modifications: 1928 – long travel valves fitted, 1943 – rebuilt as an A3, 1953 – right-hand to left-hand drive, 1957 – to 75% cut-off and 1958 – double chimney and Kylchap exhaust fitted.
Boilers fitted: 7770 from new, 7794 from September 1931, 7647 from June 1936, 8079 from September 1943, 9121 from February 1949, 9569 from June 1950, 27077 from May 1952, 27065 from October 1953, 27067 from February 1957, 27076 from 2February 1958, 27013 from October 1959 and 27049 from April 1961.
Tenders attached: 5262 from new, 5329 from June 1928, 5228 from August 1928, 5272 from April 1929, 5265 from June 1929, 5274 from September 1929 and 5570 from September 1943.
Colour schemes: LNER green from new, black fro September 1943, LNER green from October 1947, BR blue from June 1950 and BR green from May 1952.
Sheds: King's Cross from new, Neasden in June 1939, King's Cross in November 1942, Copley Hill from February 1943, New England in December 1944, Leicester Central in February 1949, Doncaster in May 1949, Grantham in May 1949, Copley Hill in May 1954, Gateshead in September 1957, Darlington in December 1958, Gateshead in June 1959, Darlington in June 1961, Gateshead in December 1961, Heaton in September 1962, St Margaret's in April 1963 and Heaton in May 1963.

Name: *Manna* then *Prince of Wales* (from 11 November 1926).
Numbers: 2553, 522, 54 and 60054,
Works Number: 1609 (built at Doncaster)
Date to traffic: December 1924.
Rebuilt as an A3: July 1943.
Withdrawn from service: Condemned in June 1964 and cut up by R A King of Norwich in 1964.
Total mileage: 1,863,000.
Modifications: 1929 – long travel valves fitted, 1943 – rebuilt as an A3, 1953 – to 75% cut-off, 1953 – right-hand to left-hand drive, 1958 – double chimney and Kylchap exhaust fitted and 1962 – trough deflectors fitted.
Boilers fitted: 7771 from new, 7695 from December 1929, 7801 from September 1932, 7798 from July 1935, 7763 from September 1936, 8084 from July 1943, 9484 from April 1946, 10543 from July 1950, 27064 from September 1953, 27058 from April 1955, 27012 from November 1958, 27027 from March 1960 and 29294 from October 1962.
Tenders attached: 5263 from new, 5264 from September 1936, 5229 from August 1941 and 5288 from September 1953.
Colour schemes: LNER green from new, black from July 1943, LNER green from October 1946, BR blue from April 1950 and BR green from November 1951.
Sheds: Gorton from new, King's Cross in January 1925, Doncaster in May 1928, Copley Hill in October 1936, Doncaster in February 1940, Grantham in March 1940, New England in October 1942, Leicester Central in February 1949, King's Cross in June 1956, Grantham in June 1957, Doncaster in September 1963 and New England in October 1963.

Name: *Woolwinder*
Numbers: 2554, 523, 55 and 60055.
Works Number: 1610 (built at Doncaster).
Date to traffic: December 1924
Rebuilt as an A3: June 1942.
Withdrawn from service: Condemned in September 1961 and cut up at Doncaster in 1961/62.
Total mileage: 2,023,000.
Modifications: 1930 – long travel valves fitted, 1942 – rebuilt as an A3, 1953 – to 75% cut-off, 1953 – right-hand to left-hand drive and 1958 – double chimney and Kylchap exhaust fitted, 1959 – small deflectors fitted.
Boilers fitted: 7772 from new, 7771 from June 1930, 7780 from June 1931, 7792 from November 1934, 7803 from June 1936, 8784 from June 1942, 9574 from July 1947, 10544 from August 1950, 27063 from November 1951, 27021 from October 1953, 27073 from June 1955, 29322 from January 1957, 29281 from June 1958 and 29301 from October 1959.
Tenders attached: 5264 from new, 5258 from March 1932, 5211 from June 1942, 5283 from November 1945 and 5286 from April 1949.
Colour schemes: LNER green from new, black from June 1942, LNER green from July 1947, BR blue from August 1950 and BR green from November 1951.
Sheds: Doncaster from new, Grantham in April 1927, King's Cross in July 1929, Grantham in October 1929, Doncaster in October 1929, Grantham in 1September 1929, Gorton in August 1939, Grantham in November 1942, Copley Hill in October 1943, King's Cross in December 1944, Doncaster in June 1950 and King's Cross in June 1956.

Name: *Centenary*
Numbers: 2555, 524, 56 and 60056.
Works Number: 1611 (built at Doncaster).
Date to traffic: February 1925.
Rebuilt as an A3: August 1944.
Withdrawn from service: Condemned in May 1963 and cut up at Doncaster apparently in 1963.
Total mileage: 1,896,000.
Modifications: 1927 – long travel valves fitted, 1944 – rebuilt as an A3, 1947 – to 75% cut-off, 1954 – right-hand to left-hand drive, 1959 – double chimney and Kylchap exhaust fitted, 1961 – trough deflectors fitted.
Boilers fitted: 7773 from new, 7767 from September 1929, 7797 from May 1932, 7792 from October 1936, 9452 from August 1944, 9978 from May 1949, 27012 from November 1950, 27078 from May 1952, 27004 from February 1954, 27017 from February 1956, 27055 from December 1957, 27068 from July 1959,
Tenders attached: 5265 from new, 5257 from July 1928 and 5269 from December 1957.
Colour schemes: LNER green from new, black from October 1942, LNER green from September 1947, BR blue from May 1949 and BR green from May 1952.
Sheds: Doncaster from new, Gorton in February 1925, Doncaster in February 1925, Grantham in October 1929, Doncaster in October 1929, Grantham in December 1935, New England in January 1936, King's Cross in February 1936, New England in February 1936, Copley Hill in February 1940, Grantham in March 1940, Doncaster in December 1941, Grantham in December 1944, King's Cross in October 1946, Copley Hill in May 1948, Doncaster in September 1951, Grantham in October 1951, Doncaster in May 1952, King's Cross in June 1952 and Grantham in February 1953.

Name: *Ormonde*
Numbers: 2556, 526, 57 and 60057.
Works Number: 1612.
Date to traffic: February 1925.
Rebuilt as an A3: January 1947.
Withdrawn from service: Condemned in October 1963 and cut up by Arnott Young of Carmyle apparently in 1964.
Total mileage: 2,141,000.
Modifications: 1930 – long travel valves fitted, 1947 – rebuilt as an A3, 1947 – to 75% cut-off, 1952 – right-hand to left-hand drive, 1958 – double chimney and Kylchap exhaust fitted, 1961 – trough deflectors fitted.
Boilers fitted: 7774 from new, 7776 from November 1930, 7768 from February 1934, 7777 from December 1936, 8083 from January 1947, 27012 from October 1952, 27030 from April 1957, 27290 from January 1960 and 29323 from September 1961.
Tenders attached: 5266 from new, 5329 from March 1938, 5262 from June 1928, 5273 from 12.41, 5284 from June 1948 and 5281 from December 1950.
Colour schemes: LNER green from new, black from December 1941, LNER green from January 1947, BR blue from July 1949 and BR green from October 1952.
Sheds: Grantham from new, King's Cross in June 1928, Grantham in June 1928, Doncaster in September 1938, Haymarket in March 1939, St Margaret's in March 1939, Eastfield in February 1940, Haymarket in December 1940, Dundee in March 1943, Haymarket in April 1943, Carlisle Canal in April 1961, Haymarket in May 1961 and St Margaret's in December 1961.

Name: *Blair Athol*
Numbers: 2557, 526, 58 and 60058.
Works Number: 1613 (built at Doncaster).
Date to traffic: February 1925.
Rebuilt as an A3: December 1945.
Withdrawn from service: Condemned in June 1963 and cut up at Doncaster apparently in 1963.
Total mileage: 1,992,000.
Modifications: 1931 – long travel valves fitted, 1945 – rebuilt as an A3, 1947 – to 75% cut-off, 1953 – right-hand to left-hand drive and 1958 – double chimney and Kylchap exhaust fitted.
Boilers fitted: 7775 from new, 7773 from May 1929, 7769 from June 1933, 7786 from July 1936, 7767 from June 1938, 7799 from July 1939, 8251 from February 1945, 8250 from March 1949, 27029 from February 1951, 27012 from April 1957, 27051 from October 1958 and 27017 from 1960.
Tenders attached: 5267 from new, 5269 from May 1929, 5270 from June 1933, 5269 from April 1934, 5211 from June 1938, 5271 from August 1941, 5289 from December 1953 and 5643 from February 1955.
Colour schemes: LNER green from new, black from April 1942, LNER green from April 1947, BR blue from February 1951 and BR green from May 1953.
Sheds: Gorton from new, Grantham in March 1925, King's Cross in November 1942, Copley Hill in February 1943, Doncaster in September 1943, King's Cross in October 1950, Doncaster in October 1950, Copley Hill in June 1954, Gateshead in September 1957, Darlington in November 1958, Gateshead in June 1959, Darlington in December 1961, Gateshead in June 1962 and Heaton in September 1962.

Name: *Tracery*
Numbers: 2558, 527, 59 and 60059.
Works Number: 1614 (built at Doncaster).
Date to traffic: March 1925.
Rebuilt as an A3: July 1942.
Withdrawn from service: Condemned in December 1962 and cut up at Doncaster apparently in 1963.
Total mileage: 2,524,000.
Modifications: 1928 – Diamond soot blower and long travel valves fitted, 1938 – speed recorder fitted, 1942 – rebuilt as an A3, 1954 – right-hand to left-hand drive 1956 – to 75% cut-off, , 1958 – double chimney and Kylchap exhaust fitted, 1961 – trough deflectors fitted.
Boilers fitted: 7776 from new, 7701 from December 1927, 7698 from November 1928, 7777 from July 1932, 7770 from August 1936, 7696 from July 1938, 7772 from December 1940, 9210 from July 1942, 8249 from July 1948, 9986 from August 1949, 27018 from December 1950, 27080 from August 1952, 27086 from July 1954, 27015 from April 1956, 27073 from January 1957, 27078 from November 1957 and 27075 from July 1959.
Tenders attached: 5268 from new, 5645 from June 1937, 5281 from December 1940 and 5284 from December 1950.
Colour schemes: LNER green from new, black from July 1942, LNER green from December 1946, BR blue from August 1949 and BR green from August 1952.
Sheds: Gorton from new, Grantham in April 1925, Gorton in September 1938, King's Cross in December 1942, New England in April 1944, King's Cross in September 1944, Leicester Central in March 1951 and King's Cross in April 1957.

Name: *The Tetrarch*
Numbers: 2559, 528, 60 and 60060.
Works Number: 1615 (built at Doncaster).
Date to traffic: March 1925.
Rebuilt as an A3: January 1942.
Withdrawn from service: Condemned in September 1963 and cut up at Darlington in October 1963.
Total mileage: 1,992,000.
Modifications: 1930 – long travel valves fitted, 1942 – rebuilt as an A3, 1948 – to 75% cut-off, 1953 – right-hand to left-hand drive and 1959 – double chimney and Kylchap exhaust fitted.
Boilers fitted: 7777 from new, 7776 from April 1928, 7769 from June 1930, 7698 from March 1933, 7769 from November 1936, 9270 from January 1942, 9446 from April 1947, 8777 from October 1948, 27054 from August 1951, 27069 from September 1953, 27024 from February 1955, 27042 from March 1957, 27021 from March 1959 and 29278 from August 1960.
Tenders attached: 5269 from new, 5253 from May 1929, 5566 from November 1936, 5270 from January 1942 and 5842 from July 1943.
Colour schemes: LNER green from new, black from January 1942, LNER green from April 1947, BR blue from January 1950 and BR green from August 1951.
Sheds: Gorton from new, King's Cross in April 1925, Doncaster in April 1927, Grantham in October 1933, Doncaster in July 1934, Grantham in March 1938, Gateshead in March 1939, Darlington in January 1952, Gateshead in August 1952, Darlington in May 1955, Gateshead in November 1955, Darlington in May 1957, Gateshead in December 1957, Darlington in December 1960, Gateshead in June 1961, Heaton in September 1962 and Gateshead in June 1963.

Name: *Pretty Polly*
Numbers: 2560, 529, 61 and 60061.
Works Number: 1616 (built at Doncaster).
Date to traffic: April 1925.
Rebuilt as an A3: May 1944
Withdrawn from service: Condemned in September 1963 and cut up at Doncaster in September 1963.
Total mileage: 2,015,000.
Modifications: 1930 – long travel valves fitted, 1944 – rebuilt as an A3, 1947 – to 75% cut-off, 1952 – right-hand to left-hand drive, October 1958 – double chimney and Kylchap exhaust fitted, 1959 – small deflectors fitted and 1962 – trough deflectors fitted.
Boilers fitted: 7778 from new, 5879 from January 1931, 7771 from December 1931, 7764 from October 1934, 7783 from June 1938, 8781 from May 1944, 8779 from November 1948, 27008 from November 1950, 27024 from August 1952, 27005 from March 1954, 27015 from March 1957, 27074 from December 1957, 27033 from October 1958, 27012 from March 1960 and 27026 from February 1962.
Tenders attached: 5270 from new, 5258 from September 1931, 5229 from March 1932, 5211 from July 1937 and 5290 from June 1938.
Colour schemes: LNER green from new, black from August 1942, LNER green from April 1947, BR blue from November 1950 and BR green from August 1952.
Sheds: Gorton from new, King's Cross in May 1925, Grantham in November 1928, New England in October 1942, Leicester Central in February 1949, Doncaster in June 1950, Copley Hill in November 1950, King's Cross in February 1951, Neasden in July 1951, Grantham in February 1953, King's Cross August 1954, Grantham in October 1954, Doncaster in February 1959, King's Cross in April 1959, New England in September 1959, King's Cross in November 1959 and Grantham in June 1963.

Name: *Minoru*
Numbers: 2561, 62, E62 and 60062.
Works Number: 1617 (built at Doncaster).
Date to traffic: May 1925.
Rebuilt as an A3: June 1944.
Withdrawn from service: Condemned in December 1964 and cut up by R.A. King of Norwich apparently in 1965.
Total mileage: 2,029,000.
Modifications: 1929 – long travel valves fitted, 1944 – rebuilt as an A3, 1947 – to 75% cut-off, 1952 – right-hand to left-hand drive, 1959 – double chimney and Kylchap exhaust fitted, 1961 – trough deflectors fitted.
Boilers fitted: 7780 from new, 7781 from March 1931, 7695 from March 1933, 7785 from March 1937, 7771 from May 1938, 7773 from February 1941, 9451 from June 1944, 9979 from July 1949, 27040 from April 1951, 27031 from October 1952, 27021 from September 1955, 27007 from July 1957, 27005 from February 1959, 27021 from October 1960 and 29301 from September 1962.
Tenders attached: 5271 from new, 5223 from July 1928, 5477 from March 1937, 5643 from May 1938, 5483 from February 1946, 5643 from March 1946, 5289 from February 1955 and 5211 from September 1962.
Colour schemes: LNER green from new, black from September 1942, LNER green from November 1947, BR blue from July 1949 and BR green from October 1952.
Sheds: Gorton from new, Doncaster in June 1925, Grantham in April 1926, King's Cross in March 1927, New England in June 1940, Gorton in July 1944, King's Cross in October 1944, Haymarket in April 1945, King's Cross in May 1945, Copley Hill in May 1948, Doncaster in September 1951, Grantham in February 1953, King's Cross in October 1955, New England in September 1961, Grantham in June 1963, Doncaster in September 1963 and New England in October 1963.

Name: *Isinglass*
Numbers: 2562, 531, 63 and 60063.
Works Number: 1618 (built at Doncaster).
Date to traffic: June 1925.
Rebuilt as an A3: April 1946.
Withdrawn from service: Condemned in June 1964 and cut up by R.A. King apparently in 1964.
Total mileage: 1,947,000.
Modifications: 1925 – E type superheater fitted, 1928 – Diamond soot blower fitted, 1930 – long travel valves fitted and E superheater removed, 1946 – rebuilt as an A3, 1947 – to 75% cut-off, 1952 – right-hand to left-hand drive, August 1958 – double chimney and Kylchap exhaust fitted, 1961 – trough deflectors fitted.
Boilers fitted: 7781 from new, 7764 from May 1933, 7799 from January 1937, 7793 from March 1938, 9486 from April 1946, 27032 from March 1951, 27008 from November 1952, 27037 from July 1954, 29294 from January 1956, 29283 from February 1959, 29295 from September 1960 and 29328 from August 1962.
Tenders attached: 5272 from new, 5267 from May 1929, 5277 from January 1937 and 5231 from March 1938.
Colour schemes: LNER green from new, black from July 1943, LNER green from May 1947, BR blue from March 1951 and BR green from November 1952.
Sheds: Doncaster from new, Gateshead in December 1925, Doncaster in September 1926, Grantham in October 1928, King's Cross in April 1938, Leicester Central August 1939, Neasden in December 1939, Gorton in February 1941, King's Cross in November 1942, Gorton in July 1944, Copley Hill in August 1944, Doncaster in January 1945, King's Cross in June 1950, Grantham in September 1951, Neasden in February 1953, King's Cross in March 1955, Neasden in March 1956, King's Cross in June 1956, Grantham in September 1956, King's Cross in October 1960, Grantham in June 1963, Doncaster in September 1963 and New England in October 1963.

Name: *William Whitelaw* then *Tagalie* from 2 August 1941.
Numbers: 2563, 532, 64, E64 and 60064.
Works Number: Built by the North British Loco Co under No. 23101
Date to traffic: July 1924.
Rebuilt as an A3: November 1942.
Withdrawn from service: Condemned in September 1961 and cut up at Doncaster in 1961/62.
Total mileage: 2,014,000.
Modifications: 1928 – long travel valves fitted, 1929 – variable FSA fitted, 1941 – Hudd ATC fitted, 1942 – rebuilt as an A3, 1948 – to 75% cut-off, 1953 – right-hand to left-hand drive and 1959 – double chimney and Kylchap exhaust fitted.
Boilers fitted: 7785 from new, 7702 from May 1929, 7788 from April 1933, 7795 from May 1941, 9116 from November 1942, 9122 from February 1947, 9981 from July 1949, 27022 from 27085 from February 1953, 27043 from January 1958 and 29314 from February 1960.
Tenders attached: 5273 from new, 5328 from May 1928, 5479 from June 1930, 5330 from July 1930 and 5584 from April 1935.
Colour schemes: LNER green from new, black from November 1942, LNER green from February 1947, BR blue from July 1949 and BR green from February 1953.
Sheds: Haymarket from new, Aberdeen in April 1935, Eastfield in November 1937, St Margaret's in July 1938, Dundee in February 1940, Eastfield in October 1940, Haymarket in December 1940, Doncaster in July 1950 and Grantham in June 1959.

Name: *Knight of the Thistle* then *Knight of Thistle* from 28 December 1932.
Numbers: 2564, 533, 65 and 60065.
Works Number: NB Loco Co No. 23102.
Date to traffic: July 1924.
Rebuilt as an A3: March 1947.
Withdrawn from service: Condemned in June 1964 and cut up by R.A. King of Norwich apparently in 1964.
Total mileage: 2,235,000.
Modifications: 1928 – long travel valves fitted, 1929 – variable FSA fitted, 1939 – Hudd ATC fitted, 1947 – rebuilt as an A3, 1952 – right-hand to left-hand drive, 1957 – to 75% cut-off, 1958 – double chimney and Kylchap exhaust fitted, 1961 – trough deflectors fitted.
Boilers fitted: 7786 from new, 7788 from July 1929, 7800 from January 1933, 7781 from November 1937, 9211 from March 1947, 8225 from July 1948, 27041 from July 1954, 27027 from October 1958 and 27062 from February 1960.
Tenders attached: 5274 from new, 5325 from July 1928, 5581 from October 1935, 5268 from June 1937, 5283 from July 1942, 5276 from January 1944 and 5285 from May 1957.
Colour schemes: LNER green from new, black from March 1944, LNER green from March 1947, BR blue from November 1949 and BR green from December 1952.
Sheds: Haymarket from new, Eastfield in February 1937, Carlisle in November 1940, Haymarket in December 1941, King's Cross in July 1950, Grantham in September 1951, New England in June 1962, Grantham in June 1963, Doncaster in September 1963 and New England in October 1963.

Name: *Merry Hampton*
Numbers: 2565, 534, 66 and 60066.
Works Number: NB Loco Co No. 23103.
Date to traffic: July 1924.
Rebuilt as an A3: December 1945.
Withdrawn from service: Condemned in September 1963 and cut up at Doncaster in September 1963.
Total mileage: 1,896,000.
Modifications: 1928 – long travel valves fitted, 1929 – variable FSA fitted, 1930 – tablet apparatus fitted, 1940 – Hudd ATC fitted, 1945 – rebuilt as an A3, 1953 – right-hand to left-hand drive, 1957 – to 75% cut-off, 1958 – double chimney and Kylchap exhaust fitted, 1961 – trough deflectors fitted.
Boilers fitted: 7787 from new, 7785 from April 1932, 7797 from February 1937, 8783 from December 1945, 9216 from January 1948, 8784 from October 1949, 27044 from January 1953, 29279 from May 1957, 29322 from October 1958, 29279 from July 1960 and 29314 from April 1962.
Tenders attached: 5275 from new, 5330 from March 1929, 5276 from July 1929, 5283 from January 1944, 5211 from December 1945, 5223 from January 1948 and 5266 from April 1962.
Colour schemes: LNER green from new, black December 1941, LNER green from December 1946, BR blue from October 1949 and BR green from January 1953.
Sheds: Haymarket from new, Gateshead in May 1928, Haymarket in July 1928, Dundee in October 1930, Haymarket in August 1931, Dundee in December 1931, Aberdeen in August 1935, Eastfield in May 1936, Aberdeen in June 1936, Eastfield in March 1937, Carlisle in November 1940, Haymarket in February 1941, Doncaster from August 1950, King's Cross in October 1950, Doncaster in October 1950, King's Cross in June 1956, Doncaster in August 1956, King's Cross in June 1957, Doncaster in November 1958, King's Cross in April 1959, New England in September 1959, King's Cross in November 1959 and Grantham in June 1963.

Name: *Ladas*
Numbers: 2566, 535, 67 and 60067.
Works Number: NB Loco Co No. 23104.
Date to traffic: August 1924.
Rebuilt as an A3: November 1939.
Withdrawn from service: Condemned in December 1962 and cut up at Doncaster January 1963.
Total mileage: 1,904,000.
Modifications: 1928 – Long travel valves fitted, 1930 – variable FSA fitted, 1930 – tablet apparatus fitted, 1935 – Flaman Speed Recorder fitted, 1939 – rebuilt as an A3, 1950 – to 75% cut-off, 1953 – right-hand to left-hand drive, 1959 – double chimney and Kylchap exhaust fitted, 1961 – trough deflectors fitted.
Boilers fitted: 7788 from new, 7785 from June 1929, 7789 from January 1932, 7767 from March 1933, 7773 from January 1934, 8226 from November 1939, 9570 from April 1947, 9568 from July 1948, 9119 from February 1950, 27059 from September 1951, 27013 from August 1953, 27059 from March 1955, 27016 from April 1959 and 29277 from April 1961.
Tenders attached: 5276 from new, 5330 from July 1929 and 5479 from July 1930.
Colour schemes: LNER green from new, black from May 1942, LNER green from April 1947, BR blue from February 1950 and BR green from September 1951.
Sheds: Haymarket from new, Dundee in August 1930, Eastfield in February 1937, St Margaret's in February 1940, Haymarket in November 1940, King's Cross in July 1950, Grantham in September 1951, Doncaster in May 1952, King's Cross in June 1952, Doncaster in October 1953, Grantham in June 1959, New England in September 1959 and King's Cross in November 1959.

Name: *Sir Visto*
Numbers: 2567, 536, 68 and 60068.
Works Number: NB Loco Co No. 23105.
Date to traffic: August 1924.
Rebuilt as an A3: December 1948.
Withdrawn from service: Condemned in August 1962 and cut up at Doncaster apparently in 1962.
Total mileage: 1,823,000.
Modifications: 1928 – long travel valves fitted, 1939 – Hudd ATC fitted, 1948 – rebuilt as an A3, 1954 – right-hand to left-hand drive, 1957 – to 75% cut-off and 1959 – double chimney and Kylchap exhaust fitted.
Boilers fitted: 7789 from new, 7786 fromDecember 1929, 7799 from January 1932, 7798 from December 1936, 8271 from December 1948, 27005 from October 1950, 27036 from March 1954, 27031 from September 1959 and 27029 from March 1961.
Tenders attached: 5277 from new, 5637 from December 1936 and 5224 from March 1954.
Colour schemes: LNER green from new, black from April 1943, LNER green from March 1947, BR blue from October 1950 and BR green from August 1952.
Sheds: Haymarket from new, Dundee in August 1930, Eastfield in February 1937, St Margaret's in November 1938, Eastfield in February 1940 and Carlisle in November 1940.

Name: *Sceptre*
Numbers: 2568, 537, 69 and 60069.
Works Number: NB Loco Co No. 23106.
Date to traffic: September 1924.
Rebuilt as an A3: May 1942.
Withdrawn from service: Condemned in October 1962 and cut up at Doncaster in May 1963.
Total mileage: 2,200,000.
Modifications: 1927 – long travel valves fitted, 1929 – Jaco regulator and Flaman recorder fitted, 1942 – rebuilt as an A3, 1954 – right-hand to left-hand drive, 1956 – to 75% cut-off and 1959 – double chimney and Kylchap exhaust fitted.
Boilers fitted: 7790 fitted from new, 7801 from March 1929, 7799 from March 1930, 7802 from June 1931, 7783 from December 1933, 7878 from February 1938, 9209 from May 1942, 8252 from January 1947, 27024 from January 1951, 27020 from July 1952, 27025 from May 1954, 27049 from April 1955, 27063 from April 1958 and 27040 from March 1960.
Tenders attached: 5278 from new, 5279 from May 1940, 5211 from July 1940 and 5258 from May 1942.
Colour schemes: LNER green from new, black from May 1942, LNER green from January 1947, BR blue from January 1951 and BR green from July 1952.
Sheds: Gateshead from new, York in 12.36, Heaton from March 1943, Tweedmouth in September 1958, Copley Hill in June 1960, Holbeck in November 1960, Copley Hill in June 1961 and Ardsley in September 1961.

Name: *Gladiateur*
Numbers: 2569, 538, 70 and 60070.
Works Number: NB Loco Co No. 23107.
Date to traffic: September 1924.
Rebuilt as an A3: January 1947.
Withdrawn from service: Condemned in May 1964 and cut up by A. Draper of Hull apparently in 1964.
Total mileage: 2,200,000.
Modifications: 1928 – long travel valves fitted, 1947 – rebuilt as an A3, , 1953 – right-hand to left-hand drive, 1957 – to 75% cut-off, 1959 – double chimney and Kylchap exhaust fitted, 1961 – trough deflectors fitted.
Boilers fitted: 7791 from new, 7803 from February 1929, 7796 from January 1930, 7803 from December 1931, 7801 from March 1936, 7775 from May 1941, 9565 from January 1947, 9572 from August 1948, 27002 from February 1952, 27009 from July 1953, 27064 from May 1955, 27020 from March 1957, 27 059 from April 1959 and 27069 from September 1961.
Tenders attached: 5279 from new, 5328 fromApril 1928, 5273 from May 1928, 5279 from June 1928, 5285 from March 1937, 5569 from March 1943 and 5477 from January 1945.
Colour schemes: LNER green from new, black from March 1943, LNER green from January 1947 and BR green from February 1952.
Sheds: Gateshead from new, York from March 1938, Gateshead from May 1946, Darlington in December 1948, Gateshead in January 1952, Darlington in August 1953, Gateshead in February 1954, Darlington in May 1957, Gateshead in November 1957, Darlington in June 1959, Gateshead in December 1959, Copley Hill in June 1960, Holbeck in November 1960, Copley Hill in June 1961, Neville Hill in June 1963 and Gateshead in December 1963.

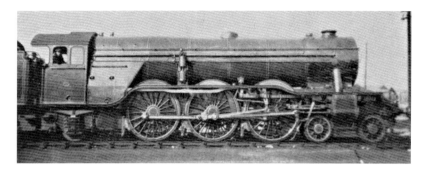

Name: *Tranquil*
Numbers: 2570, 539, 71 and 60071.
Works Number: NB Loco No. 23108.
Date to traffic: September 1924.
Rebuilt as an A3: October 1944
Withdrawn from service: Condemned in December 1964 and cut up by A Draper of Hull apparently in 1965.
Total mileage: 2,268,000.
Modifications: 1927 – long travel valves fitted, 1944 – rebuilt as an A3, 1953 – to 75% cut-off, 1953 – right-hand to left-hand drive, 1958 – double chimney and Kylchap exhaust fitted, 1961 – trough deflectors fitted.
Boilers fitted: 7792 from new, 7794 from February 1930, 7798 from February 1930, 7775 from June 1931, 7778 from November 1934, 7796 from November 1935, 7790 from October 1936, 7802 from March 1938, 9454 from October 1944, 8782 from December 1948, 8720 from July 1950, 27061 from November 1951, 27028 from August 1954, 27086 from May 1956, 27065 from July 1958, 29329 from October 1959 and 29290 from November 1961.
Tenders attached: 5280 from new, 5272 from April 1935, 5291 from January 1943 and 5263 from May 1963.
Colour schemes: LNER green from new, black from January 1943, LNER green from October 1947, BR purple from April 1958, BR blue from July 1950 and BR green from November 1951.
Sheds: Gateshead from new, York in November 1936, Neville Hill in September 1945, Gateshead in May 1946, Darlington in January 1952, Gateshead in March 1952, Darlington in September 1954, Gateshead in February 1955, Darlington in May 1956, Gateshead in November 1956, Darlington in February 1957, Gateshead in May 1957, Darlington in December 1959, Gateshead in June 1960, Heaton in September 1962 and Gateshead in June 1963.

Name: *Sunstar*
Numbers: 2571, 540, 72, E72and 60072.
Works Number: NB Loco Co No. 23109.
Date to traffic: September 1924.
Rebuilt as an A3: July 1941.
Withdrawn from service: Condemned in October 1962 and cut up at Doncaster in May 1963.
Total mileage: 2,242,000.
Modifications: 1928 – long travel valves fitted, 1947 – rebuilt as an A3, 1953 – to 75% cut-off, 1953 – right-hand to left-hand drive and 1959 – double chimney and Kylchap exhaust fitted.
Boilers fitted: 7793 from new, 7790 from June 1929, 7763 from November 1931, 7787 from May 1936, 8249 from July 1941, 8780 from March 1948, 27042 from April 1951, 27079 from June 1952, 27006 from December 1953, 27009 from June 1955 and 27080 from June 1958.
Tenders attached: 5281 from new and 5476 from October 1940.
Colour schemes: LNER green from new, black from February 1943, LNER green from March 1948, BR blue from August 1949 and BR green from June 1952.
Sheds: Gateshead from new, Heaton in March 1943, Tweedmouth in September 1958, Copley Hill June 1960, Holbeck in November 1960 and Heaton in July 1961.

Name: *St Gatien*
Numbers: 2572, 541, 73 and 60073.
Works Number: NB Loco Co No. 23110.
Date to traffic: October 1924.
Rebuilt as an A3: November 1945.
Withdrawn from service: Condemned in August 1963 and cut up at Darlington in August 1963.
Total mileage: 2,382,000.
Modifications: 1927 – long travel valves fitted, 1947 – rebuilt as an A3, 1953 – to 75% cut-off, 1953 – right-hand to left-hand drive, 1958 – double chimney and Kylchap exhaust fitted and 1961 – trough deflectors fitted.
Boilers fitted: 7794 from new, 7796 from February 1929, 7707 from December 1929, 7798 from December 1931, 7693 from November 1934, 7764 from December 1939, 9117 from November 1945, 9454 from March 1949, 27042 from June 1952, 27075 from November 19 53, 27030 from August 1955, 27005 from March 1957, 27050 from August 1958 and 27006 from February 1960.
Tenders attached: 5282 from new, 5636 from December/36, 5292 from October 1937, 5212 from October 1942, 5212 from June 1955 and 5278 from August 1955.
Colour schemes: LNER green from new, black from October 1942, LNER green from April 1947, BR blue from December 1950 and BR green from June 1952.
Sheds: Gateshead from new, York in March 1943, Heaton in May 1946 and Gateshead in June 1963.

Name: *Harvester*
Numbers: 2573, 542, 74 and 60074.
Works Number: NB Loco Co No. 23111.
Date to traffic: October 1924.
Rebuilt as an A3: April 1928.
Withdrawn from service: Condemned in April 1963 and cut up at Doncaster later that year.
Total mileage: 2,171,000.
Modifications: 1928 – rebuilt as an A3 with long travel valves, 1952 – right-hand to left-hand drive, 1956 – to 75% cut-off and 1959 – double chimney and Kylchap exhaust fitted.
Boilers fitted: 7795 from new, 8030 from April 1928, 8252 from March 1932, 8249 from March 1935, 8251 from June 1940, 8082 from July 1942, 8721 from August 1947, 8721 from August 1947, 9120 from December 1948, 27010 from November 1950, 27040 from November 1952, 27061 from September 1954, 27055 from January 1956, 27077 from October 1957 and 27041 from March 1959.
Tenders attached: 5283 from new, 5325 from April 1928, 5274 from July 1928, 5283 from July 1928 5268 from July 1942 and 5271 from January 1961.
Colour schemes: LNER green from new, black from July 1942, LNER green from August 1947, BR purple from May 1948, BR blue from November 1950 and BR green from November 1952.
Sheds: Gateshead from new, Haymarket in April 1928, Gateshead in July 1928, Haymarket in April 1937, Gateshead in February 1938, Neville Hill in December 1939, York in February 1940, Heaton in March 1943, Gateshead in November 1945, Neville Hill in February 1949, York in November 1950 and Neville Hill in December 1950.

Name: *St Frusquin*
Numbers: 2574, 543, 75 and 60075.
Works Number: NB Loco Co No. 23112.
Date to traffic: October 1924.
Rebuilt as an A3: June 1942.
Withdrawn from service: Condemned in January 1964 and cut up at Darlington later that year.
Total mileage: 2,174,000.
Modifications: 1928 – long travel valves fitted, 1947 – rebuilt as an A3, 1954 – right-hand to left-hand drive, 1956 – to 75% cut-off and 1959 – double chimney and Kylchap exhaust fitted.
Boilers fitted: 7796 from new, 7797 from December 1928, 7792 from December 1929, 7770 from January 1932, 7778 from April 1936, 9208 from June 1942, 9123 from October 1947, 27016 from December 1950, 27017 from June 1952, 27079 from April 1954, 27046 from February 1956, 27004 from December 1957, 27073 from August 1959 and 29324 from May 1961.
Tenders attached: 5284 from new, 5284 from June 1944, 5269 from July 1944, 5257 from December 1957 and 5287 from January 1963.
Colour schemes: LNER green from new, black from June 1942, LNER green from October 1947, BR purple from May 1948, BR blue from December 1950 and BR green from June 1952.
Sheds: Gateshead from new, Darlington in August 1952, Gateshead in February 1953, Darlington in October 1954, Gateshead in May 1955, Darlington in June 1961, Gateshead in December 1961, Darlington in June 1962, Heaton in December 1962, Darlington in June 1963 and Gateshead in December 1963.

Name: *Galopin*
Numbers: 2575, 544, 76 and 60076.
Works Number: NB Loco Co No. 23112.
Date to traffic: October 1924.
Rebuilt as an A3: June 1941.
Withdrawn from service: Condemned in October 1962 and cut up at Doncaster in 1963.
Total mileage: 2,141,000.
Modifications: 1928 – long travel valves fitted, 1941 – rebuilt as an A3, 1954 – right-hand to left-hand drive, 1957 – to 75% cut-off and 1959 – double chimney and Kylchap exhaust fitted.
Boilers fitted: 7797 from new, 7798 from June 1928, 7802 from November 1929, 7800 from December 1930, 7786 from June 1932, 7694 from April 1936, 9120 from June 1941, 9565 from September 1948, 27071 from March 1952, 27034 from April 1954, 27068 from September 1957, 27046 from June 1959 and 27067 from November 1960.
Tenders attached: 5285 from new, 5227 from March 1937, 5232 from March 1944 and 5262 from November 1960.
Colour schemes: LNER green from new, black from October 1942, LNER green from January 1947, BR blue from August 1949 and BR green from October 1952.
Sheds: Gateshead from new. Darlington in December 1948, Gateshead in January 1952, Darlington in March 1952, Gateshead in September 1952, Darlington in February 1956, Gateshead in August 1956, Darlington in December 1957, Gateshead in June 1958, Darlington in December 1960, Gateshead in June 1961 and Heaton in September 1962.

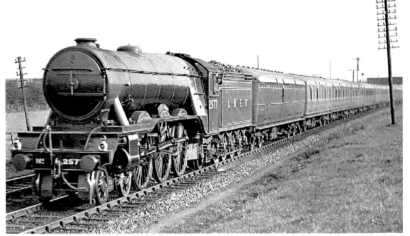

Name: *The White Knight*
Numbers: 2576,545, 77 and 60077.
Works Number: NB Loco Co No. 23114.
Date to traffic: October 1924.
Rebuilt as an A3: July 1943.
Withdrawn from service: Condemned in July 1964 and cut up by Arnott Young of Carmyle apparently in 1965.
Total mileage: 2,142,000.
Modifications: 1928 – long travel valves fitted, 1947 – rebuilt as an A3, 1953 – right-hand to left-hand drive, 1956 – to 75% cut-off, 1959 – double chimney and Kylchap exhaust fitted, 1961 – trough deflectors fitted.
Boilers fitted: 7798 from new, 7795 from June 1928, 7787 from July 1932, 7879 from October 1935, 7780 from February 1940, 8078 from July 1943, 8084 from November 1946, 9573 from November 1948, 27000 from September 1950, 27070 from March 1952, 27007 from November 1953, 27006 from June 1955, 27072 from November 1956, 27085 in February 1958, 27048 from April 1959 and 27046 from November 1960.
Tenders attached: 5286 from new, 5482 from May 1943, 5270 from July 1943, 5581 from November 1953 and 5478 from July 1964.
Colour schemes: LNER green from new, black from July 1943, LNER green from November 1946 and BR green from March 1952.
Sheds: Gateshead from new, York from November 1936, Gateshead in December 1936 and York in March 1943, Heaton in May 1946, Holbeck in February 1960, Copley Hill in June 1961, Ardsley in September 1961 and St Margaret's in June 1963.

Name: *Night Hawk*
Numbers: 2577, 546, 78 and 60078.
Works Number: NB Loco Co No. 23115.
Date to traffic: October 1924.
Rebuilt as an A3: January 1944.
Withdrawn from service: Condemned in October 1962 cut up at Doncaster in 1963.
Total mileage: 2,233,000.
Modifications: 1928 – long travel valves fitted, 1944 – rebuilt as an A3, 1953 – right-hand to left-hand drive, 1956 – to 75% cut-off, 1959 – double chimney and Kylchap exhaust fitted, 1962 – trough deflectors fitted.
Boilers fitted: 7799 from new, 7802 from April 1928, 7793 from August 1929, 7766 from November 1930. 7775 from March 1935, 7796 from July 1940, 8779 from January 1944, 9446 from November 1948, 27001 from October 1950, 27014 from May 1952, 27001 from August 1953, 27028 from June 1956, 27017 from January 1958, 27070 from February 1959 and 27007 from November 1960.
Tenders attached: 5287 from new and 5275 from May 1952.
Colour schemes: LNER green from new, black from February 1942, LNER green from February 1947, BR blue from October 1950 and BR green from May 1952.
Sheds: Gateshead from new, York in January 1937, Neville Hill in September 1945, Gateshead in May 1946, Darlington in February 1955, Gateshead in August 1955 and Heaton in September 1962.

Name: *Bayardo*
Numbers: 2578, 547, 79 and 60079.
Works Number: NB Loco Co No. 23116.
Date to traffic: October 1924.
Rebuilt as an A3: May 1928.
Withdrawn from service: Condemned in September 1961 and cut up at Doncaster apparently in 1962.
Total mileage: 1,948,000.
Modifications: 1928 – rebuilt as an A3 with long travel valves, 1953 – right-hand to left-hand drive, 1955 – to 75% cut-off and 1960 – double chimney and Kylchap exhaust fitted.
Boilers fitted: 7800 from new, 8031 from May 1928, 8249 from December 1932, 8226 from December 1934, 8027 from March 1936, 9117 from June 1940, 8247 from April 1945, 9570 from May 1950, 27050 from October 1953, 27065 from November 1956, 27000 from June 1958 and 27026 from January 1960.
Tenders attached: 5288 from new and 5277 from April 1938.
Colour schemes: LNER green from new, black from January 1942, LNER green from March 1947, BR blue from May 1950 and BR green from January 1952.
Sheds: Heaton from new, Doncaster in August 1937, Haymarket in September 1937, Heaton in January 1938, Gateshead in January 1940, Heaton in January 1945, Gateshead in May 1945 and Carlisle Canal in May 1948.

Name: *Dick Turpin*
Numbers: 2579, 548, 80 and 60080.
Works Number: NB Loco Co No. 23117.
Date to traffic: November 1924.
Rebuilt as an A3: November 1942.
Withdrawn from service: Condemned in October 1964 and cut up by A. Draper of Hull apparently in 1965.
Total mileage: 2,123,000.
Modifications: 1929 – long travel valves fitted, 1942 – rebuilt as an A3, 1946 – to 75% cut-off, 1953 – right-hand to left-hand drive, 1959 – double chimney and Kylchap exhaust fitted and 1961 – trough deflectors fitted.
Boilers fitted: 7801 from new, 7800 from January 1929, 7794 from March 1930, 7801 from April 1931, 7697 from March 1932, 7784 from June 1934, 7800 from April 1938, 7768 from February 1941, 8778 from November 1942, 9207 from August 1947, 27003 from October 1950, 27065 from February 1952, 27002 from September 1943, 27069 from March 1955, 27082 from March 1958, 27065 from October 1959 and 27079 from November 1961.
Tenders attached: 5289 from new, 5264 from June 1934, 5263 from July 1936, 5288 from April 1938 and 5229 from September 1953.
Colour schemes: LNER green from new, black from November 1942, LNER green from August 1947, BR blue from October 1950 and BR green from February 1952.
Sheds: Heaton from new, Gateshead in August 1944, Heaton in November 1945, Holbeck in May 1960, Ardsley in June 1961, Neville Hill in June 1963 and Gateshead from December 1963.

Name: *Shotover*
Numbers: 2580,549, 81 and 60081.
Works Number: NB Loco Co No. 23118.
Date to traffic: November 1924.
Rebuilt as an A3: February 1928.
Withdrawn from service: Condemned in October 1962 and cut up at Doncaster in 1963.
Total mileage: 2,052,000.
Modifications: 1928 – rebuilt as an A3 with long travel valves fitted, 1929 – ACFI fitted, 1939 – ACFI removed, 1953 – right-hand to left-hand drive, 1958 – to 75% cut-off and 1958 – double chimney and Kylchap exhaust fitted.
Boilers fitted: 7802 from new, 8029 from February 1928, 8079 from October 1932, 8080 from December 1934, 8076 from January 1936, 8224 from October 1936, 8721 from July 1941, 9514 from October 1946, 27051 from July 1951, 27086 from February 1953, 27054 from June 1954 and 29283 from October 1960.
Tenders attached: 5290 from new, 5326 from April 1928, 5290 from February 1929, 5286 from October 1936, 5280 from February 1939 and 5273 from June 1948.
Colour schemes: LNER green from new, black from September 1943, LNER green from October 1946, BR blue from October 1949 and BR green from February 1953.
Sheds: Heaton from new, Gateshead in September 1928, Heaton in March 1930, Neville Hill in December 1939, York in February 1940, Heaton in March 1943, Gateshead in November 1945 and Neville Hill in February 1949.

Name: *Neil Gow*
Numbers: 2581, 550, 82 and 60082.
Works Number: NB Loco Co No. 23119.
Date to traffic: November 1924.
Rebuilt as an A3: January 1943.
Withdrawn from service: Condemned in September 1963 and cut up at Darlington in 1964.
Total mileage: 2,194,000
Modifications: 1929 – long travel valves fitted, 1943 – rebuilt as an A3, 1954 – right-hand to left-hand drive, 1958 – to 75% cut-off, 1959 – double chimney and Kylchap exhaust fitted and 1961 – trough deflectors fitted.
Boilers fitted: 7803 from new, 7804 from January 1929, 7796 from May 1932, 7780 from July 1935, 7786 from June 1938, 9212 from January 1943, 8078 from May 1948, 8226 from September 1949, 27014 from November 1950, 27074 from March 1952, 27000 from March 1954, 27062 from June 1955, 27015 from March 1958, 27078 from September 1959 and 29310 from August 1961.
Tenders attached: 5291 from new, 5272 from January 1943 and 5226 from December 1944.
Colour schemes: LNER green from new, black fro January 1943, LNER green from May 1948, BR blue from September 1949 and BR green from March 1952.
Sheds: Heaton from new, Gateshead in June 1948, Darlington in September 1952, Gateshead in March 1953, Heaton in May 1956, Holbeck in May 1960, Heaton in July 1961, Gateshead in March 1962, Heaton in September 1962 and Gateshead in June 1963.

Name: *Sir Hugo*
Numbers: 2582, 551, 83 and 60083.
Works Number: NB Loco Co No. 23120.
Date to traffic: December 1924.
Rebuilt as an A3: December 1941.
Withdrawn from service: Condemned in May 1964 and cut up by Hughes Bolckow of North Blyth in 1964.
Total mileage: 2,109,000.
Modifications: 1930 – long travel valves fitted, 1941 – rebuilt as an A3, 1952 – right-hand to left-hand drive, 1956 – to 75% cut-off, 1959 – double chimney and Kylchap exhaust fitted and 1962 – trough deflectors fitted.
Boilers fitted: 7804 from new, 7799 from June 1928, 7803 from February 1930, 7696 from July 1931, 7704 from December 1935, 8027 from December 1941, 9513 from August 1946, 27034 from March 1951, 27016 from March 1954, 27035 from July 1935, 27033 from December 1956, 27062 from June 1958, 27030 from February 1960 and 29309 from February 1962.
Tenders attached: 5292 from new and 5282 from December 1936.
Colour schemes: LNER green from new, black from December 1941, LNER green from August 1946, BR blue from May 1949 and BR green from September 1952.
Sheds: Heaton from new, Gateshead in June 1940, Heaton in October 1940, Gateshead in June 1963.

Name: *Felstead*
Numbers: 2743, 552, 89 and 60089.
Works Number: 1693 (built at Doncaster)
Date to traffic: August 1928.
Withdrawn from service: Condemned in October 1963 and cut up at Inverurie in 1964.
Total mileage: 1,846,000.
Modifications: 1938 – fitted with speed recorder, 1955 – to 75% cut-off, 1959 – double chimney and Kylchap exhaust fitted and 1961 – trough deflectors fitted.
Boilers fitted: 8795 from new, 8253 from June 1931, 8027 from July 1933, 8254 from November 1935, 8030 from July 1940, 9512 from September 1946, 9512 from September 1946, 9115 from September 1948, 27004 from October 1950, 27073 from March 1952, 27003 from October 1953, 27018 from February 1955, 27001 from September 1956, 27072 from May 1958, 27015 from October 1959, 27086 from March 1960 and 293 29 from November 1961.
Tenders attached: 5330 from new, 5255 from February 1929, 5572 from November 1957, 5255 from December 1957 and 5254 from March 1960.
Colour schemes: LNER green from new, black from May 1942, LNER green from September 1946, BR blue from October 1950 and BR green from March 1952.
Sheds: Doncaster from new, Gateshead in March 1936, Doncaster in July 1936, Grantham in February 1941, King's Cross in May 1946, Haymarket in February 1951, Dundee in November 1960 and St Margaret's in December 1960.

Name: *Grand Parade*
Numbers: 2744, 553, 90 and 60090.
Works Number: 1694 (built at Doncaster).
Date to traffic: August 1928. In 1937 this engine was written off as a result of a crash near Castlecary when pulling the 1603 Edinburgh to Glasgow express. A replacement was quickly authorised and entered service in April 1938.
Withdrawn from service: The first No. 2744 scrapped in early 1938 following crash. Replacement No.2744 condemned in October 1963 and cut up at Cowlairs in 1964.
Total mileage: 1,917,000.
Modifications: 1947 – to 75% cut-off, 1958 – double chimney and Kylchapexhaust fitted and 1963 – trough deflectors fitted.
Boilers fitted: 8076 from new, 8075 from March 1932, 8029 from March 1933, 8247 from April 1936, 8029 from April 1938, 9453 from September 1944, 9453 from September 1944, 9977 from February 1949, 27006 from November 1950, 27062 from December 1953, 27025 from May 1955, 27006 from March 1957 and 27045 from August 1958.
Tenders attached: 5331 from new, 5273 from June 1929, 5331 from August 1932, 5273 from January 1933, 5331 from July 1933, 5267 from December 1936, 5263 attached to the replacement No. 2744 in April 1938, 5285 from February 1949, 5261 from May 1950 and 5279 from September 1959.
Colour schemes: LNER green from new, black from November 1942, LNER green from May 1947, BR blue from August 1949 and BR green from October 1952.
Sheds: King's Cross from new, Haymarket in July 1937, Doncaster in March 1938, Grantham in July 1943, New England in April 1944, Leicester Central in February 1949, Grantham in April 1949, Doncaster April 1950, Haymarket in July 1950, Dundee in November 1960, St Margaret's in December 1960, St Rollox June 1962, Eastfield in December 1962 and St Rollox in January 1963.

Name: *Captain Cuttle*.
Numbers: 2745,554, 91 and 60091.
Works Number: 1695 (built at Doncaster).
Date to traffic: September 1928.
Withdrawn from service: Condemned in October 1964 and cut up by A Draper of Hull apparently in 1965.
Total mileage: 1,562,000.
Modifications: 1956 – to 75% cut-off, 1959 – double chimney and Kylchap exhaust fitted and 1961 – trough deflectors fitted.
Boilers fitted: 8077 from new, 8028 from June 1932, 8251 from March 1937, 8028 from July 1939, 8080 from April 1945, 8077 from April 1948, 9510 from November 1949, 27044 from May 1951, 27084 from January 1953, 27017 from September 1954, 27014 from February 1956, 27010 from August 1957 and 27059 from October 1961.
Tenders attached: 5332 from new and 5480 from June 1930.
Colour schemes: LNER green from new, black from February 1942, LNER green from October 1946, BR purple from April 1948, BR blue from November 1949 and BR green from January 1953.
Sheds: Doncaster from new, Haymarket in October 1928, Carlisle in October 1928. Gateshead in May 1948, Heaton in June 1948, Gateshead in July 1958, Darlington in June 1959, Gateshead in December 1959, Darlington in December 1961, Gateshead in September 1962, Heaton in September 1962 and Gateshead in June 1963.

Name: *Fairway*
Numbers: 2746, 555, 92 and 60092.
Works Number: 1700 (built at Doncaster).
Date to traffic: October 1928.
Withdrawn from service: Condemned in October 1964 and cut up by A. Draper of Hull apparently in 1965.
Total mileage: 1,939,000.
Modifications: 1953 – to 75% cut-off, 1959 – double chimney and Kylchap exhaust fitted and 1961 – trough deflectors fitted.
Boilers fitted: 8078 from new, 8030 from July 1932, 8720 from March 1935, 8083 from August 1939, 9485 from March 1946, 27011 from November 1950, 27042 from December 1953, 27003 from March 1955, 27084 from January 1958, 27079 from November 1959 and 29272 from October 1961.
Tenders attached: 5265 from October 1928, 5326 from June 1929, 5642 from April 1937 and 5574 from November 1937.
Colour schemes: LNER green from new, black from July 1942, LNER green from June 1947, BR blue from November 1950 and BR green from August 1952.
Sheds: King's Cross from new, Gateshead in November 1936, King's Cross in December 1936, Gateshead in January 1937, Heaton in March 1943, Holbeck in May 1960, Ardsley in June 1961 and Gateshead in June 1963.

Name: *Coronach*
Numbers: 2747, 556, 93 and 60093.
Works Number: 1703 (built at Doncaster).
Date to traffic: November 1928.
Withdrawn from service: Condemned in April 1962 and cut up at Doncaster apparently in 1962.
Total mileage: 1,695,000.
Modifications: 1946 – to 75% cut-off, 1958 – double chimney and Kylchap exhaust fitted, 1961 – trough deflectors fitted.
Boilers fitted: 8079 from new, 8082 from October 1931, 8075 from May 1933, 8080 from June 1936, 9448 from April 1944, 9511 from October 1949, 27004 from May 1952, 27026 from February 1954, 27031 from September 1955, 27074 from December 1958 and 29322 from December 1960.
Tenders attached: 5226 from new, 5272 from September 1931, 5280 from April 1935, 5223 from April 1938, 5280 from June 1938, 5286 from January 1939, 5275 from February 1942 and 5287 from May 1952.
Colour schemes: LNER green from new, black from February 1942, LNER green from August 1947, BR blue from October 1949 and BR green from May 1952.
Sheds: Doncaster when new, King's Cross in March 1930, Doncaster in May 1930, Haymarket in March 1939 and Carlisle in January 1941.

Name: *Colorado*
Numbers: 2748, 557, 94 and 60094.
Works Number: 1705 (built at Doncaster).
Date to traffic: December 1928.
Withdrawn from service: Condemned in February 1964 and cut up by Henderson's of Airdrie apparently in 1964.
Total mileage: 1,516,000.
Modifications: 1947 – to 75% cut-off, 1959 – double chimney and Kylchap exhaust fitted, 1961 – trough deflectors fitted.
Boilers fitted: 8080 from new, 8077 from March 1932, 8225 from September 1934, 8078 from December 1937, 8225 from August 1939, 9118 from September 1947, 9568 from May 1950, 27076 from April 1952, 27013 from April 1955, 27034 from November 1957, 27014 from August 1959 and 27962 from August 1961.
Tenders attached: 5271 from new, 5279 from October 1941, 5261 from August 1959 and 5567 from December 1962.
Colour schemes: LNER green from new, black from May 1943, LNER green from September 1947, BR blue from May 1950 and BR green from April 1952.
Sheds: Doncaster from new, King's Cross in February 1929, Carlisle in April 1929, Haymarket in December 1947, St Margaret's in December 1961, St Rollox in June 1962, Eastfield in December 1962 and St Rollox in January 1963.

Name: *Flamingo*
Numbers: 2749, 558, 95 and 60095.
Works Number: 1707.
Date to traffic: January 1929.
Withdrawn from service: Condemned in April 1961 and cut up at Doncaster apparently in 1961.
Total mileage: 1,513,000.
Modifications: 1947 – to 75% cut-off, 1958 – double chimney and Kylchap exhaust fitted and 1961 – trough deflectors fitted.
Boilers fitted: 8081 from new, 8251 from June 1933, 8031 from July 1936, 8247 from July 1938, 9450 from June 1944, 8781 from February 1949, 27017 from December 1950, 27023 from May 1952, 29307 from February 1954, 29283 from July 1957 and 29299 from February 1959.
Tenders attached: 5255 from new, 5330 from February 1929, 5275 from March 1929, 5224 from July 1938 and 5637 from February 1954.
Colour schemes: LNER green from new, black from December 1942, LNER green from August 1947, BR blue from December 1950 and BR green from May 1952.
Sheds: Doncaster from new and Carlisle in February 1929.

Name: *Papyrus*
Numbers: 2750, 559, 96 and 60096.
Works Number: 1708.
Date to traffic: February 1929.
Withdrawn from service: Condemned in September 1963 and cut up by Arnott Young of Carmyle apparently in 1964.
Total mileage: 2,037,000.
Modifications: 1947 – to 75% cut-off, 1958 – double chimney and Kylchap exhaust fitted and 1961 – trough deflectors fitted.
Boilers fitted: 8083 from new, 8253 from November 1933, 8075 from June 1938, 9216 from May 1943, 8784 from 1February 1947, 9985 from August 1949, 27023 from January 1951, 27075 from April 1952, 27072 from November 1953, 27065 from April 1955, 27076 from October 1956, 27009 from July 1958, 27069 from January 1960 and 27014 from September 1961.
Tenders attached: 5273 from February 1929, 5331 from June 1929, 5273 from August 1932, 5331 from January 1933, 5225 from July 1933, 5327 from August 1934, 5292 from November 1936, 5329 from June 1937, 5581 from September 1937 and 5270 from November 1953.
Colour schemes: LNER green from new, black from May 1943, LNER green from December 1947, BR blue from August 1949 and BR green from May 1952.
Sheds: King's Cross from new, Haymarket in August 1937, King's Cross in September 1937, Doncaster in October 1937, Grantham in March 1939, King's Cross in October 1946, Haymarket in July 1950 and St Margaret's in December 1961.

Name: *Humorist*
Numbers: 2751,560, 97 and 60097.
Works Number: 1709.
Date to traffic: March 1929.
Withdrawn from service: Condemned in August 1963 and cut up at Doncaster in 1963.
Total mileage: 1,920,000.
Modifications: 1937 – double chimney and Kylchap exhaust fitted, 1938 – stovepipe chimney and small deflectors fitted, 1951 – rimmed double chimney fitted and 1956 – to 75% cut-off.
Boilers fitted: 8082 from new, 8254 from May 1931, 8077 from April 1935, 8252 from March 1941, 9516 from September 1946, 27041 from April 1951, 27020 from June 1954, 27079 from January 1956, 27044 from September 1957, 27067 from December 1958, 27044 from September 1960 and 29339 from February 1962.
Tenders attached: 5274 from March 1929 and 5265 from August 1929.
Colour schemes: LNER green from new, black from August 1942, LNER green from September 1946, BR blue from November 1949 and BR green from November 1952.
Sheds: Doncaster from new, Grantham in August 1942, King's Cross in October 1946, Haymarket in July 1950, Carlisle Canal in January 1954 and St Margaret's in December 1961.

Name: *Spion Kop*
Numbers: 2752, 561, 98 and 60098.
Works Number: 1710.
Date to traffic: April 1929.
Withdrawn from service: Condemned in October 1963 and cut up at Inverurie in 1964.
Total mileage: 1,719,000.
Modifications: 1956 – to 75% cut-off and 1959 – double chimney and Kylchap exhaust fitted.
Boilers fitted: 8084 from new, 8076 from August 1932, 8031 from September 1938, 8254 from July 1941, 9210 from November 1948, 9445 from July 1950, 27018 from October 1956, 27049 from April 1958, 27023 from July 1959 and 29304 from May 1961.
Tenders attached: 5326 from new April 1929, 5272 from June 1929, 5226 from September 1931, 5638 from January 1937, 5580 from October 1937, 5267 from September 1938 and 5481 from February 1943.
Colour schemes: LNER green from new, black from February 1943, LNER green from March 1947, BR blue from July 1950 and BR green from November 1952.
Sheds: Doncaster from new, Haymarket in January 1938, St Margaret's in February 1938, Doncaster in March 1938, Grantham in July 1943, New England in April 1944, Grantham in April 1944, New England in May 1944, King's Cross in August 1946, Doncaster in June 1950, Haymarket in August 1950 and St Margaret's in January 1963.

Name: *Trigo*
Numbers: 2595, 562, 84 and 60084.
Works Number: 1731.
Date to traffic: February 1930.
Withdrawn from service: Condemned in November 1964 and cut up by Hughes Bolckow of North Blyth in 1965.
Total mileage: 1,929,000.
Modifications: 1947 – to 75% cut-off, 1958 – double chimney and Kylchap exhaust fitted and 1962 – trough deflectors fitted.
Boilers fitted: 8223 from new, 8247 from June 1933, 8084 from December 1935, 8720 from November 1940, 9567 from February 1947, 27036 from March 1951, 27016 from August 1952, 27073 from January 1954, 27072 from May 1955, 27045 from October 1956, 27026 from July 1958, 27076 from December 1959 and 27001 from January 1962.
Tenders attached: 5476 from new and 5645 from November 1940.
Colour schemes: LNER green from new, black from October 1942, LNER green from February 1947, BR purple from April 1948, BR blue from June 1949 and BR green from August 1952.
Sheds: Gateshead from new, Heaton in March 1943, Gateshead in November 1945, Neville Hill in September 1949 and Gateshead in December 1963.

Name: *Manna*
Numbers: 2596, 563, 85 and 60085.
Works Number: 1733.
Date to traffic: February 1930.
Withdrawn from service: Condemned in October 1964 and cut up by A. Draper of Hull apparently in 1965.
Total mileage: 1,820,000.
Modifications: 1957 – to 75% cut-off, 1958 – double chimney and Kylchap exhaust fitted and 1962 – trough deflectors fitted.
Boilers fitted: 8224 from new, 8084 from March 1933, 8252 from June 1935, 8253 from March 1940, 9215 from April 1943, 8249 from November 1949, 27048 from June 1951, 27015 from April 1954, 29299 from November 1955, 29279 from November 1958, 29318 from June 1960 and 27039 from April 1962.
Tenders attached: 5477 from new, 5483 from March 1937, 5643 February 1946, 5483 from March 1946 and 5283 from April 1962.
Colour schemes: LNER green from new, black from April 1943, LNER green from December 1947, BR blue from November 1949 and BR green from December 1952.
Sheds: Gateshead from new, Heaton in March 1943, Gateshead in February 1944, Heaton in August 1944 and Gateshead in June 1963.

Name: *Gainsborough*
Numbers: 2597, 564, 86 and 60086.
Works Number: 1736 (built at Doncaster).
Date to traffic: April 1930.
Withdrawn from service: Condemned in November 1963 and cut up at Darlington apparently in 1964.
Total mileage: 1,794,000.
Modifications: 1953 – to 75% cut-off, 1959 – double chimney and Kylchap exhaust fitted,
Boilers fitted: 8225 from new, 8081 from December 1923, 8721 from February 1935, 9.18 from August 1940, 8776 from May 1947, 9213 from April 1949, 27027 from January 1951, 27003 from June 1952, 27014 from September 1953, 27074 from October 1955, 27046 from December 1957, 27052 from June 1959 and 29317 from January 1961.
Tenders attached: 5478 from new.
Colour schemes: LNER green from new, black from June 1942, LNER green from February 1947, BR blue from July 1949 and BR green from June 1952.
Sheds: Gateshead from new, Doncaster in March 1936, Gateshead in July 1936, Heaton in September 1939, Neville Hill in December 1939, York in February 1940, Heaton in March 1943, Gateshead in November 1944 and Neville Hill in February 1949.

Name: *Blenheim*
Numbers: 2598, 565, 87 and 60087.
Works Number: 1743.
Date to traffic: March 1930.
Withdrawn from service: Condemned in October 1963 and cut up by Arnott Young of Carmyle apparently in 1964.
Total mileage: 1,963,000.
Modifications: 1956 – to 75% cut-off, 1958 – double chimney and Kylchap exhaust fitted and 1962 – trough deflectors fitted.
Boilers fitted: 8249 from new, 8078 from November 1932, 8079 from January 1935, 8250 from October 1936, 9449 from June 1944, 9121 from August 1950, 27027 from July 1952, 27050 from November 1956, 27006 from August 1958, 29309 from February 1960 and 29306 from February 1962.
Tenders attached: 5482 from new, 5572 from October 1936, 5255 from November 1957 and 5572 from December 1957.
Colour schemes: LNER green from new, black from June 1944, LNER green from June 1947, BR blue from August 1950 and BR green from July 1952.
Sheds: Gateshead from new, Doncaster in July 1937, Gateshead in October 1937, Haymarket in October 1937, Gateshead in February 1938, Haymarket in March 1939, Aberdeen in July 1940, Haymarket in October 1941, St Margaret's in July 1960, Haymarket in November 1960 and St Margaret's in December 1961.

Name: *Book Law*
Numbers: 2599, 566, 88 and 60088.
Works Number: 1744 (built in Doncaster).
Date to traffic: July 1930.
Withdrawn from service: Condemned in October 1963 and cut up at Darlington apparently in November 1963.
Total mileage: 1,969,000.
Modifications: 1956 – to 75% cut-off, 1958 – double chimney and Kylchap exhaust fitted, and 1961 – trough deflectors fitted.
Boilers fitted: 8250 from new, 8223 from December 1933, 8250 from February 1935, 8030 from January 1936, 8081 from January 1940, 8250 from November 1944, 9209 from July 1948, 27058 from February 1953, 27084 from October 1954, 27004 from March 1956, 27075 from September 1957, 27064 from January 1959 and 27016 from June 1961.
Tenders attached: 5483 from July 1930, 5569 from November 1936, 5285 from March 1943, 5263 from February 1949 and 5291 from May 1963.
Colour schemes: LNER green from new, black from March 1943, LNER green from June 1947, BR blue from March 1951 and BR green from February 1953.
Sheds: Gateshead from new, Haymarket in October 1937, Gateshead in January 1938, Heaton in March 1943, Gateshead in May 1943, Heaton in November 1945, Holbeck in May 1960, Heaton in July 1961 and Gateshead in June 1963.

Name: *Call Boy*
Numbers: 2795, 567, 99, E99 and 60099.
Works Number: 1738 (built in Doncaster).
Date to traffic: April 1930.
Withdrawn from service: Condemned in October 1963 and cut up by Arnott Young of Carmyle apparently in 1964.
Total mileage: 2,042,000.
Modifications: 1957 – to 75% cut-off, 1958 – double chimney and Kylchap exhaust fitted and 1961 – trough deflectors fitted.
Boilers fitted: 8226 from new, 8083 from June 1934, 8079 from May 1937, 8223 from May 1943, 9982 from July 1949, 27025 from January 1951, 27026 from July 1952, 29317 from January 1954, 29306 from July 1958, 29281 from December 1959 and 27064 from July 1961.
Tenders attached: 5479 from new, 5328 from June 1930, 5232 from May 1937 and 5568 from February 1944.
Colour schemes: LNER green from new, black from December 1941, LNER green from December 1947, BR blue from July 1949 and BR green from July 1952.
Sheds: Haymarket from new, St Margaret's in January 1940, Haymarket in October 1940 and St Margaret's in January 1963.

Name: *Spearmint*
Numbers: 2796, 568, 100 and 60100.
Works Number: 1741 (built in Doncaster).
Date to traffic: May 1930.
Withdrawn from service: Condemned in June 1965 and cut up at Darlington apparently in 1965.
Total mileage: 1,927,000.
Modifications: 1957 – to 75% cut-off, 1958 – double chimney and Kylchap exhaust fitted and 1961 – trough deflectors fitted.
Boilers fitted: 8247 from new, 8078 from April 1935, 8076 from March 1937, 8077 from October 1941, 9213 from November 1947, 9117 from April 1949, 27036 from September 1952, 27066 from February 1954, 27047 from September 1958, 27057 from August 1961 and 27063 from August 1962.
Tenders attached: 5480 from new, 5332 from June 1930, 5640 from March 1937, 5275 from July 1938, 5286 from February 1942, 5283 from April 1949 and 5566 from September 1952.
Colour schemes: LNER green from new, black from February 1943, LNER green from November 1947, BR blue from November 1950 and BR green from September 1952.
Sheds: Haymarket from new, Aberdeen in April 1937, Haymarket in March 1938, Eastfield in July 1938, Dundee in October 1940, Haymarket in December 1940 and St Margaret's in January 1963.

Name: *Cicero*
Numbers: 2797, 569, 101 and 60101.
Works Number: 1742 (built in Doncaster).
Date to traffic: June 1930.
Withdrawn from service: Condemned in April 1963 and cut up by Arnott Young of Carmyle apparently in 1964.
Total mileage: 1,815,000.
Modifications: 1957 – to 75% cut-off and 1959 – double chimney and Kylchap exhaust fitted.
Boilers fitted: 8248 from new, 8082 from March 1934, 8223 from May 1935, 8776 from January 1943, 8248 from May 1947, 8080 from December 1949, 27057 from September 1951, 29281 from November 1954, 27029 from August 1957, 27083 from February 1959 and 27011 from August 1960.
Tenders attached: 5481 from new and 5571 from July 1937.
Colour schemes: LNER green from new, black from January 1943, LNER green from May 1947, BR blue from December 1949 and BR green from September 1951.
Sheds: Haymarket from new, Dundee in February 1937, Eastfield in November 1938, St Margaret's in February 1940, Haymarket in October 1940 and St Margaret's in January 1963.

Name: *Windsor Lad*
Numbers: 2500, 570, 35 and 60035.
Works Number: 1790 (built in Doncaster).
Date to traffic: July 1934.
Withdrawn from service: Condemned in September 1961 and cut up at Doncaster in 1961.
Total mileage: 1,617,000.
Modifications: 1955 – to 75% cut-off and 1959 – double chimney and Kylchap exhaust fitted.
Boilers fitted: 8776 from new, 9121 from March 1941, 8084 from November 1948, 27053 from August 1951, 27048 from May 1954, 27070 from June 1957, 27058 from January 1959 and 27001 from May 1960.
Tenders attached: 5567 from new.
Colour schemes: LNER green from new, black from April 1942, LNER green from September 1947, BR blue from January 1950 and BR green from August 1951.
Sheds: Haymarket from new, Aberdeen in March 1937, Haymarket in April 1937, Carlisle Canal in April 1961 and Haymarket in August 1961.

Name: *Colombo*
Numbers: 2501, 571, 36 and 60036.
Works Number: 1791 (built in Doncaster).
Date to traffic: July 1934.
Withdrawn from service: Condemned in November 1964 and cut up by A. Draper of Hull apparently in 1965.
Total mileage: 1,535,000.
Modifications: 1956 – to 75% cut-off, 1958 – double chimney and Kylchap exhaust fitted and 1962 – trough deflectors fitted.
Boilers fitted: 8777 from new, 9124 from January 1941, 9568 from April 1947, 9511 from July 1948, 9980 from July 1949, 27064 from December 1951, 27059 from August 1953, 27039 from December 1954, 27078 from April 1956, 27057 from November 1957, 29328 from June 1960 and 29308 from July 1962.
Tenders attached: 5568 from new and 5227 from March 1944.
Colour schemes: LNER green from new, black from August 1942, LNER green from April 1947, BR purple from July 1948, BR blue from July 1949 and BR green from December 1951.
Sheds: Gateshead from new, York in December 1939, Heaton in March 1943, Gateshead in November 1945, King's Cross in August 1947, Gateshead in September 1947, Neville Hill in February 1949, Copley Hill in June 1961, Ardsley in September 1961, Gateshead in June 1963 and Darlington in December 1963.

Name: *Hyperion*
Numbers: 2502, 572, 37 and 60037.
Works Number: 1792 (built in Doncaster).
Date to traffic: July 1934.
Withdrawn from service: Condemned in December 1963 and cut up by Arnott Young of Carmyle apparently in 1964.
Total mileage: 1,695,000.
Modifications: 1957 – to 75% cut-off, 1958 – double chimney and Kylchap exhaust fitted and 1962 – trough deflectors fitted.
Boilers fitted: 8778 from new, 8777 from August 1941, 8720 from July 1947, 10541 from June 1950, 27068 from November 1953, 27027 from April 1957, 27066 from October 1958, 27058 from July 1960 and 27004 from May 1962.
Tenders attached: 5570 from July 1934, 5261 from August 1941, 5285 from June 1950 and 5276 from May 1957.
Colour schemes: LNER green from new, black from January 1943, LNER green from July 1947, BR blue from June 1950 and BR green from March 1952.
Sheds: Haymarket from new, St Margaret's in March 1938, Haymarket in March 1939, Carlisle in February 1954, Haymarket in March 1954 and St Margaret's in November 1961.

Name: *Firdaussi*
Numbers: 2503, 573, 38 and 60038.
Works Number: 1793 (built in Doncaster).
Date to traffic: August 1934.
Withdrawn from service: Condemned in November 1963 and cut up at Darlington apparently in 1964.
Total mileage: 1,637,000.
Modifications: 1955 – to 75% cut-off and 1959 – double chimney and Kylchap exhaust fitted.
Boilers fitted: 8779 from new, 8075 from October 1953, 9512 from September 1948, 9116 from January 1950, 27038 from January 1953, 27040 from January 1955, 27018 from April 1958, 27003 from September 1959 and 27960 from June 1961.
Tenders attached: 5571 from new and 5583 from June 1937.
Colour schemes: LNER green from new, black from April 1942, LNER green from March 1947, BR blue from January 1950 and BR green from September 1951.
Sheds: Gateshead from new, Heaton in September 1939, Gateshead in November 1939, Heaton in January 1943, Gateshead in May 1943, Darlington in February 1953, Gateshead in August 1953, Darlington in August 1956, Gateshead in February 1957, Holbeck in February 1960 and Neville Hill in June 1963.

Name: *Sandwich*
Numbers: 2504, 574, 39 and 60039.
Works Number: 1794 (built at Doncaster).
Date to traffic: September 1934.
Withdrawn from service: Condemned in March 1963 and cut up at Doncaster in 1963.
Total mileage: 1,569,000.
Modifications: 1955 – to 75% cut-off, 1959 – double chimney and Kylchap exhaust fitted and 1961 – trough deflectors fitted.
Boilers fitted: 8780 from new, 9115 fromMay 1939, 9511 from September 1946, 9208 from July 1948, 9512 from March 1950, 27060 from October 1951, 27022 from March 1953, 27057 from March 1955, 27014 from October 1957, 29294 from July 1959 and 27968 from June 1961.
Tenders attached: 5573 from new.
Colour schemes: LNER green from new, black from September 1942, LNER green from September 1946, BR blue from March 1950 and BR green from October 1951.
Sheds: Gateshead from new, Doncaster in November 1935, King's Cross in March 1939, Grantham in December 1941, King's Cross in June 1950, Grantham in September 1951, Leicester Central in October 1956 and King's Cross in April 1957.

Name: *Cameronian*
Numbers: 2505, 575, 40 and 60040.
Works Number: 1795 (built at Doncaster).
Date to traffic: October 1934.
Withdrawn from service: Condemned in July 1964 and cut up by Hughes Bolckow of North Blyth apparently in 1965.
Total mileage: 1,535,000.
Modifications: 1957 – to 75% cut-off, 1959 – double chimney and Kylchap exhaust fitted and 1962 – trough deflectors fitted.
Boilers fitted: 8781 from new, 9116 from January 1940, 9119 from May 1941, 9445 from March 1947, 9447 from December 1949, 27001 from May 1952, 27035 from August 1953, 27077 from July 1955, 27079 from October 1957, 27018 from October 1959 and 27012 from March 1962.
Tenders attached: 5566 from new and 5253 from November 1936.
Colour schemes: LNER green from new, black from November 1942, LNER green from March 1947, BR blue from December 1949 and BR green from May 1952.
Sheds: Haymarket from new, Gateshead in November 1936, York in December 1939, Gateshead in December 1939, Heaton in March 1943, Gateshead in November 1945, Darlington in September 1953, Gateshead in March 1954, Darlington in August 1955, Gateshead in February 1956, Darlington in November 1957, Gateshead in May 1958, Darlington in December 1959, Gateshead in June 1960, Darlington in June 1962, Heaton in December 1962 and Gateshead in June 1963.

Name: *Salmon Trout*
Numbers: 2506, 576, 41 and 60041.
Works Number: 1797 (built at Doncaster).
Date to traffic: December 1934.
Withdrawn from service: Condemned in December 1965 and cut up by Arnott Young of Carmyle apparently in 1966.
Total mileage: 1,557,000.
Modifications: 1956 – to 75% cut-off, 1959 – double chimney and Kylchap exhaust fitted and 1963 – trough deflectors fitted.
Boilers fitted: 8782 from new, 8780 from January 1941, 9482 from December 1945, 9118 from February 1952, 27067 from February 1952, 27082 from October 1956, 27003 from February 1958, 27049 from July 1959, 27020 from March 1961 and 27024 from January 1963.
Tenders attached: 5581 from December 1934, 5325 fom October 1935, 5226 from January 1937 and 5272 from December 1944.
Colour schemes: LNER green from new, black from May 1942, LNER green from May 1947, BR blue from July 1950 and BR green from February 1952.
Sheds: Haymarket from new and St Margaret's in July 1960.

Name: *Singapore*
Numbers: 2507, 577, 42 and 60042.
Works Number: 1798 (built at Doncaster).
Date to traffic: December 1934.
Withdrawn from service: Condemned in July 1964 and cut up by Arnott Young of Carmyle apparently in 1965.
Total mileage: 1,509,000.
Modifications: 1947 – to 75% cut-off, 1958 – double chimney and Kylchap exhaust fitted, and 1962 – trough deflectors fitted.
Boilers fitted: 8783 from new, 8782 from September 1941, 9116 from August 1948, 9214 from December 1949, 27046 from May 1951, 27076 from May 1955, 27083 from September 1956, 27024 from September 1958 and 27002 from May 1960.
Tenders attached: 5582 from new, 5639 from February 1937, 5229 from November 1937, 5570 from September 1941, 5274 from August 1943 and 5260 from December 1952.
Colour schemes: LNER green from new, black from August 1943, LNER green from January 1947, BR blue from December 1949 and BR green from December 1952.
Sheds: Gateshead from new, Neville Hill in September 1945, Gateshead in May 1946, Darlington in March 1953, Gateshead in September 1953, Darlington in March 1954, Gateshead in September 1954, Darlington in November 1956, Gateshead in May 1957, Heaton in September 1962, Aberdeen in April 1963 and St Margaret's in October 1963.

Name: *Brown Jack*
Numbers: 2508, 578, 43 and 60043.
Works Number: 1800 (built at Doncaster).
Date to traffic: February 1935.
Withdrawn from service: Condemned in December 1963 and cut up by Motherwell Machinery & Scrap Co apparently in 1964.
Total mileage: 1,552,000.
Modifications: 1955 – to 75% cut-off, 1959 – double chimney and Kylchap exhaust fitted and 1962 – trough deflectors fitted.
Boilers fitted: 8784 from new, 8781 from February 1941, 9447 from January 1944, 9570 from August 1948, 9212 from April 1950, 27055 from August 1951, 27075 from November 1955, 27021 from August 1957, 27011 from February 1959, 29339 from August 1960 and 29285 from February 1962.
Tenders attached: 5584 from new, 5330 from April 1935, 5641 from April 1937 and 5256 from May 1938.
Colour schemes: LNER green from new, black from June 1942, LNER green from June 1947, BR blue from April 1950 and BR green from August 1951.
Sheds: Haymarket from new and St Margaret's November 1961.

All photos in this Appendix come from the Bert Spencer, Ronald Hillier or the author's collection.

'THEY ALSO SERVE' – MAINTAINING *FLYING SCOTSMAN* AND HER RECORDS

W hen assessing the life of a locomotive, particularly No. 4472/60103 *Flying Scotsman*, it is very easy to focus on her great deeds when out on road. A locomotive's far less glamorous life in workshops and sheds, in the hands of engineers, cleaners and many other support staff, is invariably glossed over and forgotten. Sadly, much that these men and women did, often in adverse and trying conditions, is now lost to time. But it is true to say that without these dedicated workers, much that these engines achieved would not have been possible. They literally kept the wheels turning.

Sadly, most of the records that described the work they did – the detailed maintenance files for each engine they supported and much more – have not survived. In the

An anonymous group of railway workers pose with the pride of the LNER's fleet. When recording the lives of locomotives such as this it is easy to forget the important contribution made by these men and women. (BS)

1960s, when steam was coming to an end on Britain's network, a decision was taken to destroy these 'superfluous' records without any true consideration of their historic value. Luckily a number of people, such as W.B. Yeadon, were wise

to this wholesale destruction and retrieved some records before it was too late. In due course, much of this material ended up at York in the National Railway Museum's archives or in the hands enthusiasts. By these diverse means sufficient

In some ways an engine cleaner's life was the hardest of all on the railways. Out in the open in all weathers clambering over a locomotive preparing it for the day ahead. For this there was very little protective clothing, least of all gloves to protect their skin from the hazards of handling chemical agents and such like. The dangers of these conditions to health were obvious with, at best, colds and other infections resulting or, at worst, such things as dermatitis and cancers forming over time. Here this publicity photo for No. 4472 catches a glimpse of a cleaner's life. In due course, many of these men will become firemen then drivers – an equally hard life, but at least, with the Pacifics, on a covered footplate. (BS)

No. 4472 undergoing a General Repair at Doncaster with her nameplate on display for what was undoubtedly a publicity photo. (BS)

paperwork could be gathered to allow historians to build up a picture, albeit with many pieces missing, of the lives of those in workshops and sheds and what they did each day – in peace and war.

The working conditions here were as hard, dirty and dangerous as only heavy industries can be when left unprotected by legislation and Government controlled inspection. And to make matters worse the living conditions 'enjoyed' by most people in Britain during the 1920s and '30s would now be considered unacceptable. So, it was perhaps no surprise that child mortality ran between 10 and 14 per cent each year during this period (7 per 100,000 in 2020) and life expectancy was 59 to 62 for women and 55 to 58 for men in the decade between 1920 and 1930.

For those involved in maintaining and preparing engines and rolling stock there was little to lighten the load or reduce the adverse effects of this work on their health and well-being. Accidents and deaths in service were a regular occurrence and statistics easily reveal the scale of the problem and the range of illnesses and occupational diseases that afflicted these workers. It is probably true to say that few of the people lucky enough to reach retirement age went on to enjoy long and healthy lives after that, due to their working and living conditions. Nevertheless, they were not a group of workers to shirk their responsibilities. Far from it, in fact. Industrial disputes though increasingly common in the 1920s and '30 were still fairly rare in the LNER's workshops. The one exception to this was the 1926 General Strike. However, this was an event of national importance where many union members were driven to protest by observing how the mine owners shamefully treated their work force. In some cases, they reduced wages by as much as 50 percent from an already low level and presided over a death/injury rate that made other industrial workers and leaders recoil in horror. Or, as Bert Spencer later put it, 'at rates comparable with those faced on the Western Front in the Great War'.

So, the LNER's workshops and sheds were manned by a steadfast and honourable group of workers who should be remembered and admired for their contribution to the company's story. In a limited way we can do this by observing and understanding the few papers that have survived. Here an engine's Record Cards provide a clue, especially when accompanied by an understanding of life in heavy industry, with all its risks. Luckily many of these cards have survived in public and private hands, and through them we can observe and appreciate the cycle of life in workshops and sheds in the heyday of Flying Scotsman and her sisters.

Sadly, few sets are complete, but for No.4472 sufficient have survived to allow us a glimpse of all the work undertaken to keep her moving and, in some cases the names of some of those who oversaw the work. It isn't a day-to-day account of life in the workshops, but it is as close as we are likely to get so long after the event.

The two Forms 3340 above, which are No.4472's earliest surviving records, carry quite a complete locomotive history – where based and when, maintenance programmes, modifications, some general technical detail, mileages and so on. It is thought, though not confirmed, that the 3340's may have been retained and kept and updated by staff at the running sheds, so remained close to a locomotive wherever it was based throughout its life.

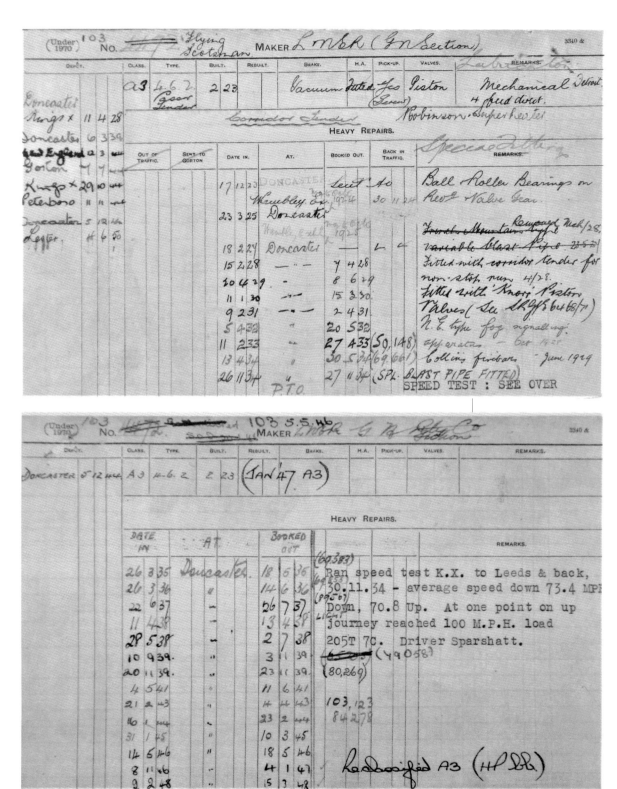

L.N.E.R. DONCASTER WORKS.
(G.N. SECTION.)

Engine 103 502

Class A.1.

"Flying Scotsman"

ENGINE REPAIRS.

Received at Works: Date sent for	District	Tender	Date of Arrival	Erecting Shop Date In	Out	Chargeman	Bay	Paint Shop Date In	Out	Despatched into Traffic Date	District	Tender	Repairs
	King's X	5324	6/4/32	8/4/32	11/5/32	L. Williamson	4	11.5/32	17.5/32	May 20/32	London	5324	G.
	London	5324	23.2/33	3.3/33	13.4/33	L. Williamson	4	19.4/33	24.4/33	April 27/33	London	5324 1.	G.R.
	King's X	5324	19.4.34	23.4.34	18.5.34	A. Strangward	4	18.5.34	28.5.34	May 30.34	London	5324 2.	G.
	King's X	5324	24-26 11.34							June 9.34	London	5324	Here for Exhibition L. Purposes
	King's X	"								Nov 27.34	London	5324	L.
	King's X	5324	27.3.35	30.3.35	8.5.35	H. Strangward	4	8.5.35	15.5.35	May 18.35	King's X	5324	2.
" "	"	5324	25.3.36	31.3.36	9.5.36	L. Williamson	4	13.5.36	13.5.36	June 14.36	" "	5324	30.3 H.
" "	"	5324	19.10.36							Oct 20.36	" "	5290	Change Tender
" "	"	5290	25.6.37	26.6	17.7			17.7	22.7	July 24.37	" "	"	H
" "	"	5290	12.4.38	13.4	16.4	Parker				13.4.38	" "	5290	Light
" "	"	"	27.5.38	28.5	25.6	Strangward		28.6	30.6	July 2.38	" "	5642	Heavy
" "	"	5640	18.9.39							Nov 3.39	Doncr.	5640	Heavy
" "	"	"	20.11.39	"Blowdown"						Nov 23/39	–	–	–
Doncaster	"	"	10.5.41							June 11.41	" "	"	"
"	"	"	27.2.43							Apl. 3.43	" "	"	"
"	"	"	5.2.44							Feb 23.44	" "	"	Light

In due course, Doncaster Works introduced an unnumbered form to record what happened in the workshops and when. These appear to have run alongside the 3340s but were kept at Doncaster Works. This example came to me via the good work of Sheffield Railwayana Auction House. Presumably other examples covering the engine's life may have survived.

Engine No. E60103 ~~HH72 502~~ **Class** ~~A10~~ A3 **Stock** GN.G.C./G.N ~~N50~~ 5640 **TENDER**/~~TANK~~

FAILURE STATISTICS — BOILERS

Date	Defect No.	Cause No.	P. or F.	Section reporting failure		Date	Defect No.	Cause No.	P. or F.	Section reporting failure	
							Blr. No.			N of B.II	Built by
6·1·45	26	16	P.	N.E.							
19/1/45	16	3	P.	W.			~~329~~		P.	E (N)	
2/8/46	38	16	P	W			~~405~~		P		
5/6/48	38	14	P	W							
4·2·49	1	15	P	W			813		P.		
6·4·49	105		P	W.							
28·4·49	409		P.	W		14·3·5	27015		SH.		
12·4·49	113		P.	W.		6·4·56	27074		S.H	Doncaster	
7·6·49	403		P.	E (W)		7·10·55	27007		"	"	
4·7·49	807		P.	—		13·7·57	27011		SH		
16·8·49	Toll 2011		P.	—		24·1·59	27044		SH		

OTHER INFORMATION

Converted A10 to A3 4/1/47   21/1/46 Reconditioned.
                                5/5/46 "

Sold to Mr A.F. Pegler 15·1·63.   When Cond. See 16/3/61   32164
of 1·3·60 also 7·3·60

BR 11500 Locomotive Statistics

Engine No. 60103 **Class** A3 2 **Wheel Type** 4-6-2 **TENDER**/~~TANK~~

Tractive Effort _____ lbs. **Section/Area Stock** GN _____ **Built** 1923

REPAIR STATISTICS

Date W.E.			Heavy repairs				Light repairs		
Out of traffic	Sent to shops	Out of shops	Works	Days under repair	Time	Miles	Works	Days under repair	REMARKS
					Y. M.	since previous heavy repair			
6·60	3·60	24·3·60			1 2		Doncaster	14	P.V.
7·60	6·7·60	9·8·60	Doncaster	29	1·6	85,317			
2·61	14·2·61	4·3·61			·6	37,039	Doncaster	16	
11·61	21·11·61	16·12·61			1·3	81,404	Doncaster	15	P. & E ...
4·62	25·4·62	2·6·62	Doncaster		1·8	98,331			
	25·6·62		Done						

It seems that in the 1940s, possibly under the influence of the Ministry of Transport's central control and before nationalisation, a closer, more controlled system of statistical analysis of each engines performance was set up. The aims of this new system were obvious – to ensure each engine spent as little time as possible in the works, but also to identify the reasons why this was so and any trends that might require action to correct. The deteriorating condition of Gresley's three cylinder engines fitted with his conjugated valve gear would have been one likely area of concern requiring monitoring.

The coming of BR in 1948 changed the nature of the railway business in Britain and saw the establishment of a new corporate identity and a standardisation of the many accounting systems they had inherited from the Big Four companies. This was none more so than in the way the lives of locomotives were recorded. For maintenance work undertaken at sheds and shops, the Form BR 11500 was introduced

Sold to Mr A.F. Pegler. 15.1.63.

BRITISH RAILWAYS
THE RAILWAY EXECUTIVE

ENGINE RECORD CARD

BR.9215 2/

E. ~~ON~~   Region Division   Name *FLYING SCOTSMAN*   Number **60103**

Class(S.R.) *YP*   Type *A3*   Built by *Doncaster*   Date *Feb. 1923.*

~~Robinson..~~

PASSENGER TENDER SUPERHEATER*   Wheel arrgt. *4-6-2.*   Wheel base (E. & T.) *60* ft. *10⅝* ins.

~~MIXED TRAFFIC~~ *

~~FREIGHT TANK NON-SUPERHEATER~~*   Type of motion *Wal/Gresley*   Diameter of driving wheels *6* ft. *8* ins.

Engine and Tender—Weight in working order T. *156* C. *12* Empty *114* *12*   Overall height from rail level *13* ft. *1* ins.

No. of cylinders *3*   Dia. *19* ins.   Stroke *26* ins.   Overall length over buffers (E. & T.) *70* ft. *5⅛* ins.

Class of boiler *94a.*   No. of tubes { *43* Large / *121* Small }   Dia. *5¼* ins. / Dia. *2¼* ins.

Heating Surface *3398.3* *1454* sq. ft.

Boiler pressure *220* lbs. per sq. inch.   Tractive effort at 85% B.P. *32,909* lbs.   Firebox { Steel / Copper* } grate area *41.25.* sq. ft.

Radius of minimum curve *6* chains (or _____ chains dead slow)   Feed Pump†   L.& R.H. Drive

Brakes† *Vacuum*   Valves† *Piston*   Tablet Catching Apparatus† _____

Injectors (Type & Size) { R.H. ~~Live 4/x~~ *Footstep Ext.* 10 mm / L.H. ~~Exhaust 10 x/x~~ *Footstep Fine 11* mm } Mechanical Lubrication* { Cylinders _____ / Axle Boxes }   Atomiser Lubrication / Sight Feed Lubrication / Fountain Lubrication

Axle Boxes (coupled wheels)† ~~Bronze~~

C.W.A.* { Front end / Tender end / Both ends }   SANDING* { Steam / Mechanical / Back / De-sanding }   WATER PICK-UP APPARATUS*   { Forward direction / Both directions / Internal fittings / only }   ROLLER BEARINGS*   { Bogie† _____ / Truck† _____ / Coupled† _____ / Tender† _____ }   MANGANESE LINERS*   { Bogie / Truck / Coupled / Tender }

Double

SPECIAL FITTINGS*

Drop/Rocking grate   ~~Hopper ashpan~~   ~~Self-cleaning smoke box~~   Smoke box deflector plates   ~~Spark arrester~~   Blast pipe†

Revg. gear { Screw *Smith-Stone* / Lever / Power *Speed-Indicator* }   Speed indicator   ~~Push and Pull fitted~~   { Vac. C.R. / Air C.R. / Mech. C.R. }   ~~Vacuum pump~~   ~~Continuous blowdown~~   Blow-off cock   ~~A.T.C.~~   A.T.C

~~Trip cocks~~   ~~Condenser~~   ~~Sand gun~~   Gangway doors *E & T*   ~~Storm sheets~~   ~~Back cab~~   ~~Limousine cab~~

~~Tender weather boards~~   Coal bunker access doors   ~~Coal rails~~   ~~Coal pusher~~   Fitted for snow-plough   Regulator { ~~Smoke box~~ _____ / Dome } †

Single 3/52

OTHER NON-SPECIFIED DETAILS:—

Above and opposite: In a final cycle of reporting, the BR Form 9215 (Engine Record Card) was introduced apparently across all Regions of BR in the early 1950s and remained in place until the end of steam. Judging by the number for each engine that have survived, several copies of each were produced with virtually the same information on each card. This suggests that sheds and workshops maintained their own copies. As a brief summary of each class, the modifications made, where based, time in workshops, tenders attached and more they are an invaluable record of locomotives under BR's management.

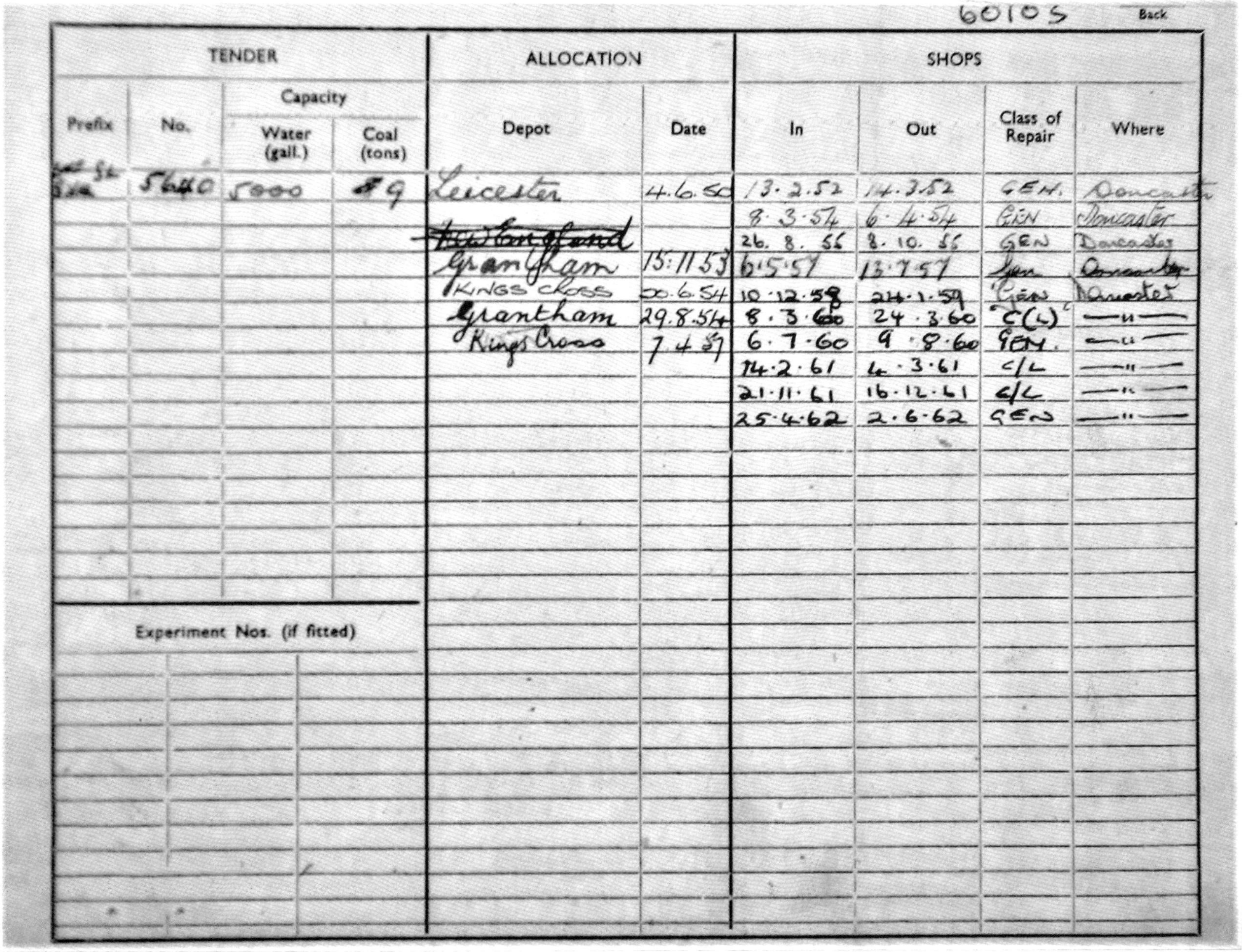

60105   Back

TENDER				ALLOCATION		SHOPS			
Prefix	No.	Capacity		Depot	Date	In	Out	Class of Repair	Where
		Water (gall.)	Coal (tons)						
St	5640	5000	9	Leicester	4.6.50	13.2.52	14.3.52	GEN.	Doncaster
						8.3.54	6.4.54	GEN	Doncaster
				~~New England~~		26.8.56	8.10.56	GEN	Doncaster
				Grantham	15.11.53	6.5.57	13.7.57	Gen	Doncaster
				Kings Cross	30.6.54	10.12.58	24.1.59	Gen	Doncaster
				Grantham	29.8.54	8.3.60	24.3.60	C(L)	—"—
				Kings Cross	7.4.57	6.7.60	9.8.60	GEN.	—"—
						14.2.61	4.3.61	C/L	—"—
						21.11.61	16.12.61	C/L	—"—
						25.4.62	2.6.62	GEN	—"—

Experiment Nos. (if fitted)

The end result of all the labour of staff in workshops and sheds – an immaculate, highly polished engine ready to begin another high profile journey along the East Coast Mainline. (BS)

Appendix 4

1470/4470 GREAT NORTHERN – THE A1 THAT GOT AWAY

Being the first of a major new class of locomotive would normally bestow on that engine some special status and, perhaps, ensure that it received a fair amount of publicity during its life time.

Not so Gresley's prototype A1, No.1470/4470 *Great Northern*, which is even more surprising when considering the huge advance in design it represented when first appearing in 1922. But almost from the first, its reputation and status

was eclipsed by her sister engines, most notably No. 1472/4472 *Flying Scotsman.*

Conjecture always tends to cloud any true assessment of history and apocryphal stories, that soon take on the status of 'evidence', are often

Above left and above right: **Although a** significant locomotive in railway history, 1470/4470 *Great Northern* was a remarkably 'camera shy' engine throughout her life. Whilst *Flying Scotsman* has been captured in hundreds if not thousands of photographs, and to a lesser extent a number of the other A1/A3s, 1470/4470 seems to have been rarely pursued by cameramen. The pictures above are two rare examples from the 1920s and '30s. (BS)

added to confuse or distort how we view or interpret past events. This was none more so than in the case of *Great Northern*, though in her first few years all seemed to be relatively plain sailing for this engine and class mates. The only real issue that seems have courted controversy concerns the locomotive's comparatively low profile at this time when other engines were attracting so much more attention.

Bert Spencer probably came closest to explaining this when he wrote:

Great Northern as an experiment was a success but in service the engine was not thought to be one of the better performers and, if my memory serves me well, was not particularly popular with the footplate being, at times, a poor steamer. The engine

improved when modified with the long travel valve, as did the remainder of the class.

In terms of being used on big occasions its name, which harped back to a bygone age, probably did not sit happily with the LNER's senior managers, so may account for its comparatively quiet life. For this reason, it was based at Doncaster virtually until rebuilt.

Right, opposite and overleaf: 1470/4470's Record Cards, which were acquired a few years ago through Sheffield Railwayana Auctions, having failed to be preserved by BR in the 1960s, give an indication of the locomotive's life between 1922 and when rebuilt as a Class A1/1 Pacific in 1945 under Edward Thompson's management and Edward Windle's direct guidance (THG)

L.N.E.R. DONCASTER WORKS. (G.N. SECTION.) "GREAT NORTHERN."
ENGINE REPAIRS.

Engine **4470**
Class **A1**

Received at Works				Erecting Shop				Paint Shop		Despatched into Traffic			Repairs
Date sent for.	District.	Tender.	Date of Arrival.	Date In.	Out.	Chargeman.	Bay.	Date In.	Out.	Date.	District.	Tender.	
Cont'd.													
6/26	Doncaster	5211	3.6/26	June 4/26	June 12/26	Parker J	A	—	—	June 8/26	Doncaster	5211	L.R.
5.3/27	"	"	4.3/27	Mch 4/27	Apl 9/27	"	A	12.4/27	28.4/57	Apl 30/27	"	"	G.R.
"	"	"	13.10/27	—	—	—	—	—	—	Oct 13/27	"	"	NOT. TO COUNT.
3/28	"	"	29.3/28	Mch 30	May 23	Williamson	A	25.5/28	4.6/28	June 8/28	"	5227	
	"	5227	25.10/28	Oct 26/28	Oct 29/28	"	A	20.6/29	25.6/29	Octr 30/28	"	"	L.R.
9.5/29	"	"	7.5/29	May 11/29	June 19/29	Parker J	A	25.7/29	31.7/29	June 29/29	"	"	
6/30	"	"	10.6/30	June 12/30	21.7/30	Wilson J	A	" 30	" 30	Aug 7/30	"	"	G.R.
"	"	"	24.10/30	24.10/30	11.11/30	"	A	4.12/31	10.12/31	Nov 12/30	"	"	L.R.
23.9/31	"	"	23.9/31	28.9/31	1.12/31	"	A	18.5/33	23.5/33	Dec 17/31	"	"	G.R.
"	"	"	6.4/33	7.4/33	1.5/33	Parker	A	30.1/34	5.2/34	May 25/33	"	"	G.R.
"	"	"	29.12/33	3.1/34	23.1/34	Parker	A	8.1/35	12.1/35	Feby 8/34	"	"	H.R.
"	"	"	29.11/34	30.11/34	5.1/35	G.Wilson	A	15.4.36	20.4.36	Jan 16/35	"	"	G.R.
"	"	"	5.3.36	6.3.36	9.4.36	H Strangward				Apl 22.36	"	"	H.R.
"	"	"	15.1.37	14.1		G.Wilson		19.2	24.2	Feby 27.37	"	5582	H.R.
"	5582		29.11.37	Blow Down app.						Dec 2.37	—	—	L.R.
"	"		2.3.38	4.3	26.3	Wilson		28.3	31.3	Apl 2.38	—	—	Heavy.

This seems to be a measured, prosaic account reported by someone who was knowledgeable and close to the centre of action without an axe to grind and able to view events in a balanced way, so may be believed. However, it was a minor issue by comparison to the one that appeared to engulf *Great Northern* in 1945 as a result of Edward Thompson pursuing a company plan for a standardised fleet of locomotives. As the CME's Assistant, Spencer was close to the action and simply described what happened when it was decided to rebuild No. 4470. His words give no hint of any controversy or

| Engine No. **4470** | | | | L.N.E.R. DONCASTER WORKS *Great Northern* | | | | | | | | | | 3 |
| Class. ~~A1~~ ~~A10~~ ²⁵/⁴/45 A.1 ²⁵/⁹/45 | | | | | | | | | ENGINE REPAIRS. | | | | | |

Received at Works.				Erecting Shop				Point Shop.		Despatched to Traffic				
Date sent for.	District	Tender	Date of arrival	Date		Chargeman	B a y	Date		Date	District	Tender	Repairs.	
				In	Out			In	Out					
—	Donc.	5582	17.4.39							May 20·39	Donc.	5582	Heavy	
	"	"	5·3·40							Mar 30·40	"	"	"	
	"	"	8·1·42							Feb 14·42	"	"	"	
	"	"	20·11·43							Dec 24·43	"	"	"	
	"	"	1·5·45							Sept 25·45	"	"	Rebuild	
	"	"	1·10·45							Oct. 6. 45	"	"	Adj	
	"	"	22·11·45							Dec 13·45	Kings X	"	Light	
	"	"	10·1·46							Jan 21·46	"	"	"	

disagreement when plans for this engine were being considered or actioned:

4470 Great Northern, was rebuilt in 1945 to test the efficacy of some elements of the standardisation programme. This conversion was deemed a success and work soon began on what Thompson and Windle hoped would be the standard Pacific and in 1946 the first of the A2/3s, as they were called, appeared.

Received wisdom would have us believe that in an act of spite, Thompson, once he became CME in 1941, deliberately chose to undo Gresley's work, destroying his legacy in the process. The rebuilding of the P2 2-8-2s as

Pacifics was the first manifestation of this plan, with the reconstruction of *Great Northern* the next stage. If so, why should Thompson have set out on such a course of action?

It has been suggested that Thompson felt bitter over the way Gresley had condemned then prematurely scrapped all five of Vincent Raven's North Eastern Railway Pacifics in the late 1930s. This, or so the story goes, was an injustice that was supposed to have festered in Thompson's mind, especially as they were his greatly admired father-in-law's final engines. So, when an opportunity arose, he took his revenge by 'destroying' Gresley's Pacific masterpiece, which had been built in 1922 as a rival to Raven's 4-6-2s.

But if there was any truth to these stories, then Thompson would have chosen a far more important target for his attention rather than one tired old engine – the A4s or A3s for example. Yet he did nothing, kept these engines largely as they were and even promoted their continued use in his standardisation plans. This lack of meddling in either design suggests that pay back was not his motivation when considering the future of *Great Northern*.

For reason that aren't clear, this is a story that has grown over the years, gradually gaining momentum seemingly based on conjecture as much as facts. So where might the truth lie and is it now possible to unravel

these distant events to reach any supported conclusions? To do this, we have to go back to 1944 when Gresley's pioneering A1s were all approaching twenty years old or more and their condition deemed poor after five years of an exhausting and bloody war. At the time there were undoubtedly discussions over the future of many locomotives as the end of the conflict was glimpsed and firm planning for the future could recommence

Like most engines of the time, the A1s had suffered from the heavy demands placed on them during the war and the lower maintenance standards resulting from pressure of other work and lack of trained staff to service them. Inevitably,

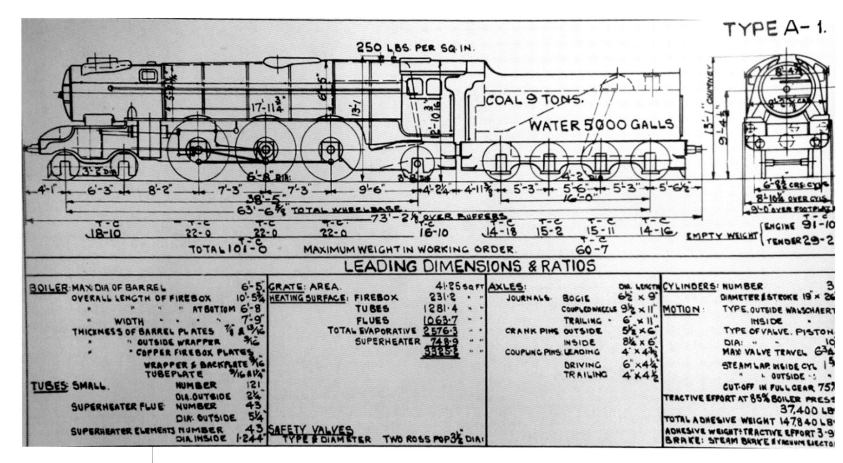

The new A1/1 as it appeared in 1945/46 with small deflectors added either side of the chimney to aid smoke-lifting. (THG)

high performance engines such as the Pacifics would have suffered more than others types because they tended to be worked to their maximum capacity over prolonged periods. In the meantime, some of them had been modified to reflect the changes introduced when the A3s appeared in late 1928. These conversions had begun in July 1927, but moved forward at a snail's pace with the majority of the engines only being modified under Thompson's management. Within this programme, *Great Northern's* upgrade to A3 standard was not given a high priority, even though by 1944 she was reported by Richard Hardy, then a draughtsman at Doncaster, as being

'… an average old tub with nothing much to write home about at that time – a low pressure A1 rarely used on the heaviest jobs'. To which Bert Spencer added,'with a known problem with her conjugated, 2-1 valve gear that the war had exposed very graphically'.

So, despite being the first of Gresley's Pacifics, she seems to have become no more than just another engine and in this guise was an obvious choice for rebuilding or even scrapping, if her condition was thought poor enough.

So, if we ignore the question of malice, the chief issue in this debate seems to be the practical question of how to upgrade this 'old tub' or whether to scrap her and build

new. In the event, Thompson chose to reconstruct her, or one of her sisters, to test out his and Windle's developing ideas on locomotive construction, rather than simply let her become another A3. On face value neither of these two options seems particularly contentious, so it is the choice of 4470 that appears to have raised eyebrows because another, less historically important engine might have filled the bill better.

For those critical of Thompson's actions, there is an unconfirmed report that he deliberately selected 4470 against the advice of Edward Windle, his Chief Draughtsman, who preferred to use another engine instead. But in the absence

of any written word from Windle, this is impossible to verify. The only reliable source of information that can be quoted with any certainty is Richard Hardy, who was involved in the project to rebuild *Great Northern*. With regard to any objections raised by Windle or his fellow draughtsmen to the choice of this engine he recorded:

The drawing office team were a hard bitten group of engineers and never a word did I hear regarding the selection of No. 4470 for rebuilding. Most of them, including Windle, were steeped in the Gresley tradition but the choice of this engine meant nothing to them at the time. As for me I was a 21-year-old and full of romantic ideas about engines, footplatemen and running sheds – the practical life. I was acquainted with 100s of engines on a personal basis from Pacifics to C12s, GN Atlantics and all the lusty Great Central designs. So if anybody should have got uptight, it should have been me – and I never gave it a second thought….she wasn't one of the best anyway.

Maybe Edward Thompson did refuse to change the number that had been submitted to him, based on which engines were due for a heavy general repair. When a locomotive was required for a special event or for rebuilding the Running Superintendent, in this case George Musgrave, would be asked to nominate an engine. It is quite likely that a tidy minded clerk at Gerrard's Cross put together the number of the first of the bunch and why not? A letter would be written, the selection approved and by the time the news reached Thompson, the die had been cast. It is possible that Windle did remonstrate with ET over the choice and it is equally possible that his chief told him that 4470 was Musgrave's choice and that would have been an end to it. We have no means of knowing otherwise today but this is how a choice would normally have been made and how railwaymen behaved in the real world. Apart from anything the war was still at its height and the pressure was so intense on ET that I doubt if he had enough time to eat or rest let alone plot such an act.

Wherever the truth might lie, No. 4470 was selected, potentially the first of a number of A1s that

The transformation of No. 4470 is nearly complete and a new class of Pacific emerges at Doncaster in September 1945 to be fired up for the first time. To some that work was a sacrilege but the engine was, to me at least, striking in appearance and still demonstrably a Gresley engine. (RH)

In due course, and before nationalisation of the railways took hold, the small smoke deflectors on 4470 were replaced by these larger versions which gave the engine a distinctive and, to me, a more balanced look. As part of the Pacific development programme streamlining re-entered the debate. But after some experiments authorised by Thompson, the matter was quietly dropped by Peppercorn, when becoming CME, who, it seems, prefered to discontinue Gresley's work in this field. (BS)

might eventually be rebuilt as A1/1s, presumably with the remaining A1 to A3 programme being dispensed with. Planning took some months and in due course drawings and a diagram appeared, incorporating many of the ideas that Thompson and Windle had been developing over the previous two years. And when she re-appeared in September 1945, the modifications were only too apparent, although the change to three-cylinders with three independent sets of Walschaert valve gear was well hidden from view. Not so the double blastpipe, containing a Kylchap exhaust,

the outside cylinders set back behind the front bogie and a longer smokebox. Due to space restrictions, the middle cylinder could not be placed parallel to the outside cylinders so was set further back. This created a need for new, longer frames similar to those used on the A4 except for the wheel spacings at the front. As a result the engine's wheelbase was increased to 38ft 5in making it even longer than the Gresley P2s. To complete the picture, a 107 type boiler was fitted, presumably because it had proved so successful on the A4s. To this was added a hopper ashpan, similar to that used on the four

A2/1 Pacifics built in 1944/45. This proved very popular to the users who now did not need to get under the engine to clear out the ashpan.

Most of Thompson and Windle's developing ideas were incorporated in the new locomotive, with very little of the original engine being used in the rebuilding process. So, to all intents and purposes it was a new engine, but with looks in the Gresley style, or, as one commentator succinctly put it, 'a cartoon version' and in this shape she went into traffic to begin evaluation. However, first impressions must have been good because a month later an order was

No 60113	"GREAT NORTHERN"	Maker	L.N.E.R (G.N.R) Doncaster	LNER 6231/8/46 250	59

Depôt	Class	Type	Built	Rebuilt	Brake	H.A.	Pick-up	Valves	Lubricator
King's Cross									
To North.	A.1/1	4.6.2.	4	22					
Eastern Area 24.7.47	altered to A.1/1 25.1.48. Heavy Repairs								
Gateshead									
Haymarket 2.8.47									
King's Cross 18.9.47									
Peterboro 4.6.50									
Grantham 9.9.51									

Date in	At	Booked out	Back in Traffic	Remarks	Special Fittings
5 7 46	Doncaster	11 7 46			
19 9 46	"	25 9 46			
28 3 47	"	5 47			
15 6 47	"	21 6 47			
11 8 48	"	1 10 48	G		
15 9 49	"	6 1 50	G	75705	
3 5 50	"	11 5 50	C.L.		
2 6 50	"	16 50	c/L		
18 4 51	"	18 5 51	H/I 76104		
20 11 51	"	4 12 51	c/L		

This Record Card highlights the early years of 4470, then re-numbered 113 and finally 60113, as she began life as the solitary A1/1. Between 1945 and 1951 she would be on tour round five sheds before finally settling at Grantham for six years. After a brief sojourn to King's Cross in 1957, she will then spend the rest of her life at Doncaster where she will be condemned in 1962 and cut up during February the following year. (THG)

placed authorising construction of sixteen new Pacifics using, it would seem, the A1/1 template as a basis for their design. These engines finally appeared during Peppercorn's tenure, by which time the A1/1 design had been reworked resulting in Peppercorn's A1 Pacifics. It appears to have been decided at about the same time to let the A1 to A3 programme continue with no effort being made to remove the conjugated valve gear and replace it with three independent sets of Walschaerts at the same time. And in this condition they remained in service until withdrawn and scrapped in the 1960s.

Before the railways were nationalised in 1948, the LNER introduced a new numbering system which saw *Great Northern* go from 4470 to 113 in October 1946 and then 60113 under BR ownership. (RH)

CONDEMNED

BRITISH RAILWAYS THE RAILWAY EXECUTIVE **ENGINE RECORD CARD** **60113** BR.9215

19-11-62

E.GN. — Region/Division — Name *Great Northern* — Number 60113.

Class (M.P.) 8P — Type A1/1 — Built by *Doncaster* — Date *April 1922*

BALL JOINTS

~~PASSENGER TENDER SUPERHEATER~~ *
~~MIXED TRAFFIC~~ *
~~FREIGHT TANK NON-SUPERHEATER~~ *

Wheel arrgt. 4 - 6 - 2 — Wheel base (E. & T.) 63 ft. 6½ ins.

Type of motion *Walschaerts* — Diameter of driving wheels 6 ft. 8 ins.

Engine and Tender—Weight in working order T. 159 C. 8 Empty T. 119 C. 18 — Overall height from rail level 13 ft. 1 ins.

No. of cylinders 3 — Dia. 19 ins. Stroke 26 ins. — Overall length over buffers (E. & T.) 73 ft. ins.

Class of boiler 107

Heating Surface ~~3385~~ 3282 sq. ft. — No. of tubes { 43 Large * Dia. 5¼ ins. / 121 Small Dia. 2¼ ins. }

Boiler pressure 250 lbs. per sq. inch. — Tractive effort at 85% B.P. 37,397 lbs. — Firebox { Steel / ~~Copper~~ * } grate area 41.25 sq. ft.

Radius of minimum curve 5 chains (or ___ chains dead slow) — ~~Feed Pump~~† ___ L. H. Drive

Brakes† *Steam Vac: Ejector* Valves† *Piston* — ~~Tablet Catching Apparatus~~†

Injectors (Type & Size) { R.H. *Exhaust* 10 m/m *Foot Step* / L.H. *Live* 11 m/m ___ }

Mechanical Lubrication* { Cylinders ___ Atomiser Lubrication / Axle Boxes ___ ~~Sight Feed Lubrication~~ / ~~Fountain Lubrication~~ }

Axle Boxes (coupled wheels)† *Bronze*

C.W.A.* { ~~Front end~~ / Tender end / ~~Both ends~~ } — SANDING* { Steam / ~~Mechanical~~ / Back / ~~De-sanding~~ } — WATER PICK-UP APPARATUS* { ~~Forward direction~~ / ~~Both directions~~ / ~~Internal fittings~~ / only } — ~~ROLLER BEARINGS~~* — { ~~Bogie~~† / Truck† ___ / Coupled† ___ / Tender† ___ } — MANGANESE LINERS* — { ~~Bogie~~ / Truck / ~~Coupled~~ / ~~Tender~~ }

DROP — HOPPER ASHPAN — SPECIAL FITTINGS*

~~Drop/Rocking~~ grate — ~~Hopper ashpan~~ — ~~Self-cleaning smoke box~~ — Smoke box deflector plates — ~~Spark arrester~~ — Blast pipe

Revg. gear { Screw / ~~Lever~~ / ~~Power~~ } — Speed indicator *SMITH STONE SPEED INDICATOR.* — Push and Pull fitted { ~~Vac. C.R.~~ / ~~Air C.R.~~ / ~~Mech. C.R.~~ } — ~~Vacuum pump~~ — ~~Continuous blowdown~~ — Blow-off cock — ~~A.T.C.~~ ATC

~~Trip cocks~~ — ~~Condenser~~ — ~~Sand gun~~ — Gangway doors *& T* — ~~Storm sheets~~ — ~~Back cab~~ — ~~Limousine cab~~

~~Tender weather boards~~ — Coal bunker access doors — ~~Coal rails~~ — ~~Coal pusher~~ — Fitted for snow plough — Regulator { ~~Smoke box~~† / Dome † } SINGLE

OTHER NON-SPECIFIED DETAILS:—

S.T. ~~BRACKETS ONLY~~

* Delete items not applicable.   † State type.

Above and opposite: **Great Northern's** final record card covering her life from 1949 to 1962 when withdrawn from service and scrapped. (THG)

With his retirement only a few months away, Thompson was undoubtedly eager to see this new engine tested in action before he departed. Apart from any assessment by those charged with its daily operation that would have been passed to him, the engine also ran some coal and water consumption comparison trials against two A4s – first No. 4466 *Sir Ralph Wedgwood* during 1945/46 and then No. 31 *Golden Plover* in 1947. The results seemed to favour the 'new' engine, though the gap was a very slight one indeed. However, the knowledge that she had been successfully tested

Back

TENDER				ALLOCATION		SHOPS			
Prefix	No.	Capacity		Depot	Date	In	Out	Class of Repair	Where
		Water (gall.)	Coal (tons)						
LNE 2WHK	5587	5000	8	Grantham	9.9.51	19.9.49.	6.1.50:	GEN:	DONCASTER:
				K. Cross	15.9.57	3.5.50:	11.5.50:	C(L):	DONCASTER:
				Doncaster	13.10.57	2.6.50:	21.6.50:	C(L):	DONCASTER:
						19.4.51:	18.5.51:	I(H):	DONCASTER:
						20.11.51:	4.12.51:	C(L):	DONCASTER:
						20.7.52	21.8.52	G	—
						25.11.53	13.1.54	G	—
						15.12.54	26.1.55	C/L	DONCASTER
						24.2.55	18.4.55	G	DONCASTER
						20.4.55	22.4.55	Adj	DONCASTER
						11.1.56	1.2.56	N/C	DONCASTER
						7.8.56	8.9.56	C/L	DONCASTER
						18.9.56	20.9.56	Adj	DONCASTER
						7.1.57	18.1.57	N/C	—
						15.4.57	31.5.57	GEN	DONCASTER
						24.9.57	8.10.57	C/L	DONCASTER
						20.2.58	5.3.58	N/C	DONCASTER
						2.4.58	19.4.58	C/L	DONCASTER
						15.9.58	8.10.58	C/H	DONCASTER
						4-5-59	17-6-59	GEN	Donc. 105,7,18
						21-3-60	21-3-60	N/C	DONCASTER
						5-7-60	14-7-60	N/C	DONCASTER
						7-12-60	2.2.61	GEN	Donc 89184

Experiment Nos. (if fitted)

60113

against the cream of Gresley's engines must have pleasing nonetheless. At the same time, it provided some re-assurance that the effort had not been wasted, had some genuine engineering value and answered any criticisms that may have come his way suggesting that the work might have been unnecessary.

In terms of performance and downtime, due to maintenance needs, the engine's first twelve months of service showed a moderate amount of time in the workshops – six brief visits for minor maintenance, not unusual for a new engine. After that, any maintenance issues or breakdowns that arose seemed to have been no better or worse than any other engine of the Pacific type, though time spent in the workshops may have been slightly greater

Not at her cleanest for the prestigious Yorkshire Pullman, but *Great Northern* still looks impressive nonetheless on a sunny day at King's Cross in May 1948. She will soon lose her No. 113 and LNER tender markings to become British Railway's No. 60103. (RH)

due to locomotive's uniqueness. Perhaps of greatest concern was an apparent weakness in the front end of the frames caused, it seems, by their length, vibration and the positioning of the cylinders. Strangely enough this reflected a problem found with Stanier's Princess Royal Pacifics, which had a similar stretched look and outside cylinders positioned aft of the leading truck. To correct this defect, the front frames were cut back and new sections fitted, but this didn't eradicate the problem entirely and the high stresses imposed still caused problems. It was a problem that was only truly resolved when Tom Coleman took the design and developed it into the Princess

Coronation Class. Peppercorn would, as CME, find a similar solution when later building more Pacifics for the LNER.

As an experiment, the 'Great Northern' project proved of some value and was part of a process which would evolve into Thompson's A2/3s and Peppercorn's A1s and A2s in time. But was the programme the cultural vandalism that some have suggested? Richard Hardy appears to have thought not, and I tend to agree with him, primarily because there is no real corroborating evidence to show that Thompson had any ill-intent. But what of Bert Spencer, who was a more senior witness to these events?

As might be expected from a mature, experienced and wise man, his comments are balanced and measured, if not non-committal. Later in life he wrote:

The main effort in developing the locomotive fleet was applied by Windle. Thompson certainly set him some broad guidelines but then allowed the Chief Draughtsmen to interpret them as he saw fit. Peppercorn did likewise and both men seemed pleased with the outcome. All six P2s became Pacific class A2/2s during 1943/44, then the last four V2s appeared as 4-6-2s [designated A2/1s] in '44 and a Gresley A1, 4470 Great Northern, was rebuilt in 1945 to test the efficacy of some elements of the standardisation programme. This conversion was deemed a success and work soon began on what Thompson and Windle hoped would be the standard Pacific and in 1946 the first of the A2/3s, as they were called, appeared.

There were long discussions about converting all the remaining A1s to A2/3s or simply completing their modification to A3 standard, as had long been planned. For reasons of cost Thompson chose the latter course and this programme was given much added weight.

The future of the A4s also came up and Windle was keen to de-streamline them when removing Gresley's conjugated valve gear. Thompson was not prepared to sanction these changes and preferred to keep them as they were.

His description of Windle's role in the process is perhaps the most interesting because Spencer seems to see him as the prime mover behind each development. If so, this assessment rather negates any criticism of Thompson if destruction of Gresley's legacy was his true motive. Also of interest are his words '… this conversion was deemed a success …' suggesting that he may not have agreed with this conclusion or, more likely, played no part in the test and evaluation process so felt unable to pass a personal opinion.

We shall never really know where the truth lies in this case and whether Thompson bore a grudge that affected his reasoning and his actions. However, there is one more point to consider in this debate and this concerns his publicly expressed views on Gresley. If he was truly embittered, surely he would have left some critical trace of his feelings. Yet, as he recorded later, he greatly admired Gresley and thought him 'the greatest British locomotive engineer since Churchward'. These are hardly the words of a nemesis, but a principled and conscientious man. However, he wasn't blinded to Gresley's shortcomings and respected less his predecessor's often inflexible approach to the question of cylinder numbers and conjugated valve gear which seemed to dominate his designs. By comparison, Thompson was prepared to look more widely, select the best from Gresley's work and experiment with other ideas in an effort to improve the breed. He wasn't always successful and lacked the design skills of his predecessor but at least he tried hard in very difficult circumstances.

With Thompson's departure in June 1946 on a well-earned retirement, Arthur Peppercorn took up the reins for three years and completed the Pacific programme begun so many years before. *Great Northern* remained a singleton but was gainfully employed until her service came to an end in 1962. The problems created by her long frames and the position of her three cylinders were never, or so it seems, entirely resolved. This impacted on the engines riding quality and, in turn, her maintenance needs, though to what degree is unclear. However, her availability and reliability were not significantly impaired by this issue, and she became just another Pacific in a very large stud of the type running along the East Coast Mainline on a variety of turns, both high and low profile. But the end of steam was in sight and in the early 1960s the non-standard elements of her design probably meant that she would be an early candidate for withdrawal. This proved to be the case and so the 'A1 that got away' was condemned and scrapped where her life began in 1922 and where she was re-born twenty-three years later.

On his copy of this photo Bert Spencer has simply written '*Great Northern* now in BR livery at Doncaster in the 1950s' but gives no other details. In his extensive collection of papers and photographs this rebuilt engine is a constant feature suggesting an underlying interest in the project that saw her go from Gresley's A1 to Thompson's A1/1. (BS)

Appendix 5

1 MAY 1928 – 4472's PERFORMANCE – 'NOT AS GOOD AS IT COULD BE'

When reading the various accounts of 4472's many triumphs, one might be forgiven for thinking the engine and the non-stop Flying Scotsman service, with which she will always be associated, were praised by all from the beginning. For the first run, this was not the case. In Chapter 3, I recalled events on 1 May 1928 when 4472 pulled the inaugural train from London to Edinburgh. On board that day was a Mr Ballam, who appears to have been a senior member of the LNER's staff, possibly from the General Manager's Department. His role that day was to report on the train's performance and present his findings to Ralph Wedgwood, the General Manager, apparently without reference to Gresley or the CME's Department while doing so.

From the papers that have survived, this appears to have been a role Ballam often undertook. For example, on 10 February 1928 he was on board 'an experimental train' of 445 tons, including dynamometer car, running from York to Edinburgh, pulled by A1 2568 *Sceptre*. His role on this occasion was to measure the engine's performance in terms of water/coal consumption, speeds attained and maintained, ride quality and so on. So, he was obviously thought qualified for such work.

While many praised Gresley and the LNER for their great achievement, Ballam wrote and submitted a somewhat critical Memorandum that same evening which latched on to the overall speed of the service. For the sake of historical interest and accuracy it is reproduced below in its entirety.

Tuesday 1 May 1928 and 4472 gets underway from King's Cross with a large crowd to witness her departure. The inaugural non-stop run was successful, but not everyone on board that day was pleased, as the correspondence reproduced here bears witness. (BS)

Memorandum 1st May 1928

Subject: Flying Scotsman – 1000 am ex-King's Cross Non-stop to Edinburgh

I travelled from King's Cross to Waverley by the above train today, the inaugural run of the down '*Flying Scotsman*'.

Composition and Weight of the Train

The train consisted of 12 vehicles, 3 in the front for Aberdeen and the remainder for Edinburgh, weighing in all approximately 400 tons. The vehicles were marshalled in the following order from the engine:

Aberdeen – Brake Third.
Third.
Compo.
Edinburgh - Third.
Restaurant Third.
Kitchen.
Restaurant First.
First.
Third and Hairdressing
   compartment.
Third.
Third.
Brake Van.

The train was fairly well filled, there being 39 first and 166 third class passengers on leaving King's Cross.

Locomotive Arrangements

Pacific engine 4472 '*Flying Scotsman*' worked the train throughout with the following crew:

King's Cross–Tollerton – Driver
   Pibworth (King's Cross).
Fireman Goddard (King's Cross).
Tollerton–Waverley – Driver
   Blades (Gateshead).
Fireman Morris (Gateshead).

Running

It is satisfactory to be able to record that there were no stops of any description between King's Cross and Waverley and only one or two checks due to the permanent way. Three minutes were lost on the bank up to Potters Bar but Peterborough was passed 1½ minutes early and from that point the train was on or before time for the remainder of the journey. I have detailed point to point timings of the run throughout, but it is sufficient to remark that after what seemed a comparatively slow journey, the train pulled up at Waverley at 6.2pm, 6 minutes ahead of W.W.T time and 13 minutes early by public time.

General Observations

If it is the aim of the LNER to provide the maximum comfort on their trains between London and Edinburgh, that object has certainly been achieved in these latest '*Flying Scotsman*' developments, but my chief impression of the journey is the slowness of it. I am not sure that this may not be partly due to the exceptional smoothness of the running so that one is really moving faster than one thinks, but at the same time, even with an arrival time in Edinburgh at 6.2pm this average speed is under 50 miles per hour. Certain sections of the journey seem exceptionally slow, as for instance between Durham and Newcastle where 21 minutes is allowed for the 14 miles, chiefly downhill, but I doubt if the speed exceeded 60mph at any point. I am aware, of course, of the 8¼ hours understanding with the LMS, but it is quite clear, I think, that we shall have to face pretty caustic criticism from the public, and various remarks I overheard on the train confirm this belief. On the present working the '*Flying Scotsman*' hardly justifies its name.

At the bottom of this Memo Wedgwood has written 'Noted. We must do better' above his initials. For Gresley, it seems, there were no such qualms. According to Spencer:

The Chief was well satisfied with the performance of the locomotive, the working of the new tender and the performance of the footplate crew. Any question of scheduling or attainment and sustaining higher speeds was a matter for the Operating Department to sort out. It was felt that the engines could easily meet a much faster schedule, if so desired.

So ended another successful day for Gresley and his team. By any standard the engine had performed well, as did Shotover running in the other direction. Credit for this success must go to the CME, but a large share must also go to his assistant, Bert Spencer, who was determined to improve the breed by resolving the long lap issue.

It is 6.2pm at Waverley Station on 1 May 1928 and 4472 pulls into the platform slightly earlier than planned. For Gresley, the day was a great success, but for others, such as Ballam, more remained to be done in terms of speed and scheduling. (RH)

REFERENCE SOURCES

The National Railway Museum (Search Engine)
Records Consulted
Corr/LNER/1 to 6.
Calc/LNER/1
Loco/LNER/1 to 9.
Spec/Don/7.
Spec/LNER/1 to 7.
Test/LNER/1 to 10.
The R. Bond Collection.
The E.S. Cox Collection.
The R. Riddles Collection (donated by author).
The Immingham Collection (donated by author).
The E. Thompson Collection.

Other Collections Consulted
Institution of Mechanical Engineers, London.
T.F. Coleman/M Lemon.
A. Ewer.
R.H.N. Hardy.
R.A. Hillier.
D. Neal.
N. Newsome.
B. Spencer.
R.A. Thom.

Publications
IMechE/ILocoE *Journal*
The Engineer
The Gazette various dates.
The *Meccano Magazine*
Steam World
Stephenson Society Journal

Books
Allen, J.R. and Bursley, J.A., *Heat Engines; Steam, Gas, Steam Turbines and Their Auxiliaries* (1941).
Bannister, Eric, *Trained By Sir Nigel Gresley*, Dalesman (1984).
Bond, R., *A Lifetime With Locomotives* (1975).
Brown, E.A.S., *Nigel Gresley. Locomotive Engineer"* Littlehampton Book Services (1961)
Bulleid, H.A.V., *Master Builders of Steam*, Ian Allan, (1963).
Bulleid, H.A.V., *Bulleid of the Southern"* Littlehampton Book Services (1977).
Bush, D.J., *The Streamlined Decade*, George Braziller (1975).
Chapelon, A., *La Locomotive a Vapeur* (1952).
Coster, P., *Book of the A3 Pacifics*, Irwell Press (2003).
Coster, P., *Book of the A4 Pacifics*, Irwell Press (2005).
Coster, P., *Book of the V2 2-6-2s*, Irwell Press (2008).
Cox, E.S., *Locomotive Panorama Vols 1 and 2*, Ian Allan (1965/66).
Cox, E.S., *Chronicles of Locomotives*, Ian Allan (1967).
Cox, E.S., *Speaking of Steam*, Ian Allan (1971).
Dalby, W.E., *The Balancing of Engines* (1920).
Dalby, W.E., *British Railways: Some Facts and A Few Problems* (1910).
Grafton, P., *Edward Thompson of the LNER*, Oakwood Press (1971 & 2007).
Hillier-Graves, T., *Gresley and His Locomotives*, Pen and Sword Transport (2019).
Hillier-Graves, T., *Gresley's Master Engineer – Bert Spencer* Pen and Sword Transport (2023).
Hillier-Graves, T., *Gresley's Silver Link*, Pen and Sword Transport (2022).
Hillier-Graves, T., *Peppercorn. His Life and Locomotives*, Pen and Sword Transport (2021).
Hillier-Graves, T', *The A4s After Gresley*, Pen and Sword Transport, 2023
Hillier-Graves, T., *Thompson. His Life and Locomotives*, Pen and Sword Transport (2021).
Hillier-Graves, T., *Tom Coleman. His Life and Work*, Pen and Sword Transport (2019).
Hardy, R.H.N., *Steam in the Blood*, Littlehampton Book Services (1971).
Haresnape, B., *Gresley's Locomotives*, Ian Allan (1981).
Holcroft, H., *Locomotive Adventure Vols 1 and 2*, Ian Allan (1962).
Hughes, Geoffrey, *Sir Nigel Gresley*, Oakwood Publishing (2001).
Martin, S.A.C., *Edward Thompson. Wartime CME*, Strathwood, Ltd (2022).

McKillop, Norman, *Top Link Locomotives*, Thomas Nelson and Sons (1957).

Nock, O.S., *The Gresley Pacifics*, David and Charles (1973).

Nock, O.S., *Locomotives of Sir Nigel Gresley*, (1945).

Pope, A., *Wind Tunnel Testing* (1947).

RCTS, *Locomotives of the LNER – Vols 2A, 2B & 6B* (1973 & 1983).

Rogers, H.C.B., *The Last Steam Locomotive Engineer*, Allen and Unwin (1970).

Rogers, H.C.B., *Thompson & Peppercorn. Locomotive Engineers*, Allen and Unwin (1979).

Rogers, H.C.B., *Transition from Steam*, Allen and Unwin (1980).

Townend, P.N., *East Coast Pacifics at Work*, Littlehampton Book Services (1982).

Townend, P.N., *Top Shed*, Ian Allan (1975).

Yeadon, W.B., *Yeadon's Registers* – Nos 1,2,3,4,5,8,9,10 and 25 (various dates).

Photographic Sources/Credits

B Spencer (BS), R Hillier (RH), Author (THG), D Neal (DN) and J. Constantine (JC).

In producing photographs for this book some preservation work has been necessary. In some cases, their sepia finish, foxing and dilapidated condition could not be entirely overcome. However, because they are often rare pictures or have some historic significance they have been included despite their condition. I hope this doesn't spoil your enjoyment of this book.

Copyright is a complex issue and often difficult to establish, especially when a photograph or document exists in a number of public and private collections.

Strenuous efforts have been made to ensure each item is correctly attributed, but no process is flawless, especially when many of these items are more than 70 years old with photographers or authors long gone. If an error has been made, it was unintentional. If any reader wishes to affirm copyright, please contact the publishers and an acknowledgement will be included in any future edition of this book, should a claim be proven. We apologise in advance for any mistakes we have made.

A number of documents held by the NRM, other institutions and private individuals have been quoted in this book. My thanks to them all for permission to use this material. The same goes for authors and publishers of various books and articles referred to in the text. We are so very lucky in Britain to have so many sources to tap when studying our history.

INDEX